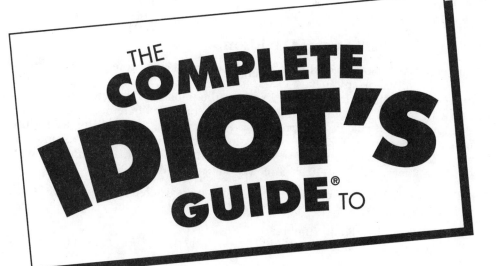

THE COMPLETE IDIOT'S GUIDE® TO

Change Management

by Jeff Davidson

ALPHA

A Pearson Education Company

This book is dedicated to the change masters of the world, who strive to make things better, safer, more just, or more enjoyable.

Copyright © 2002 by Jeff Davidson

THE COMPLETE IDIOT'S GUIDE TO and Design are registered trademarks of Pearson Education, Inc.

International Standard Book Number: 0-02-864217-1
Library of Congress Catalog Card Number: 2001094710

04   03   02   8   7   6   5   4   3   2   1

Interpretation of the printing code: The rightmost number of the first series of numbers is the year of the book's printing; the rightmost number of the second series of numbers is the number of the book's printing. For example, a printing code of 02-1 shows that the first printing occurred in 2002.

Printed in the United States of America

Publisher
Marie Butler-Knight

Product Manager
Phil Kitchel

Managing Editor
Jennifer Chisholm

Senior Acquisitions Editor
Renee Wilmeth

Development Editor
Michael Koch

Production Editor
Katherin Bidwell

Copy Editor
Michael Dietsch

Illustrator
Jody Schaeffer

Cover Designers
Mike Freeland
Kevin Spear

Book Designers
Scott Cook and Amy Adams of DesignLab

Indexer
Lisa Wilson

Layout/Proofreading
Svetlana Dominguez
Susan Geiselman

Contents at a Glance

Contents

xi

16 Jump Starting to Total Immersion   175

17 Going Cold Turkey   185

Appendixes

Foreword

Welcome to your guide to managing change in businesses and organizations. It's no small feat for you to have picked up this book and decided to tackle the change-beast head on! Let's face it, all around us, every organization is facing more change than it probably chose to contend with. Researchers tell us that society experienced more change in the last five years than most people previously experienced in their lifetimes.

From Jeff Davidson's own research, we know that more information is generated on earth in a single minute today than a person could take in the rest of his or her life! Technology breakthroughs are introduced at a frightening pace. There are more products and services available now than someone a hundred years ago could have possibly imagined. Every place you turn, you're confronted with more change, new information to consider, more instructions to learn, more to incorporate into your life. As Jeff Davidson so aptly puts it, "Has there ever been a generation in the history of the earth that was confronted by more competing for its time and attention?" Understandably, organizations are feeling the effects. And, here's the great opportunity for you, managers who are effective in dealing with change.

Unlike the masses who make their way through each day trying to do their best but often getting frustrated or upended by change, by picking up this book, you have chosen to take a careful look and a systematic approach to managing change in your career and, by extension, in your life.

You are in good hands. Jeff Davidson has written six books in *The Complete Idiot's Guide* series, including *The Complete Idiot's Guide to Managing Your Time*, *The Complete Idiot's Guide to Managing Stress*, *The Complete Idiot's Guide to Assertiveness*, *The Complete Idiot's Guide to Reaching Your Goals*, and *The Complete Idiot's Guide to Reinventing Yourself*. As with all *Complete Idiot's Guides*, proven subject matter experts are chosen to deliver high-quality information in a palatable and often humorous form.

What you're going to learn will have great application, but the lessons won't seem like drudgery—often they'll seem more like fun! Jeff Davidson tackles the subject of managing change with a comprehensive, encyclopedia-like, down-to-earth style that hundreds of thousands of readers have come to know and enjoy.

Jeff has been a professional speaker since 1983 and a book author since 1985. All the while, he has learned how to hone and refine his ability for researching and collecting the latest data, and then codifying his observations and insights to yield breakthrough information to his readers. The result—an aptly assembled, smooth-reading text that takes you from where you are to where you want to be.

Jeff's primary focus at all times in assembling this book is to craft a user-friendly plan that you can easily understand and apply. Jeff's capacity for devising personal systems for accomplishment will work well for you the first and every time you put them into practice.

Often in his own career and life, Jeff wonders how some people get through the day. He sees career professionals who seemingly cannot manage their own offices characterized by papers and piles strewn all over. People seem besieged and beleaguered by change as evidenced by the equipment they accumulate and then don't use, an inability to maintain their schedules, and, in some cases, ineptness at managing their domestic lives. Like standing at the conveyor belt, as Charlie Chaplin did in *Modern Times,* too many managers are fearful that they cannot keep pace.

When you're "dancing as fast as you can," as Jeff observes, attempting to proceed at an even more rapid pace is not the solution. Temporarily, you need to slow down .... Slow down long enough to observe the big picture of what is happening in your organization and your career. Slow down long enough to rethink systems for accomplishment. Slow down to chart a new course, devise a new path, or craft a new, manageable way of proceeding.

Jeff has constructed this book so that you can proceed at a manageable pace without getting sidetracked by trivia or attempting to do too much at once. His ever-vigilant focus is on offering you proven approaches and fresh perspectives to managing change while maintaining productivity and balance. In this regard, succeeding in the workplace and having peace of mind are not mutually exclusive goals; they are simultaneously achievable (and necessarily so).

Jeff offers time-honored principles from antiquity to leading-edge techniques for effectively managing change and ultimately becoming a master of it. As you set out to read and digest the material in this book, be sure to assemble the tools that will help you to get the most out of it. This might include a highlighter or felt tipped pen, stick 'em pads, paper clips, bookmarks, everything and anything that will enable you to better absorb and apply the material. Jeff encourages his readers to copy selected pages as necessary or desirable. (Fear not, this is not a violation of copyright law.)

Give yourself the opportunity to read this book in a quiet setting away from distractions. This may be difficult to do, but if you want to extract the best from this book, reading it at your own pace, free from interruption is recommended. Managing change is a challenging issue so you should give your undivided attention to the topic.

I am enthusiastic and optimistic about the progress you can make on the journey you are about to undergo. The material that Jeff has provided here, along with your resolve to become an effective change manager, all but guarantees your success! May you get so good at managing change that you become a role model for others.

—Bob Nelson, Ph.D.

Bob Nelson is the author of *1001 Ways to Reward Employees* and *1001 Ways to Energize Employees.*

Introduction

Change—is there a single word that better encapsulates the measure of our careers and our lives? Do you feel as if things would be a whole lot simpler if you were making strides in your career in say, the early 1970s, instead of the early twenty-first century?

By now, you've figured out that ever-increasing change is here to stay. Moreover, it's not likely that society will return to a time when the pace of life moves along at an even keel, or when what you learned yesterday will be good far into the infinite future.

The larger the challenges and changes you face, the more important it is for you to realize that human physiology changes very slowly. In fact, as a species we've been in progress for tens of thousands of years. Yet, the reality of our times dictates that each of us be more fluid and more open to new procedures and systems for effectiveness in the workplace and beyond.

This book is about successfully managing change in your company, in particular, deftly managing specific change campaigns.

What This Book Is Not

Change campaigns are akin to projects. However, this book will not cover the same ground as books on project management. The focus here is on the managerial and leadership aspects of successfully directing change campaigns, including understanding the nature of corporate change, approaches to change management, the human dynamic, and big picture concerns.

Many good books on project management are available, including my own, *The 10 Minute Guide to Project Management* (Alpha Books, 2000). Such books encompass key topics for a venture's success such as developing action plans, the work breakdown structure, planning tools, task scheduling, software programs, budgeting, and reporting.

A Brief Rundown

Part 1, "The Basics of Change Management," focuses on helping you learn the basics of surviving change. **Part 2, "The Four Approaches to Change Management,"** discusses four basic notions of how people behave. In this part, I discuss that while every organizational culture is different, by classifying change environments into one of four basic categories, you have a better chance of being able to devise an appropriate change management plan. In **Part 3, "Leading Through Organizational Change,"** I'll focus on common issues that you're likely to encounter and offer you a variety of methods of prevailing. **Part 4, "Ensuring a Successful Campaign,"** is all about innovative approaches to ensuring a successful campaign. **Part 5, "Making Change Work for You,"** takes a novel look at honing and refining your skills as a change manager. Finally, **Part 6, "Broadening Your Understanding,"** illuminates the work of change gurus. It also exposes some change management pitfalls, and concludes with a look at why change managers often proceed as if tomorrow will be pretty much like today, perhaps with a few little differences here and there, and how to blast through that trap!

Extras

Sprinkled throughout the text are some special boxes that will help you through each chapter. These sidebars are shown here so that you will be familiar with them as you encounter them in the text:

Word Power

These are words or groups of words related to change that merit special attention.

Change Master

These are pithy and profound observations offered by a "mythical" sage.

Proceed

These are recommendations, tips, and action steps that you'll want to act upon right away while your energy level is high and the fish are jumpin'.

Factoid

These are timeless principles, Internet-age realities, or dyed-in-the-wool facts on which you may rely.

Be Wary

These are areas where you may want to proceed with caution. They represent pitfalls to avoid and proverbial land mines to step around, such as trying to incorporate too much change into your routine at once, allowing yourself to be besieged by information, or responding to fads as opposed to long-term trends.

Now, without further ado, you may flip to Chapter 1 and launch into your change management quest. Or, if you're the curious type, you'll read on to find out whom I have aptly chosen to acknowledge.

Acknowledgments

The fine folks at Pearson Education know how to acquire, edit, produce, promote, and sell books! They have proven this to me for more than seven years, and I feel privileged to be involved in such a relationship. My continuing thanks and praise to Renee Wilmeth, senior acquisitions editor at Pearson Education, and Marie Butler-Knight, publisher, for their vision, insights, and strategies. Without them, this book could not become a reality.

Thanks as well to Michael Koch for his wonderful editing, pithy observations, and wry humor, and to the production team at Alpha Books for putting up with my last-minute changes.

A tip of the hat to Sheree Bykofsky, Janet Rosen, Toni Boyle, Ed Keyes, Jesse Wacht, Dr. Gerry Faust, Bill and Nancy Lauterbach, Emory Austin, Dr. Rosabeth Moss Kanter, Rachelle Schifter, Jeffrey Gitomer, Ray Leone, Rebecca Morgan, Art Berg, Keith Harrell, Geno Auriemma, Anson Dorrance, Ralph Nader, Colin Powell, Zorica Henderson, Teresa Brown, Mark French, Kalle Lasn, Dr. Charles Petty, Terry Brock, Margaret Hickey, Billy Joel, Winifred Gallagher, Dr. Hazel Henderson, Dr. Aggie Jordan, Tom Hanks, Kevin Costner, Bill Brooks, Ty Boyd, Anne Walters, Lorna Riley, and Dr. Sarah Layton. These people have all been empowering, inspiring, or helpful in some way.

Another tip of the hat to Brent Winter, Sharon Askew, Christie Koch, Jessi Bromwell, Ian Zook, and Beth Lynn Hocutt for their editing, proofing, and all-around excellence. Thanks to Sue Davidson for her transcription and word processing ability.

Finally, thank you to Valerie Davidson, age 11, whose name is now in about 12 books and who helps Daddy to master the nuances of change management on a daily basis.

Trademarks

All terms mentioned in this book that are known to be or are suspected of being trademarks or service marks have been appropriately capitalized. Alpha Books and Pearson Education, Inc., cannot attest to the accuracy of this information. Use of a term in this book should not be regarded as affecting the validity of any trademark or service mark.

Part 1

The Basics of Change Management

While it may be hard for you to conceive right now, you can become comfortable with change, or at least embrace it to the degree that it doesn't represent as much of a disruption to you and your organization as you imagine.

Philosophically, you might as well attempt to get as comfortable with change as you can, for indeed, none of us can avoid it. The future will present accelerating change in practically every arena of life.

Chapter 1

No More Standing Still

In This Chapter

➤ Change means doing things differently

➤ The quest for stability, balance, and predictability

➤ Industry waits for no one

➤ The old order never goes quietly

➤ Effective change managers earn the most

If you coast, you roast. Today, the nature of society, the importance of technology, and the flow of information govern any business or organization. We will witness large-scale ongoing change on a regular basis such that as soon as three years from now, all businesses and organizations will operate differently. In this chapter, I'm going to cover the topic of change in general and how you as a career professional cannot escape its clutches.

Change Means Doing Things Differently

Change refers to a significant difference in what was before. This could mean doing things in a new way, following a new path, adopting new technology, installing a new system, following new management procedures, merging, reorganizing, or any other highly significant, disruptive event.

The change to which I refer does not represent smooth progression, a highly antici-pated development, or an incremental approach for getting from point A to point B.

Change Master

The kind of change I am discussing cannot be handled by some existing formula or repre-sent an off-the-shelf fix. If doing what you have done before or doing some variation of what you've done before alleviates a problem, that's fine, but that isn't change manage-ment as defined and discussed in this text. The kinds of change campaigns you will be managing are far-reaching. They impact people and resources and represent something unprecedented in the organization, department or divisions, and subsequent operating procedures.

Change Is Significant, Prolonged, and Disruptive

Change as referred to here is significant, prolonged, and often disruptive. It represents a departure in whole or in part of what came before it. It might include venturing into completely new territory, facing something unexpected, making a major course redirection, or getting up to speed in record time with insufficient resources.

This change is the kind that you don't necessarily seek, but recognize as a possible el-ement in your career journey.

Change Is a Continuous Process of Alignment

Writing in *Industrial Management* (May/June 1997), authors Lisa Kudray and Brian Kleiner define change management as the "continuous process of aligning an organi-zation with its marketplace—and doing it more responsibly and effectively than com-petitors."

For an organization to be aligned, say the authors, "the key management levers—strategy, operations, culture, and reward—must be synchronized continuously." They observe that, "managers need to remember that they are changing, manipulating, and rearranging a variety of both human and non human elements."

The Quest for Stability, Balance, and Predictability

Human beings by nature, tens of thousands of years in formation, seek out stability, balance, and predictability. Oh sure, we want thrills at the amusement park, and entertainment that titillates, but in general the human organism craves *homeostasis*— a state in which a person's or thing's relationship to the environment is stable.

Longitudinal studies of human physiology have confirmed that people are at their best when they get regular amounts of sleep, sufficient amounts of exercise, and balanced and nutritious diets. Married people tend to live longer than single people, have fewer illnesses, and spend less time in long-term care facilities. Likewise, those with supportive families and friends, and a predictable social structure, tend to be happier and healthier and have greater longevity.

Factoid

Whether or not they realize it, virtually all human beings seek order and stability most of the time.

Taking It to the Suites

Human beings bring their inherent inclinations into the workplace and hence all businesses and organizations are dramatically affected by the tens of thousands of years of human psychology and physiology. It is human nature to resist change, even though for particular individuals at particular times this may not seem to be the case.

Curiously, in the early years of the twenty-first century, growing numbers of people recognize that constant change is starting to become the norm, particularly in business and organizational environments. From CEOs to front-line workers, and virtually everyone in between, more and more people are now recognizing that in spite of a multicentury predisposition to resisting change, we are now in an era in which constant change is the norm. This might continue to be so for the duration of the existence of the human species! What a predicament!

Proceed

To everyone in the workaday world, there has never been a more crucial time to develop change management skills. The fact that you're reading this book signifies that you comprehend the need to develop a skill that is the antithesis to the human organism. Or, maybe you find yourself in trouble at work and recognize that you need to do something about it—fast—or the situation might become hopeless.

Being Hired to Manage Change

Here is a realization worth considering as you proceed in your career; today, you are essentially hired,

Change Master

Today, everyone with the title of manager, in one form or another, has to be a change manager. Whether or not you have considered it, you manage change all the time, be it through people, technology, information, or other resources.

paid, and retained for managing change. In a large measure, you have earned your living thus far, and certainly most recently, for being a change manager.

Maybe you have managed change effectively, but there is always room for improvement. In the future, a larger percentage, if not all, of what you do will involve it. In essence, you will likely earn 100 percent of your future income as a result of your ability to effectively manage change.

Viewed from this perspective, it makes sense to learn as much as you can about being an effective change manager. This includes reading books, not only this one, but others after it. It also includes taking courses, becoming a keen observer, practicing new behaviors, adopting new techniques, and being more open to the input of others than you have been in the past. As the following table explains, today, every viewpoint, every assumption, and nearly everything about society is subject to changing views.

Changing Views

Old View	New Realizations
More choices never hurt.	*More choices have profound implications.* Children who face 48 flavors of jellybeans vs. 10, or purchasing agents who face 850 options vs. 6, expend considerable mental energy simply to make a choice.
There are victimless crimes. (Marijuana advocates argued that smoking it was a victimless crime.)	*There are no victimless crimes.* If you smoke, drink, or are otherwise chemically dependent, others pay through increased health insurance, your tardiness and absenteeism, and innumerable other social costs.
Out of sight, out of mind.	*What we cannot see can harm us.* We are now aware of the need to conserve and recycle. A growing number of people understand that there are social costs of discrimination.
Women are inferior in math and science. Men do not nurture their young.	*Au contraire!* Sex roles in society are influenced by many factors; both sexes have the capacity to be proficient in many of the skills traditionally viewed as exclusive to the domain of the opposite sex.

Old View	New Realizations
Only manipulative women succeed in business.	*As with men, women in business succeed for a variety of reasons.* Many are working to succeed despite difficult circumstances, that is, the pressure of being a single mother and breadwinner.
Raising a family is neither work nor a full-time job in and of itself.	*Successfully raising a family is among the most demanding feats in society.* Some people are blessed with the ability to succeed both professionally and domestically.
Nature and wildlife are valuable in terms of what they can provide to us.	*Nature and wildlife are valuable and worthy in their own right.* We now appreciate that they still exist. The supreme challenge of our era will be to preserve what nature took millions of years to create.

Industry Waits for No One

"Wouldn't it be nice," as goes the old Beach Boys' song, if things stayed relatively the same in your job, while allowing you to look forward to raises, advances, and promotions? Wouldn't it be nice if you could read one or two books and take one or two courses every couple of years and gain the information and skills you needed to continue to be successful on the job?

Wouldn't it be nice if you had a totally stable environment in which you reported to experienced, effective bosses? A work environment in which you could count on your staff showing up on time, being energetic and enthusiastic, doing the job, and then going home?

Wouldn't it be nice if customers or clients weren't becoming increasingly demanding? If you could count on their loyalty for years, instead of having them switch alliances with the click of a mouse?

Wouldn't it be nice if the technology you work with today continued to improve but in bite-sized increments that you could easily master? Wouldn't a host of other developments be nice—all of which protect you from having to confront major, challenging, or disruptive change?

Unrelenting Change

None of the above is going to happen. In all likelihood, the opposite will be the case. As the future unfolds, you will find yourself in a broad array of work situations in which the players keep changing, the situations get more challenging, you are asked

Be Wary

Time after time, we witness organizations, particularly large organizations with heavy investments in equipment, industry, or marketing positions, that seem unwilling, unable, or perhaps totally unaware of the need to change direction. Are you employed in such an industry?

to do more with fewer resources, your staff is temporary or nonexistent, and customer loyalty nearly becomes an antiquated concept.

At times, it seems as if everything is up for grabs. Industry waits for no one. All businesses, organizations, industries, and professions are subject to unrelenting change.

Building a Better Widget?

Drawing on the graduate business school mythological product—the widget—suppose your company has a long and proud history of selling the A-1 widget. Soon you discover that the A-1 widget is no longer in demand. Other products offered by competing companies have replaced it, the manufacturing process for producing it is too costly, or emerging factors in the external environment have all but rendered the product a relic of the past.

Suppose that every member of the management team recognizes that much of the organization's history and identity, not to mention sales revenue, is tied to the A-1 widget? So, they resolve to undergo a dramatic change. They decide to upgrade the raw materials used in producing the A-1 widget. Now it's "new and improved," but somehow it doesn't help to alleviate the problem. So, they employ a variety of other strategies:

➤ They make changes in the factories that produce the widget.
➤ They beseech the sales staff to increase its effectiveness.
➤ They convene a task force to study the widget.
➤ They undertake research to see if the widget can be used in other ways.
➤ They increase advertising to induce customers to re-embrace the new widget.
➤ They hire an advertising agency to give the widget a new image.
➤ They design a training course for widget users (which no one signs up for).
➤ They rename the widget, calling it a wudget.
➤ They disseminate articles on the value of the wudget.
➤ They make a bigger, more versatile wudget.
➤ They install wudgets in social and charitable organizations.
➤ They increase the R&D budget to further enhance the wudget's performance.
➤ They assemble a focus group to learn how people are using the wudget.

➤ They design wudget add-ons to enhance the overall product.

➤ They retool their factory to produce the new, improved wudget.

➤ They initiate quality circles to discuss how to produce more wudgets per day.

➤ They invite the press to the main plant to view wudget production in person.

➤ They decide to return to the original product name, the A-1 widget.

When sales continue to flatten, they hire a lobbyist in Washington to push for easing regulations that would result in lower costs of widget production.

➤ They study foreign markets where widgets might prove to be popular.

➤ They lure away the product development vice president from a rival widget maker.

➤ The new vice president announces that he is committed to reviving widget sales.

Embracing Change? Not

The above example is a bit dramatic, but leaves no doubt that this is an organization not prepared to embrace change. You might scoff and say that no group would act like this, but think again ....

How often have certain companies and entire industries in our society lingered long after visible signs of market disapproval, social condemnation, government intervention, lawsuits, and, perhaps most tellingly, the rise of considerably superior alternatives? The tobacco industry and cassette tape recording manufacturers are obvious examples.

The Old Order Never Goes Quietly

While services such as Napster raced ahead in violation of copyright laws, the powerful software it employs enabled millions of users to share data with one another anonymously. Such software will be applied in a variety of settings and industries. This will enable the administrator to generate large revenues as a result of the advertising placed on the site. Legal hurdles are real and need to be heeded.

One of the many lessons you can learn from Napster is that the old established order with a huge power base does not go away quietly. Even if the record industry is able to easily generate *more* revenues and higher profitability as a result of per song fees or monthly subscriptions via music sharing services such as Napster, it may take years before the industry deals with it. The powers that be are wedded to CDs, packaging, shipping, warehousing, and the industrial-age trappings that are part and parcel of the world in which they dwell. They fear recording artists will bypass them altogether.

9

As a change manager, you should ...

➤ **Contemplate the inevitable.** The power structure would prefer to ignore that music is now digital. This is a clear case of the Internet irrevocably changing an entire industry. Once people discover the awesome power of saving, storing, ar ranging, manipulating, and controlling their song bases, they will never return to what came before. Yet, this is only beginning to sink into record executives' minds.

You can make the argument that there will be continuing profits for selling items long after their heyday. Today, more than 100 years after the introduction of the automobile, buggy whips still sell; there aren't many of them, but the in-dustry is alive and well. The question for you, your team, your company, and your organization is: Do you want to sell the equivalent of buggy whips five or ten years, or even *one* year, after the automobile takes hold on the economy?

➤ **Distinguish strategic design from strategic neglect.** It's one thing to carve out a strategic niche that says, "Our company will continue to be the leader in buggy whip sales even as the automobile dominates the landscape." It is quite another to sell buggy whips by default as the world passes you by.

Proceed

If you're an established business entity, what changes may be in store for your industry as a result of the Internet? Contemplate the inevitabilities and you can stay ahead in the game.

Even in the case that you choose to become the buggy whip industry leader, you and your team will still have to embrace broad-sweeping, dis-ruptive changes to achieve and maintain market position. The nature of your product and the consumers to whom you sell differ more than those of the buggy whip manufacturers of 100, 50, 20, 10, or even 5 years ago.

➤ **Maintain a dual focus.** Presuming you're in an organization or industry that recognizes the vol-ume and frequency of change occurring in the external environment, you, as a career profes-sional, need to maintain a dual focus. This means that at any given time, on any given day, you're an alert, effective, responsible, forward-thinking employee. At the same time, you maintain a sharp focus on the big picture of your own career.

Effective Change Managers Earn Big Bucks

Considering how people are compensated in society, sometimes it seems as if wages and bonuses are distributed unfairly. Yet, there is a pattern to it. In baseball, for example, the home-run hitter is likely to make more money than the nonslugger. Why? For one, the home run counts as a run itself, and the team that scores the most runs wins the game. The home run also automatically scores anybody else on base, presuming they touch all the bases on their paths toward home.

The fans enjoy seeing home runs, and this brings them out to the ballpark. Hence, the owner's gate revenues increase. Home-run hitters also make for more lucrative television contracts between the club owner and the TV networks.

The Vicissitudes of the Season

In baseball, the superlative fielders, the power or control pitchers, the swiftest base runners, and so forth, tend to earn more than their counterparts. Why? They are managing change—weather, travel, crowds, and the pitches. They are meeting fierce competitors head on and helping their teams win about 58 percent to 65 percent of the team's games.

Word Power

Vicissitudes are the up and down variations in an event or observable phenomenon.

Consider the high price the consultants who may walk the halls of your organization command. They work for prestigious firms, perhaps out of New York, Boston, or Chicago, with long histories of success. Their pay greatly exceeds the typical worker in your organization. Why do they command such fees? Because they have the ability to keenly focus on the situation at hand and identify the critical factors for success.

Bargaining for the Best

This is also the case with high-level negotiators (see Chapter 21, "Leapfrogging and Picking Spots"). They are brought in to strike a bargain with the opposition. The negotiation lasts for days, exhausting all participants and emotionally frazzling everyone. When the agreement is struck, it needs to be one that all sides can live with.

You only entrust the very best problem solver to sit at the table for you, and you pay him or her larger amounts of money. Something must change in the situation that necessitates two sides getting together and coming to a resolution; otherwise, everybody loses.

Big Challenge, Big Pay

The CEOs who receive million-dollar salaries and multimillion-dollar bonuses are the subject of feature articles in magazines and newspapers. Some writers lament that pay scales are totally out of whack with contribution. Whether or not that is the case, why is there such a great disparity between the pay of top officers in a corporation and that of middle managers or line supervisors?

Proceed

Change managers earn the big bucks. It behooves you to become an effective change manager not solely because your predicted stream of career income will rise, but because higher levels of compensation in and of themselves usually correlate with the ability to handle significant, prolonged, and disruptive situations invariably brought about by change.

The top officers address the fundamental challenges confronting the organization, change-management issues such as deciding in what direction to proceed in the future. They devise plans that provide answers to the following questions:

➤ How can we meet competition?

➤ What product or services should we launch?

➤ How can we improve customer service?

They deal with issues related to remaining viable, generating revenues, and earning profit.

In essence, those who take on huge challenges are change managers. No challenge stays the same, whether it's one baseball team playing another or one corporation fending for itself in a highly competitive arena. The competition will not stay the same. The external environment will not stay the same. The fans, or customers, will not stay the same in terms of their expectations, their loyalties, how much they are willing to pay, what they expect, and what they are willing to endure.

Pick Up the Mantle

You're not a baseball player or the CEO of your organization—you're a manager or an aspiring manager. You reached your present post by proving yourself to be effective. You faced problems of varying sizes and complexity, and, for the most part, were able to generate effective solutions.

Perhaps you never regarded yourself as a change manager, but all the while that's what you've been progressing toward. Every course you took, every book and article you read, all the training experience and observations you made have prepared you to arrive at your present point—a manager or potential manager.

Now comes the more formal process of focusing specifically on increasing your skills in managing the types of change your organization confronts.

The Least You Need to Know

➤ Regardless of your industry or profession, in a few years, you will be operating very differently than you are today.

➤ Whenever you encounter the term *management*, think of *change management*.

➤ The wise career professional maintains a dual focus at all times—being a professional, highly effective worker for his or her employer and keeping an eye on the big picture of his or her career.

➤ Change managers make the most money because they demonstrate the ability to handle challenging issues.

➤ Today, you are most likely paid for managing change, be it through people, technology, information, or other resources.

Chapter 2

Change Scenarios

In This Chapter

➤ Undertaking successful change campaigns

➤ Sizing up the corporate culture

➤ Facing restructuring and downsizing campaigns

➤ Incorporating new processes

➤ Instilling a sense of ownership

➤ Making an organization conducive to change

All organizations confronting change share some common concerns and challenges. As a change manager, you might find yourself heading up any one of a number of change campaigns. In this chapter, I address fundamental issues common to all organizations and change managers, and highlight a number of change situations that you may actually encounter.

Undertaking Successful Change Campaigns

The most successful change campaigns are comprehensive—no stones are left unturned; all of the steps, interim goals, and final outcomes are achieved.

Change campaigns may affect a small part of an organization or the entire organization. In any case, something is irrevocably altered—the organization, department, or division can't go back to what came before, how people used to do things, or "standard operating procedure."

Change Is an Unnatural Act

If you are feeling a little shaky about undertaking that change campaign, and the sponsor behind you seems a little scared (but is totally committed to the project), relax. Such feelings are par for the course. You are in that rare air of managers who need to commit to behaviors that "constitute an unnatural act," while running a little scared about the change campaign overall.

Be Wary

By many estimates, less than a third of actual change campaigns proceed according to plan and generate precisely the intended results.

Andrew Grove, the much-quoted chairman of Intel Corporation and previously the corporation's president and CEO for more than 10 years, observes that many changes hit organizations "in such a way that those of us in senior management are among the last to notice."

Michael Porter, a professor at Harvard University and the author of *Competitive Advantage,* observes that large-scale change within an organization represents an unnatural act. "The behavior required to sustain advantage, then, is in many respects an unnatural act for established firms." Porter says, "Few companies make significant improvements in strategy changes voluntarily. Most are forced to. The management of companies that sustain competitive advantage always run a little scared."

Be Wary

Staying where you are will ultimately lead to ruin, especially in an ultra-competitive environment.

In their book, *Surfing the Edge of Chaos: The Laws of Nature and the New Laws of Business,* authors Richard Pascale, Mark Millemann, and Linda Gioja argue that "equilibrium is a precursor to death." Organizationally, this means staying put is a risky proposition. If you regard the change you are about to manage as risky, consider that in the broad scope of things, it's probably *less* risky than staying where you are.

The Situational and Psychological Components of Change

In a sense, change can be viewed as both psychological and situational. The psychological aspects of change relate to all of the perceptions, emotions, and reactions that people experience when being involved in a change campaign and when coming to terms with the new situation after the change has been implemented. William Bridges, author of *Transitions* and the follow-up book *Managing Transitions,* says:

➤ Before beginning something new you have to end what has been.

➤ Before becoming a new person, you must let go of the old identity.

➤ Before you can learn the new way, you have to unlearn the old way.

The situational component of change relates to new ways of proceeding, new policies, new processes, and new roles. We'll examine the "people" component of change in Chapters 4, 5, 10, and 11. For the balance of this chapter, we'll look at the situational components of change.

Which Road, O! Cheshire Cat?

Change campaigns can take the form of helping top management to decide on strategic alternatives. When faced with three possible paths that an organization can take, for example, it's not uncommon to commission someone from within or hire an outside consultant. They can conduct a campaign that assesses the benefits and costs, both short and long term, to pursuing each of the three possible paths.

Like a scout in the Old West galloping along several miles ahead of the wagon train to ascertain which path will be best for the group, the change manager who serves as strategic scout plays a critical role for the sponsor and for the organization.

Pick the wrong path, and the company could miss lucrative opportunities, or worse, find itself in dire straights. The problem with all scout work in change campaigns is that all the study, analysis, and data in the world never truly prepare a company for how it is going to be once it actually embarks on a chosen path.

If you are chosen to head up such a campaign, invariably it's indicative of the trust and confidence that top executives have in you!

Change Master

The greater the departure the paths represent from the organization's operating history, the more crucial the findings of the change manager and the change management team.

Factoid

Virtually all large corporations today routinely have studies under way that provide critical insights and perspectives to top managers so that they can make their best decision as to the future direction of the company.

A Cornucopia of Change Management Situations

You might also find yourself heading up change campaigns to accomplish one or more of the following: Is your company expanding, adding branches, or relocating its headquarters? If such events represent singularities—that is, they are not part of your normal procedure—then the move is probably best facilitated by a task force headed by a change manager.

Depending on the size and scope of the change, you may find yourself visiting new locations; meeting with architects, engineers, and designers; visiting city planners; contacting commercial real estate firms; and evaluating proposals from van line companies among a host of other activities.

Still other types of change might include adopting a new quality management system, revising a mission, restructuring a specific operation, making a major purchase, or some other fundamental and radical reorientation in the way an organization, department, or division operates.

The Customer As Initiator

It is entirely possible that one of your customers serves as an initiator of change if he or she has a vested interest in the new product or service offering and is willing to serve as a guinea pig to help you perfect your innovation. Such customers are invaluable for many reasons.

All market researches, studies, calculations, and computer models never quite yield the same insights and experience of testing what you have done in the field, away from your facility. This test customer potentially serves as an advocate who can influence an initiating sponsor.

Change Master

Any innovation, improvement, new product or service has a higher chance of success if you can test it, in the field, with a real life end user.

The customer could serve as a target of change (see Chapter 3, "Charting the Players," for details), because he or she is the one who will be most directly affected by what you and your staff have been toiling over. In some respects, the customer can also serve as a bystander since, unlike the typical end user, the customer will have some definitive view as to what further modifications may be necessary.

Test customers can be individuals as well as businesses. Customers like these are worth their weight in gold. You want to cultivate such relationships. Where else on this earth are you going to get someone who is willing to play along with you, literally providing you the real-life "laboratory" that is so sorely needed for most innovations?

Even if you fail miserably, you still have confined operations and limited expenditures so that the failure is not as public and expensive as it might be if you were to launch the imitative market wide.

Sizing Up the Corporate Culture

Many organizations today are seeking some variation of cultural change such as increasing the diversity of the work force, converting to a flatter organizational structure, helping professional staff balance work and family life, altering and extending the lines of communication, or even developing a new operating philosophy and corporate image.

Be Wary

The longer your organization has existed, the harder it is to change.

What is corporate culture? Drawing on anthropology, it is communicable knowledge for humans coping within a particular environment that is passed down for the benefit of subsequent generations. If you are a change manager, it is crucial that you understand the culture of the organization, department, or division where you are attempting to make a change.

Many regard culture as the benefits and values that unify an organization and help determine how things get done. Inducing cultural change can take many years, hundreds of thousands of dollars, outside consultants, and team members working at full bore to implement. Cultural change may necessitate that the change team undertake an organizational needs analysis, an organizational goals and strategy session, and polls and surveys to establish baseline data.

For purposes of this book, cultural change represents too big an issue to tackle. I'm going to stick to more bite-sized change campaigns, the type that you're likely to be assigned to manage.

Be Wary

By some estimates, changing the culture of an organization can require five to seven years or more. With such a gargantuan venture, often the initiating and even the sustaining sponsors (see Chapter 3) are no longer on board when and if the project ever comes to fruition. Team members change, departments and divisions change, even change managers may come and go during this long scheme.

Facing Restructuring and Downsizing Campaigns

Restructuring or downsizing represents a huge change initiative, although not on the order of changing an organization's culture. If you're slated to manage a downsizing campaign, as unpalatable as the project may seem and unpopular as you may prove to be within your organization, fortunately, the time horizon is limited. Three months, six months, a year at the worst—and the campaign is usually over.

Slim Down, Beef Up

Over the years, articles in publications such as *The Wall Street Journal* and *Business Week* have discussed that companies with a predisposition to downsize often find themselves to ramping back up after having wielded the unemployment axe too freely. Hence, the term *rightsizing* began appearing in business literature a few years back.

Word Power

Rightsizing is determining the appropriate staffing levels within an organization based on both a short- and a long-term perspective.

A variety of other widely used terms such as restructuring, reorganization, rationalizing, de-layering, and de-hiring have made their way into the halls of large organizations. In such change situations, you want to ensure that eliminating staff within your organization is done for the express purpose of meeting specific objectives and/or fostering growth, and not as an expedient, cost-cutting reflex.

No matter how you slice it, many large companies have been reducing permanent staff size for many years. But have they been successful as a result of the cuts?

➤ White Associates conducted a survey of 1,005 downsized companies and found that 68 percent were not successful in increasing their profits.

➤ The University of Wisconsin conducted a study of Fortune 100 companies and found that over a five-year period, downsizing resulted in diminished financial performance.

➤ The Society for Human Resource Management conducted a study of 1,468 companies and found that in more than 50 percent of the companies downsizing had contributed to a deterioration of productivity.

➤ The American Management Association reports that over a 14-year period, two thirds of U.S. companies that had downsized did not experience an increase in productivity, and 55 percent did not improve operating profits.

Be Wary

Many companies find that while downsizing might temporarily satisfy shareholders who have a vested interest in seeing that the company's financial statements remain strong, ultimately, as management guru Tom Peters says, "You can't shrink your way to greatness."

Boost Employee Morale

As a result of downsizing or other organization-shaking initiatives, you might find yourself slated to manage a change campaign designed to rebuild trust or confidence within an organization.

While a downsizing situation is not the sole criteria for a change initiative to rebuild trust or confidence, it has happened frequently enough over the last decade and a half to have become the *cause célèbre*.

Those surviving downsizing often take on a guarded posture—they don't share information freely with others, are less likely to be effective team members, and are reticent to make sacrifices for the organization. The challenge of rebuilding trust in such situations is gargantuan.

Some change agents have investigated a range of options including initiating daycare services, providing health club memberships, offering consulting services, and allowing flextime. Some organizations have relied on messages from top officers through company reports, specially produced videos, and letters to staff that convey personal concerns.

Change Master

Removing large numbers of employees, seemingly justified by current conditions or corporate strategy, can damage the health and vitality of an organization as remaining employees become leery. They have to bid farewell to friends they have known for years and then wonder if they, too, will be next on the chopping block.

Capitalize on Constituencies

A variety of companies today find themselves facing diversity issues and have not approached the situation creatively. By failing to address immediate challenges, such companies often find they experience both internal moral problems with employees, as well as problems in the marketplace.

Customers are often quick to voice their displeasure with the company's hiring and firing procedures when a pattern of discrimination or unfairness is detected. As a change manager, given the challenge of incorporating the best and most effective elements of diversity into your organization, department, or division, how might you proceed? Among many strategies, you might hold employees accountable for their technical, professional, and personal development and work to create an organization, department, or division based on trust and respect.

Be Wary

One consultant says to "get rid of the term 'diversity.'" What you are really doing is capitalizing on your employee and customer constituency. This means focusing on complying fully with all equal opportunity employment laws and implementing everything that brings your organization into full compliance with these laws.

Change Master

In many instances of downsizing, the best fix is time and success. When a year or two passes and people sense that the organization has achieved a measure of stability, or if a company has several profitable quarters in a row, the existing staff start to look on the downsizing days as the "bad old days."

Factoid

In many companies, planned obsolescence of their own products is an ongoing function that occurs at a pace that seems frightening to outsiders.

Think Twice Before Closing Out a Product or Service Line

Depending on how long you have been offering a particular product or service, its cessation may necessitate a change campaign. After all, there are plenty of issues to be resolved:

➤ What are the ramifications of withdrawing items from the marketplace that a built-in constituency relies on?

➤ Do customers require continuing parts and supply services?

➤ Is a trade-in program desirable to induce them to upgrade?

Sony estimates that its shelf life for products will dwindle to 18 days. Its mission is to make its own products obsolete because its newer products will be so superior.

Why would Sony do this? Suppose it could make a breakthrough every 18 days. Doesn't it wreak havoc on its employees, distribution systems, and customers to continuously come out with new products? The answer is a big, fat yes. At the same time, if Sony doesn't constantly improve what it's offering, then its competition will do it in.

Incorporating New Processes

One of the most confounding issues facing organizations is when to adopt new processes, particularly in regards to high technology. A manager at one company, for example, lamented that his company was grappling with installing DSL connections to the Internet.

A few months after the change took place, he learned that for not much more cost or effort, T1 lines could have been installed and would have yielded a dramatic increase in speed and download capability. From this experience he concluded that half the time you think you have to do something immediately, your best strategy would be to hold on and take a longer look.

Don't Bleed Needlessly

Peter de Jager, reachable at Managechange@technobility.com, observes in his online change-management newsletter:

> There is hardly ever a need to be on the bleeding edge even in a fast-paced environment.
>
> If you reasonably seek to stay on top of technology development, you won't miss the trends. Even the daily newspapers will give you sufficient information to see where things are going, and how fast," he says. "Once you decide that your competitors are starting to benefit by adapting to change, it is probably the right time to start looking at it yourself.

He is speaking, of course, about adapting to basic technology that is ancillary to your primary product or service offerings. If you're in business specifically to offer a competitive advantage to your clients or customers via technology, the observation doesn't hold.

Find the Trailblazer

When the process you are charged with installing does not represent a first for your industry, you have the option of finding the trailblazer.

➤ Who else in the industry has made such an installation?

➤ Can you read about it?

➤ Can you study it?

➤ Can you visit the installation?

➤ Can you talk to staff who maintain it? And if not,

➤ Can you talk to customers who benefit by it?

Often you have a variety of ways to determine (for nonleading edge changes) if the change you are contemplating for your company makes good sense based on other organizations' experiences.

In Virgin Territory

If you're treading in completely new territory, i.e. no one else has incorporated a given process and the change will position you as an industry leader, then understandably your change campaign carries high risk and commensurate high reward. It is exceedingly difficult to undertake an accurate market study for a product or service offering that does not currently exist. (That's why you see so many similar movies and TV shows!) The same holds true when attempting to incorporate a new process.

23

Incorporate New Technology

Perhaps there is some new hardware or software item that offers tremendous operating advantages to your organization, department or division, and it's ultimately to everyone's benefit to have this new technology incorporated as soon as possible. This would necessitate the development of a training schedule, follow up, and feedback.

Many organizations have longstanding departments whose mission is to provide such training as the benefits of adopting new technology become apparent. Some organizations outsource this function. Smaller companies often don't have the means, and hence handle such scenarios through individual change initiatives.

Be Wary

You can ask people how they would respond to the change, but the replies must be taken for what they're worth—merely conjecture. Management literature is strewn with examples of change campaigns launched following survey data that represented nothing more than conjecture on the part of respondents.

Instilling a Sense of Ownership

Employee stock operating plans (ESOP) give staff the opportunity to participate in the ownership of the organization where they are employed. In contrast, the sense of ownership discussed below is psychological, not financial.

Employees need and want to believe that their efforts on the job will be instrumental in the future success of the organization. This sounds like "Management 101" stuff, but unless employees have a sense of ownership in regards to the work that they do, the goals that they strive for, and the overall success of the company, then they're merely putting in time, i.e. punching a clock.

Vital Companies, Vital Involvement

Vital organizations, the kind that are cited in books such as *The 100 Best Companies to Work For in America,* by Robert Levering and Milton Moskowitz, find ways to get employees involved in the work and the affairs of the organization on many levels. Your job as change manager might involve any one of the following:

➤ Developing an interorganizational campaign that raises the level of employee pride.

➤ Encouraging greater participation among employees in company sponsored community involvement or volunteerism.

➤ Cross-training employees to expand their awareness and appreciation for what other parts of the company does.

➤ Tapping the insights and opinions of employees through focus groups, the results of which are widely known to be communicated directly to top management.

Cultivate the Ownership Feeling

The behaviors and activities of one inspirational leader can have a profound effect on the staff of an entire organization and dramatically increase individual's sense of corporate "ownership."

Much of what employees feel in the way of ownership springs from the behavior of top executives. Perhaps the result of your campaign will be to formulate a strategy whereby top executives …

➤ Interact with employees on the floor more often.

➤ Greet them by name.

➤ Solicit their advice.

➤ Make special requests.

➤ Offer invitations.

Making an Organization Conducive to Change

Corporations can actually make themselves more conducive to change. Accenture (formerly Anderson Consulting) regards the *capacity to change* as being analog—change "assets" can be assembled, warehoused, and drawn on as required.

Clues All Around

Often there are solid indications as to an organization's receptivity and capability to respond to and manage change:

➤ Your company is lauded in the business press.

➤ Market share remains stable or is even increasing.

➤ Productivity is on the rise.

➤ Expenses remain under control.

Word Power

The **capacity to change** is the ability of an organization to initiate and successfully achieve change on an ongoing basis.

These may seem like simple indicators, and they are. Behind them is the fundamental notion that in an era of rapid change such as this one, simple indicators of health over the long term indicate many positive developments. For example, that the firm is …

➤ Continually making appropriate decisions.

➤ Adapting to crucial changes as the needs become apparent.

➤ Making anticipatory changes before tangible needs are apparent.

Companies That Stand Out

In their book, *Built to Last: Successful Habits of Visionary Companies,* James Collins and Jerry Porras, professors at Stanford University, embarked on a journey to determine what precisely makes some companies exceptional, forward-thinking, and responsive to change.

The companies that Collins and Porras studied had exceedingly long track records, unlike the ones studied by Tom Peters and Robert Waterman in *In Search of Excellence.* The 18 stellar companies under examination shared several traits:

➤ They were regarded as leaders in their respective industries.

➤ They were routinely praised by the business press and general public.

➤ They had been in business for an average of nearly a *century.*

➤ They had outperformed the composite stock market since 1926 by 1,500 percent.

Three characteristics, however, proved to be most influential:

1. These phenomenal companies had a continual focus on improvement. They did not rest on their laurels. They did not wait for the wolf to be knocking on their doors. They sought out change with regularity.

2. They maintained core values that remained immutable despite current fads in society. Almost like an organic entity, they developed the processes for thriving and transferring knowledge of their best practices and procedures to their offspring, thereby ensuing long-term survival.

3. They pursued a range of objectives, one of which includes being profitable, although that is not even a primary objective. Remarkably, over the long-term, these companies proved to be more profitable than their competitors, most of who were driven primarily by generating revenues.

While other bright meteor companies come and go, companies conducive to change seem to have an organic, balanced, service-minded approach that transcends the ages and keeps them vibrant and, in many cases, dominant within their industries.

If you're employed by such an organization, you tend to know it. And you're lucky!

The Least You Need to Know

➤ Much of the change that businesses or organizations face leads to common concerns. Often, you have the capability to draw on what trailblazers have done to guide you in your thinking.

➤ Restructuring or downsizing often has a destructive effect and does not result in the desired outcome.

➤ Instilling a sense of ownership among employees or staff is a frequent challenge faced by change managers, which potentially yields tremendous payoffs.

➤ Closing out a product or service line can be a delicate undertaking.

➤ Exceptional companies with long track records of success are service, rather than revenue, focused and develop an organic approach to change that helps ensure the long-term survival of the corporations.

Wanted:
Players
for a
RADICAL
LIFE
CHANGE
Auditions Today.

Chapter 3

Charting the Players

In This Chapter

➤ Enhancing your view of your environment

➤ Making sense of your environment

➤ Finding sponsors for your change campaign

➤ Slipping into the role of a change agent

➤ Interacting with players in a change campaign

➤ Looking at the bystanders

The more you read about managing change, the more you run into conflicting testimonies. Some books suggest that the players in a change process have limited roles and limited interplay.

As you're about to learn, the "players" in a "change campaign" most definitely play dynamic roles and impact each other greatly.

Who Moved My Bifocals?

One highly popular book, which shall remain nameless, suggests that a "scout" type of player seek out change to help an organization enhance its organizational vision. She enjoys working within an organization that recognizes change and adapts accordingly. A second player, according to this book, likes to scamper about getting things done, presumably taking action based on a new corporate vision. Such a player needs a lot of guidance so that he doesn't scamper off in the wrong direction.

A third player is primarily concerned with working in a safe place and changes reluctantly only when his or her sense of security is threatened. Some of these players can't change in a timely manner and thus become dead weight in an organization and have to be let go.

A fourth player, according to this popular text, reflexively resists change but is open-minded enough to take some chances. She knows how to work with others, keep the situation light, and adapt as needed.

While this lexicon of players may provide insights for some change situations, for the purpose of conducting a successful change campaign, it is ineffective. It falters in addressing the crucial interplay between sponsors, change agents, advocates and well-wishers, targets, and bystanders.

Other books suggest that you can't manage change because "change just happens." That might be true for certain types of change at certain times; however, the type of change we're focusing on in this book is that which *you fully intend to manage*—change campaigns that have specific beginnings and, if they're handled correctly, specific endings.

The change may come about as a result of any one of the variety of change scenarios discussed in Chapter 2, "Change Scenarios." Or it may spring from the *plethora* of other circumstance that have developed in your organization, company, division, branch, or team, such as refining operations, having to make a move, or overcoming some dilemma.

Be Wary

No matter how popular a title, the text provides only momentarily satisfying nuggets about potential roles played by targets of change. It fails completely to address the roles of sponsors and change agents.

Word Power

A **plethora** of something means a surplus of it.

Making Sense of Your Environment

One of your major responsibilities is to understand the basic roles people play and the dynamics of their interaction. Relax, you've untangled far more complicated situations. As a newborn, you faced the challenge of making sense of the sights and sounds surrounding you.

Much of what you heard started off as gobbledy gook until you were able to incorporate what you heard into the structure of language. Slowly you began to form words and later whole sentences. A simple word such as *Momma* was likely one of the first things you said. Later, you tried more complex polysyllabic words.

Incorporating the Basics

Your foods were undoubtedly strained peaches, pears, plums, and other mush. As you developed teeth, you began to eat more solid and complex foods. Your first toys were simple, often brightly colored, washable, safe, and durable. You could bang them, pound them, drop them, or kick them. Little by little you drew on basic skills. You started walking by first leaning on the side of a couch or whatever else was available.

Soon, you took a step. Finally, you walked across your living room without help. You fell many times, but usually you got up and optimistically began again.

The Players and the Scorecard

Concurrently, managing a change campaign necessitates incorporating the basics:

➤ Who are the various players?

➤ What are their roles?

➤ How do they interact?

It has been said in sports that you can't tell the players without a scorecard. Understanding the people dynamics of a change situation is as important as anything else you can possibly know. Here is your scorecard.

Finding Sponsors for Your Change Campaign

Sponsor refers to any higher-up in your organization or group who has the authority or power to initiate, approve, and oversee a change campaign. In the simplest example, a sponsor is your boss, who tells you to do XYZ. In reality, your boss may be simply one in the chain of command who passes instructions on to you.

In all cases, the initial or ultimate sponsor first considers what is impacting the organization, what potential risks lie ahead for both taking action and not taking action, what alternatives might be available, and what possible results might occur following each alternative.

As the Sponsor Goes ...

Many management guru types believe, with good reason, that the major factor in the failure of a change campaign to achieve the desired result is a lack of management commitment, that is, the sponsor not following through on his or her original intent. Others point out that sometimes the focus of the change campaign can simply be off the mark from the outset. In either case, the sponsor's influence and unmistakable mark color the entire change campaign.

In his book, *Managing at the Speed of Change,* Daryl Conner observes that sponsors ...

➤ Decide which changes will happen.

➤ Communicate new priorities to the organization.

➤ Provide the proper reinforcement to assure success.

Change Master

Although a sponsor may be vigorously enthusiastic at the start of a change campaign and disappear during its execution, the sponsor is nevertheless primarily responsible for establishing a climate in which the desired changes can take effect on time and within budget.

Be Wary

Usually it is difficult enough for targets of change to handle and report on assigned responsibilities. To be intermittently hit with changes from the top is simply asking too much.

Sustaining Sponsors Pick Up the Ball

Sometimes, the initiating sponsor gives way to what Conner calls the *sustaining sponsor.* The initiating sponsor may be a person or group high up in the company, who after giving his blessing to the change campaign is completely removed from the situation. In such cases, without a sustaining sponsor, the change campaign could quickly become jeopardized.

The sustaining sponsor recognizes the need to intermittently monitor the change process, lend crucial support to the successful completion of the campaign, and serve as a sounding board to the change agent.

Cascading Sponsorship, Not Cascading Change

Here is an important distinction to understand about sustaining sponsorship. As the locus of sponsorship shifts within an organization, the mission and operating procedures of the change campaign and change team itself do not necessarily vary to accommodate the style and whims of the latest sponsor. If this was the case, no change team would likely remain intact or be effective by the time a third or fourth sustaining sponsor emerged.

Concurrently, all sponsors participating in a cascading form of sponsorship need to understand that asserting themselves and injecting newly favored elements into a change campaign increase the probability of failure. The sustaining sponsor needs to restrain him- or herself if ...

➤ The change campaign has been designed properly from the outset.

➤ The action plan is solid.

➤ The right change manager has been selected.

➤ A talented team is in place.

A sustaining sponsor's primary role becomes that of supporting the change that is in effect. He or she upholds the entity that was designed to see it to successful resolution.

The Deity Who Pulls the Strings

Because the role of sponsor is vital to a change campaign, and the sponsor is often invisible to the majority of participants in the campaign, both change agents and those assigned to actually carry out the work of the campaign sometimes assume a false sense of efficacy. That is, they proceed as if they need no sponsorship.

Sponsors need to understand that if they take on more change than they can effectively handle, they put specific change campaigns in jeopardy. They also convey to others in their organizations that they are ineffective leaders. In that sense, as Daryl Conner observes, "they lose twice."

Slipping into the Role of a Change Agent

This is where you come in. You are a manager, a team leader, or some kind of task-force supervisor. Your role is to manage and lead the change campaign, achieving a desired objective with the resources that are provided.

As a change agent, you can find yourself under a lot of pressure. You report to people who are expecting great things of you, and you manage a staff that needs to be continually educated to understand what it must do. Change agents at greatest risk are perhaps those who find themselves in new positions. You may find yourself in an organizational culture that is simply not responsive to your style of management.

Change Master

Effective change agents have to be skilled in a variety of areas. They must have the abilities to establish an action plan, supervise others, monitor results, diagnose problems, and, perhaps most challenging of all, improvise, improvise, improvise.

Being Charged with Change

A leading executive recruitment firm in Chicago undertook a client search for a top manager. The client organization spent $280,000 (a large but not unusual sum) in finding and hiring an individual whose role would be to effect change, that is manage a series of change campaigns. The manager was fired within a year because he wanted to make too many changes!

The skills and experience of a change agent can dramatically impact the success or failure of a change campaign and even how responsive his or her own organization and sponsors are to change.

Mess with Success

To be a successful change agent, you need to have a large variety of skills, traits, and aptitudes. Successful change agents ...

➤ **Have staying power.** Have stamina and persist in the face of disappointment, roadblocks, and initial failures, rising almost like a phoenix from the ashes to build commitment to a change campaign to a desired objective.

➤ **Are masters of timing.** Craft a plan that allows for real-world contingencies, down time, ramp-up time, and the interplay of people and resources to their full and intended effect.

➤ **Are empathetic.** Listen to the needs and concerns of the change campaign team or targets who are directly involved in implementation of the desired change.

➤ **Anticipate resistance.** Understand that resistance is a normal human response to a change situation and welcome it, rather than run from it. Understand through experience or intuition that the apparent lack of resistance can signify a deeper, underlying problem.

➤ **Are adept at regular reporting.** Understand the need to keep all those on the change campaign informed on a regular basis because it is their responsibility, and because it quashes rumors, doubts, and second-guessing.

➤ **Provide feedback.** Beyond regular reporting, recognize the need to offer feedback on a continuing basis to those who require it, especially in pursuit of excellence on the job, in support of the overall change campaign.

➤ **Maintain a fence of objectivity.** Comprehend the needs and goals of everyone involved in a change campaign.

➤ **Give credit to the group.** Continually acknowledge the efforts of the change campaign team as opposed to taking sole credit for achievements.

Change Master

Change agents often have to be Renaissance–type men or women, the kind of people who bring a variety of skills, insights, knowledge, common sense, and intuition to a change campaign.

Intermittently provide rewards and incentives for change team participants as a way of encouraging and inspiring them for the duration of the campaign.

➤ **Become students of the organizational climate.** Beyond simply understanding their own department or division's operating procedure, environment, and culture, effective change agents make it their business to understand these same elements within any organizations the change campaign encompasses.

For example, if the change campaign involves a merger with another company, the effective change agent learns everything he or she can about the company with which the organization will be merging.

The Roles Can Vary

At various times within a change campaign, you, as change agent, may play more than one role. It is highly likely that you will adopt the posture and behavior of advocate, that is influencing your own sponsor, formally or informally, about particular points that are important to you.

It is also possible for you to be a sponsor to the same people that you supervise. After all, if their participation in a change campaign is so far removed from the initial or sustaining sponsor that they have no inkling of this person or group, in addition to the role of change agent, you might also represent sponsorship to them. Who else will they accord the role of sponsor, even if they know that there is somebody back in the corporate office who started it all?

Dealing with Advocates and Well-Wishers

An advocate might be a person or a group who fully supports a change but doesn't have any authority or power to put it in motion. From this standpoint, the role of advocate or well-wisher can be the most frustrating in the change process. He wants something to change, but, from a formal standpoint, he can't do anything about it. Informally, advocates do have their day.

Well-wishers are somewhat akin to advocates. They agree wholly or partially with what you're seeking to accomplish. They may or may not be vocal in their support. Nevertheless, it may be to your benefit to keep them in the loop.

Proceed

Within your own sphere, it makes sense to identify the advocates and well-wishers. Even if they don't have a formal role in a change campaign, having them on your side, keeping them informed, and benefiting from the influence that they can exert are all to your advantage.

As an example, I served as president of Carolina Speakers during a recent fiscal year. During that time, I was a sponsor of change, empowering my board to work with targets, generally our membership, to achieve desired results. At times, I was also a change agent myself and sometimes a target, that is, the one who ended up undertaking the tasks in pursuit of a desired objective.

If an advocate happens to be friends with a sponsor, she has the opportunity to influence the sponsor and hence indirectly effect change. If a change agent knows that an advocate or well-wisher is the friend of a sponsor or has the ear of a sponsor, it may enable the advocate to have influence over the agent as well.

Sometimes advocates try to influence the *targets* of change but this more than often backfires. Targets report to change agents who report to sponsors. When advocates try to influence targets without the *aura* of sponsorship, they are not likely to get very far.

Advocates could come from anywhere. They could be board members themselves, general members, past presidents, and particularly longstanding members, including a few who were involved in the founding of the chapter. These patron and matron saints may not have had any official status in terms of enacting change, but they certainly had their influences (more on this in Chapter 4, "Dealing with Resistance").

In my experience, when there were specific things I wanted to achieve, and I knew there was a good chance of getting the support of these well-wishers, I made sure they were in the information and reporting loop. The conversations they had with one another and their friends among the membership, largely through phone calls and e-mail, often generated enough buzz to provide a requisite amount of support of my overall objective.

Word Power

An **aura** is an atmosphere or a climate, and, on a personal basis, an air or undercurrent.

Factoid

It is possible that both your staff and others share the role of targets of change to varying degrees.

Working with Targets of Change

I referred to targets in Chapter 2, so by now you have a pretty good understanding of who they are and what they do. Daryl Conner explains that the term *target* "is used because these people are the focus of the change effort and play a crucial role in the short- and long-term success" of a change campaign.

Your staff or change management team can be the sole targets of change for the change campaign that you are managing. Or, they may simply be aiding you as a conduit of change that impacts some other population that serves as the targets of change.

It would be cumbersome to make this clarification repeatedly throughout the book. For purposes of "shorthand," unless otherwise spelled out, targets of change will refer to the staff assembled to participate in the change campaign, while it is recognized that far larger populations can serve as targets of change in a real-world change campaign scenario.

Hereafter, the term *targets* refers to specific individuals, a team, or even a large group, who are charged with executing the tasks that will result in the desired objective during a change campaign.

Your primary role as a change agent working with targets is to educate them so they understand why the change needs to be achieved, what their roles are, and how to best proceed.

By using the principles espoused by Dr. Aubrey Daniels in his book *Bringing Out the Best in People,* a change agent can dramatically increase the probability of influencing targets so that they will turn in consistently excellent performances (see Chapter 10, "Preparing Your Team for Change," and Chapter 11, "Leading Your Team Through Change").

Proceed

Your prime objective in working with targets at all times is to increase the likelihood of success of the change campaign.

Be Wary

The most fundamental error made in change campaigns is presupposing that a change agent can give instructions to targets who don't report to him or her. Clear, simple lines of authority reporting and responsibility work best.

Interacting with Players in a Change Campaign

The most fundamental interrelationships in a change campaign are those of targets reporting to change agents who report to sponsors. Any other alignment, and there are many including triangular, circular, square, and so forth, is likely to cause problems.

No Sponsor Pain, No Gain

Unbeknownst to change agents, targets, and even advocates and well-wishers is the level of sacrifice that a sponsor must sometimes endure to see a change campaign through to completion. Beyond the legitimate power to initiate a change campaign, the sponsor must have, as Conner says, "a level of discomfort with the status quo that makes change attractive."

In other words, unless the sponsor is experiencing fits and starts about a certain situation, and unless the situation poses a significant, perceivable threat, then the sponsor probably won't muster enough impetus to initiate the change campaign, authorize the change agent, and support the change agent as might be necessary.

A View from Afar

The sponsor has to have an unimpeded view of what changes need to occur. He or she also has to have a comprehensive awareness of the organization's assets that would be drawn on to effect a change. These usually break down to human resources, monetary funds, facilities, and equipment, all allocated over some palatable time period.

Effective sponsors are not new to change. They understand that to see a change campaign to fruition, often they have to give up something else. Each campaign and each objective comes with a price or an opportunity cost, which essentially means that less attention or no attention may be given to other issues.

Enduring for the Duration

In many cases, the sponsor will have to convey an unwavering level of support for the change campaign and the activities of the change agent while having the mental and emotional strength to resist undertaking short-term activities that could possibly impede or are inconsistent with the long-term desired result. The more important the change campaign, and the longer its duration, the greater the level of persistence required by the change sponsor.

It is relatively easy for someone in authority to provide sponsorship for a change. It is quite another story to fully support a change agent to the degree required to dramatically increase the probability of success of the mission.

Be Wary

If you find yourself managing a campaign backed by a sponsor of questionable commitment, you have your work cut out for you.

Sponsors Without the Resolve

Many sponsors don't understand the full ramifications of their initiating role and long-term responsibilities. Hence, the business world is full of change agents who feel as if the engine driving the vehicle of change is operating on only a couple of cylinders. Often the predictable results are misdirection, misallocation of resources, and abandoned projects.

Certainly projects get abandoned for good reasons (see Chapter 5, "Stay Sane, Manage the Pain"). Frequently, however, projects cease because the underlying support structure was faulty.

Looking at the Bystanders

A bystander is anybody who happens to get wind of a change campaign in motion. Bystanders could represent:

➤ Shareholders of the organization

➤ Staff not assigned to the project

➤ The general public

➤ Newspaper reporters

➤ Politicians and pundits alike

Bystanders have no formal role in the change campaign. Depending on their status and influence over formal players within the change campaign, a bystander may rise to the level of advocate or well-wisher.

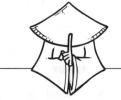

Change Master

The wise change agent tries to anticipate where and when bystanders to a campaign may become more or less mobilized. As you might imagine, this is far easier said than done.

A newspaper reporter who hears about a company's change campaign, for example, might write an article that praises or criticizes the efforts, which may have an effect on the campaign itself. Likewise, other parities who seemingly have little or no role to play may emerge at opportune or inopportune moments.

A company that engages in a campaign to revamp its environmental policy and procedures may be dramatically influenced by an outside environmental group that gets wind of the company's campaign and charges that it is far too little and inadequate. (More will be discussed on these kinds of scenarios in future chapters.)

Understanding the people dynamics of a change campaign is the most illuminating and challenging task of all!

The Least You Need to Know

➤ Since your earliest days you have been well adept at learning the basics, be it talking, eating, walking, or any other vital function.

➤ Behind any successful change campaign is a sponsor who is sufficiently motivated to see the change through to its conclusion.

➤ To be successful as a change agent, you need a committed sponsor and the authority to instruct targets who will carry out the action.

➤ Advocates and well-wishers do not have a formal role in change campaigns, but may certainly influence sponsors and even change agents and targets.

➤ Targets do the work necessary to achieve the desired result. A good change agent can make a dramatic difference in targets' overall effectiveness.

➤ Understanding the people dynamics of a change campaign is fundamental.

Chapter 4

Dealing with Resistance

In This Chapter

➤ Understanding fear of the unknown

➤ Starting over is often difficult

➤ Anticipating and welcoming resistance

➤ Practicing what you preach

➤ Securing a commitment to change

With all the changes in your world, industry, and market, there is simply no more standing still. At one time or another, all organizations share some common concerns and challenges, such as rebuilding trust, instilling a sense of ownership, shifting strategic focus, or adapting to new management. The various players in a change situation—including sponsors, change agents, advocates, well-wishers, targets, and bystanders—and how they interact with one another as a change ensues, make the difference between a winning campaign and something less desirable.

On your path to becoming an effective change manager, recognize that the natural human response to change is resistance. People become attached to familiar ways of doing things, even ways they initially regarded as cumbersome, costly, or ineffective.

Individuals resist change; teams and groups resist change; whole organizations resist change. Going further, entire societies, entire continents, world religions, even the broad swath of humanity reflexively resist change. Remember, the word "change" as used throughout this book means significant, challenging, and disruptive change.

> **Change Master**
>
> In essence, life is a series of attempts to resist change in any form, incorporate the change, and then resist any new changes.

Fear of the Unknown

The resistance people exhibit when they're confronted by change is derived in part from fear of the unknown. My sister worked for years in a battered women's shelter. Time after time she would meet victims who shared their tales of misery, being beaten and abused by an out-of-control spouse or mate. Such mates then relented hours or days later professing sorrow for their actions. Then, the cycle would continue, until one day the battered woman showed up at the shelter.

My sister wondered why such women didn't leave these relationships. After endless rounds of battering, hearing apologies, and then being battered again, surely these victims knew the situation was not going to change. Yet, most had extreme difficulties doing what observers thought to be a much-needed change—leaving the relationship.

The Hardship of Making a Better Life

These victims were afraid of starting over in a new community, finding new homes, seeking new work, and living on their own. As difficult as it was to endure the battering, they perceived greater hardship upon leaving their relationships. The same situation occurs in companies, communities, even in entire cultures.

John Kenneth Galbraith, a noted economist from Harvard, wrote *The Nature of Mass Poverty*. While researching his book, he visited four continents to determine why some civilizations remain poor. He wondered why some groups had stayed poor for centuries.

> **Word Power**
>
> To **accommodate** poverty or any other condition is to tolerate the situation as the only alternative.

Galbraith found that poor societies *accommodate their poverty*. As hard as it is to live in poor conditions, unfortunately people find it more difficult to accept the hardship—the challenge—involved in making a better living. Hence, they accommodate their poverty, and it lingers from year to year, decade to decade, and even century to century.

Resistance Despite Awareness

You likely don't face anything like those situations mentioned above, yet the demons keeping you or your team from embracing change may be just as onerous.

When an individual *knows* and *understands* that a change will be for the better, he or she is still likely to resist for factors such as these:

➤ Embracing the change will take time and effort that the participants may not be willing to invest.

➤ Taking on something new largely means giving up something else, and that something else is familiar, comfortable, and predictable.

➤ Annoyance or fear of disruption may prohibit people from taking the first step even when it is widely acknowledged that the net result will be to their extreme benefit.

➤ If the change is imposed externally, as opposed to internally derived, resistance may endure as a result of ego-related issues.

Be Wary

People resist change most of the time, even in this era in which presumably people are already acclimated to change.

A Tale of Resistance

In 1981, I was working for a management consultant firm in the Georgetown section of Washington, D.C. We employed a staff of 40 people. At the conclusion of each consulting engagement, we had to write a report for the client. This was the most cumbersome, labor-intensive aspect of the job.

I had been in consulting for five years and had written my share of reports. I was looking for ways to do my work faster and easier. One of the staff consultants had a pocket dictator he used occasionally to dictate letters. I asked him if I could momentarily borrow it and he said, "Sure." I became proficient within about two minutes and surmised that nearly anyone could do the same. I asked him if I could borrow it for the day if he wasn't going to be using it and he said, "Go ahead."

Armed and Potent

Our office was equipped with transcription equipment, although hardly anyone knew it. I decided to dictate my very next report. I loathed writing longhand, my

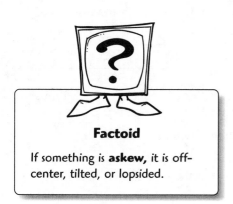

Factoid

If something is **askew,** it is off-center, tilted, or lopsided.

handwriting wasn't very good, and it took me forever. When I started using the dictation equipment, miraculous things happened.

Soon, I was able to do my job in 30 percent of the time that it used to take. Incredibly, my 40-hour workweek now only required 12 hours.

Something seemed *askew*. Here was a device that worked so well and so easily, and no one knew about it. I told my co-workers of this miraculous equipment. I suggested that everybody adopt it. I sang the virtues of dictation equipment to my boss as well. Surprisingly, nobody took me up on my suggestions to give dictation a try.

Let Resistant Dogs Lie

Everyone was attached to writing reports longhand and then submitting them for word processing. So, I became silent. I decided that I would refrain from functioning as an advocate of dictation equipment within my office. If others didn't want to accept a new way of doing things that could vastly improve their productivity and their lives, so be it. I wouldn't be stopped from excelling.

For the next three years, I used dictation equipment extensively. I dictated every single thing that I needed to write and save on computer. One of our office administrative staff transcribed the mini cassettes.

With a weekly average of 28 hours freed, I used the time to read, research, or help others in the office. I got large raises and was promoted several times during this three-year period. By 1984, I was the third-ranking professional in the company. I supervised eight people directly, was a project director as well as a project manager, and ultimately was given the title Vice President of Marketing.

It's Your Option

I could have ordered my staff to use dictation equipment, but I refrained. Instead, I conducted sessions in which I demonstrated how to use the equipment. I let everyone get familiar with it and then let them decide whether they would use dictation equipment to do their reports or revert back to longhand.

Around this time, PCs were starting to appear in offices in large numbers. Some people started typing their reports and that was a bit faster than writing, but still woefully inefficient compared to dictating.

All eight of my staff reverted back to longhand writing or, in a few cases, typing on a computer. No one had anything to do with dictation equipment except perhaps to appease me. I let it go. I knew that the productivity of my staff was less than what it could be. However, my projects were still turning out well, coming in on time and under budget. I was still getting promoted, earning bonuses, and considered a superstar in the firm.

Adopt and Win

To this day, I am amazed at the *diffidence* people show in embracing change even when given instruction, follow-up, encouragement, time to make the transition, and every other opportunity to embrace the new way of doing things.

Looking at the larger question, how many of us, throughout the day, week, or month shun alternative means of accomplishment when the advantages yield such productivity that there is no comparison to the old way? How many individuals don't want to hear about new days of proceeding in their careers and their lives in ways that would make dramatic differences?

Most of the *Breathing Space* principles contained in my book of the same name and which I discuss at my presentations will make dramatic differences in people's lives. Those who adopt *Breathing Space* principles routinely write to me, sometimes three, six, or nine months after my presentations to tell me that the benefits they have received have had a cascading effect. The benefits have increased since the time they first started adopting them.

Word Power

Diffidence is the same as reluctance or caution.

Anticipating Resistance to Change

As a change manager, you may have observed that the moment people are required to make a change in their behavior, predictable phenomena are likely to occur.

Some or all of your staff will bemoan what they have to forsake. This occurs even when they didn't like what they were doing before! People form irrational, if fleeting, attachments to the way they have been doing things.

Proceed

Even if you do not intellectually and emotionally agree with your staff's viewpoint, give them validation to their feelings. That will prove to be a most helpful gesture in inducing them to move on to what is next.

45

➤ Some of your staff will feel uncomfortable if they try to embrace the new measure.

➤ Some will feel ill at ease and perhaps actually manifest physical illness.

➤ Some may feel awkward.

Your job is to acknowledge them for the "sacrifices" that they will have to make and to commiserate with them for enduring the hardship of changing over.

To give you the experience of what it might be like for your troops, if you're wearing shoes with laces, untie one of your shoes right now. Re-tie the shoe but switch hands.

Be Wary

Even the most minor of changes has the potential to throw someone off kilter.

If you normally hold the strings with your left hand and make the bow with your right hand, hold the strings with your right hand and make the bow with your left hand. That will feel awkward.

Alternatively, if you're wearing a belt, take it off and put it on in the opposite direction, securing it at the same loop as before. You feel different, don't you? This isn't the way you wear your a change manager, you may have observed that the moment people are belt.

How long would it take you to feel comfortable tying your shoelaces the opposite way? It could be days, weeks, or even months. How about reversing the direction of you belt? You could probably adjust in a few minutes.

So it is with asking your staff to incorporate various changes. Nearly all are likely to cause some feeling of awkwardness, even if for a few moments. Some changes will have a lingering effect. Some will make your people feel self-conscious for days on end.

An effective change manager anticipates resistance at the outset of a change campaign. He or she almost welcomes resistance because it's a sign that the change process is unfolding.

Be Wary

Consider the situation in which change perceived to be burdensome, demanding, or difficult meets with little resistance on the part of those charged with executing it. If anything, such a situation would be cause for alarm, because people were masking their reactions.

Putting Your Money Where Your Mouth Is

When you understand what your troops are enduring, potentially you can be a far better manager of them. In the movie *The Battle of the Bulge*, the German commander, played by Robert Shaw, was served a lavish meal one evening. The meal came during a time when rations for his men had to be cut back. He waved away the server in effect saying, "Bring me the same level of rations that my men are receiving."

This commander understood the importance of sharing the experience that his targets of change were experiencing. He could have easily eaten the lavish meal and justified having such a feast. After all, as the commander of the troops, he would need to be mentally sharp; he would need to have the full benefits of a highly nutritious meal.

He could still empathize with the troops. He could intellectually surmise what it must be like to ingest 40 percent of one's normal caloric intake. He could *postulate* on the ramifications of lower levels of proteins in their diet. He could talk with others about calorie deprivation. Perhaps he could read about it, make notes, and even plot a course of action.

Word Power

To **postulate** is to surmise, assume, or guess.

None of these maneuvers, however, would give him the insights that would naturally accrue as a result of him having the same meal that they had.

You and Your Targets

What about you? Are you prepared to have the same meal as your targets of change? Or are you going to rationalize the situation, claiming that you have the intellectual and emotional capacity to empathize with their experience? The old adage, "Do as I say, not as I do," can be the death knell for the change manager who erroneously believes that he has extended capacity for understanding the blight of others.

As mottos go, "Walk a mile in my moccasins" and "Practice what you preach" are far more cogent.

Change from Afar

If you are managing people who are reporting to you from different locations, chances are that each participant is going to feel as if he or she is incurring the change alone! Managing change is challenging enough when a group meets at the same location. It is magnified when targets of change report in from somewhere else via e-mail, phone, and fax.

Under such a scenario, your task is to be more supportive and available than you would otherwise presume that you would have to be.

You may be the only sounding board for individuals experiencing tumult. If they haven't been participants in a change campaign before, at least knowingly, then they

Factoid

People going through an ordeal together generally are better able to cope with the rigors of the experience than those going through it alone.

Word Power

Reintegration means reassimilation or reconsolidation.

are likely to feel as if their burden is unique. "Nobody understands the trouble I've seen." This is all the more reason to periodically convene the group so that they can share their observations and insights.

One Is the Loneliest Number

When U.S. troops began returning from World War II, they were assembled in large numbers, consigned to ships, and over several months, slowly sailed home. During the time on board, they got to reflect with one another, and mentally and emotionally prepare themselves for *reintegration* into civilian society.

Conversely, U.S. troops departing from the Vietnam War came home one at a time, injured or in a hurry. They came via jet planes that transported them in less than 24 hours from a hellish environment back to the world they had left. There was little or no transition time, no camaraderie with people who had shared a like experience, no time to mentally and emotionally prepare for reentry into the civilian world.

The World War II vets came home, got married, had children, and bought houses. The Vietnam vets often couldn't have relationships, even with themselves, and incurred a high rate of drug abuse and suicides.

United We Stand

Analysis of plane crash survivors in remote locations or people simply stuck for hours on elevators indicate that their respective blights were lessened because of the companionship.

Conversely, it takes a rare individual to succeed alone in the face of disruptive change. Following World War II, periodically lone soldiers emerged who had been stranded on remote islands for 10 or 12 years, believing that the battles were still ongoing. Now we know that such real-world survivors are a unique breed. They are able to survive without one of the most comforting aspects of an ordeal—the capability to commiserate with others.

Fortunately, your staff members have you to guide them through their darkest hours.

Inducing Commitment

If there were no such thing as resistance, people could commit in a nanosecond. Whatever plans you laid out, once understood, could be acted upon swiftly. Daryl Conner sees commitment and resistance as two sides of the same coin.

A High Initial Outlay

Initially, your time and energy investment to en-sure commitment is high.

If you don't take work to build commitment (see Chapter 10, "Preparing Your Team for Change") at least at first, it will seem as if you have gotten a free ride. Resistance among your staff doesn't seem to be significant. Wait a moment! As the campaign proceeds, resistance mounts. Now, any efforts that you make to shore up commitment need to be far greater than at the outset, had you recognized the importance of securing commitment early on.

As the project commences, you can maintain com-mitment with relatively less strenuous efforts if you made strident efforts to maintain it at the out-set.

> **Be Wary**
>
> If you don't do all that you can to ensure commitment early in the campaign, then resistance is sure to rear its head, and make you pay in ways that are far more taxing than the efforts you need to take at the outset to increase commitment.

Who Wants to Pay the Price?

Why don't more change managers pay the price of securing commitment early? For one, it's a huge task, and implementation can be exceedingly slow. It can feel as if you are not getting anywhere. Also, some change managers are lulled into thinking that resistance simply won't be a significant factor later on in the campaign.

Conner says that securing commitment among targets early on wins "bodies and souls," whereas failing to do so may win "bodies but not souls."

Conner points out that "many times, the way people are approached—rather than the change itself—is what causes resistance." He's observed that targets are likely to respond in such situations by saying things like the change itself wasn't so bad, but the way it was foisted upon them ruffled a lot of feathers.

Slow Down

One of the paradoxes of initiating a change cam-paign in light of the need to secure commitment and ward off anticipated resistance is that often the first thing that you need to do is slow down.

> **Change Master**
>
> A successful change manager is willing to make efforts to de-velop strong commitment posi-tions to his or her team and indeed his or her entire cam-paign for project success rather than simply gaining compliance, which ultimately may be fleeting.

You temporarily slow down to manage a campaign that will unfold at a rapid pace. In my book *Breathing Space: Living and Working at a Comfortable Pace in a Sped-Up Society*, I discuss the concept of slowing down at length and how a variety of career and life benefits accrue.

By slowing down you open up the possibility of developing synergistic working relationships, better communication, and more involvement among staff. While it is natural for change managers to jump into a campaign and want to be at full speed in short order, the reality proven throughout the ages is that the most effective change campaigns often start at a measured, deliberately slow pace. By starting at a slow pace, the change at hand can be approached and ultimately incorporated at an accelerated pace.

The Least You Need to Know

➤ The resistance people exhibit when they're confronted by change is derived in part from fear of the unknown.

➤ When you understand what your troops are enduring, potentially you can be a far better manager of them.

➤ Managing change is challenging enough when a group meets at the same location. It is magnified when targets of change report in from yonder.

➤ If you don't do all that you can to ensure commitment early in the campaign, resistance is sure to rear its head.

➤ To secure commitment and ward off anticipated resistance, often the first thing to do is slow down.

Chapter 5

Stay Sane, Manage the Pain

In This Chapter

➤ Campaigning for change

➤ Crossing the pain threshold

➤ Avoiding the pain of a spectacular failure

➤ Dispensing pain in small measures

➤ Understanding the need for pain management

In my earlier book, *The Complete Idiot's Guide to Reinventing Yourself,* I defined personal reinvention as a departure from what came before or a notable embellishment of something already in place. Reinvention includes getting started on the new you; getting your mind in gear for change; renewing your physical self; or revitalizing your career, your relationships, and other aspects of your life.

Moving from Point A to Point B

Within a company, change can be defined in much the same way. You want to move from Point A to Point B. Point A is where you are. Point B is the desired outcome that you want to achieve, or that's been imposed on you. For confronting significant, challenging, disruptive change—the kind that we've discussed in this book—the process can't be left to chance.

You increase your success of moving from Point A to Point B by effectively managing a change campaign. During the campaign, many things are in transition. People don't feel comfortable—they resist. The change campaign represents upset for many people; it is a departure from what they were doing.

Proceed

The effective change manager helps people adopt new operating procedures, exhibit new behaviors, and develop new attitudes that all support progress toward the desired outcome.

Be Wary

In business, many companies want to keep offering the product or service that has brought them healthy profits in the past. Yet, as competition strives to offer superior products or services, and as the marketplace becomes more aware of opportunities to upgrade products and services, there is simply no standing still.

In *Managing at the Speed of Change*, Daryl Conner notes that keeping a change campaign moving forward "is only possible when the pain of the present state exceeds the cost of the transition state." For example, it would be exceedingly costly to abandon your car if it were stuck on a railroad track. As a train approaches, it would be even more costly to not abandon the car!

Is it expensive to develop new products or services, particularly on a continuing basis? You bet. However, it is more expensive to stay where you are.

Moving On in Discomfort

Even when people fully, intellectually embrace the need to change, the tendency to slip back to what they were previously doing is powerful. The keystrokes you're familiar with or the buttons you used to push no longer get the desired results. What's worse, you're not sure what will give that result.

Change managers—and by osmosis, targets of change—who are most effective in executing a change campaign, understand and accept the need to *move on* even when it's uncomfortable.

Pain Is a Great Motivator

In *Awaken the Giant Within,* Tony Robbins contends that personal pain management is the greatest single motivator for people to achieve what they want. By extension, pain management applied to a change team may be the greatest single motivator for the group to achieve the desired objective.

Robbins suggests that after deciding what you truly want, determine what's preventing you from having it now. Then get leverage by associating massive pain with maintaining the status quo and massive pleasure with experiencing the desired change now.

Unless you associate sufficient amounts of pain with your current situation, in a week, a month, or a year you will find yourself right where you started. You likely will be surrounded by all of the unpleasant aspects of your current situation, because you won't muster sufficient impetus to break through the transition state to get to the desired end result.

Passing Along the Pain

Since change campaigns are initiated by sponsors, and sponsors inherently feel some level of pain, it behooves the sponsor to convey an appropriate level of pain to the change manager, who will then convey such to the change targets. If an organization, department, or team seeks to change because they will lose out on a fun or interesting opportunity otherwise, will the level of pain be sufficient? In most cases, the answer is "no."

If failing to make a change will result in some minor upset, hurt feelings, or other temporary negative situation, then once again, the pain level is insufficient to stage a change campaign that will be carried all the way through to the desired end.

Crossing the Pain Threshold

What, then, constitutes appropriate and sufficient pain? How much is enough to motivate a sponsor to initiate change, to cause a change manager to feel the heat, and to pass on the intensity to the targets of change on whom the responsibility falls? As it turns out, the answer is not crystal clear. Pain is subjective. The amount of pain and the form it takes impact people differently.

Frustration or Dissatisfaction

The owner of an underachieving baseball team who is frustrated with the team's performance and is dissatisfied with being the "cellar-dwellers" of the league has sufficient incentive to make drastic changes. A new manager is hired. Expensive trades are in the works to get top players.

Be Wary

Your reflexive action in the face of change is to gravitate back to what did work—the old software. At least you knew where you stood when you pushed this button versus that one.

Proceed

When considering any goal, Tony Robbins says, you have to consider where you are as *intolerable*, a place where you *simply cannot stay.*

Be Wary

Personally, as well as group-wide, if the level of pain is not high enough, there will be no change.

There is usually more off-season trading among clubs who did poorly than among those who did well, except in the case of clubs located in media centers such as New York and Los Angeles where revenues are always high, and they are always able to go out and get the best players. In basketball, during the heyday of the Chicago Bulls, the nucleus of the team remained intact for several years. Only the role players seemed to come and go.

In our baseball example, perhaps the owner feels he isn't getting sufficient support from the fans, and that by moving his ball club to a more attractive location, he could enjoy a larger fan base and more revenues, and hence better players could be obtained.

Factoid

In the business world, frustration and dissatisfaction can show up as a result of loss of market share, loss of industry position, and even loss of prestige.

Fear and Anxiety

Never underestimate the power of fear as a motivator to change. Psychologists will tell you that following a person's divorce, he or she has the greatest incentive to get back into shape if more than a "few pounds" have been added over the years. The newly divorced person fears that he or she will not attract a mate commensurate with his or her desires.

While married, this person may have had little incentive to shed pounds. Once back in the singles' market, the pounds come off relatively easily compared to any previous weight reduction campaign.

Proceed

An organization-wide fear can be harnessed by sponsors and change managers to great effect. It is not as if they brought about the situation, but they sure can make use of what has occurred.

So, too, organizations that fear for their viability as a result of virtually any stimulus are inherently primed for change. Initiating sponsors have fewer hurdles to clear to get a change campaign in place. Sustaining sponsors more readily have the ear of change managers, who, in turn, more readily have the attention and participation of staff.

Surprise or Shock

Sometimes pain comes all at once:

➤ The advertising agency that loses a major account that had sustained the firm for years.

➤ The manufacturer who faces a crippling lawsuit when environmentalists bring an airtight case to court.

➤ The airline CEO who discovers his major competitor has just acquired another airline and now will easily dominate in several key markets.

Sudden pain is often the hardest for firms to contend with. The immediate inclination is to "do something" and to do it right away.

The Growing Realization

This form of pain falls some place between frustration and dissatisfaction and shock and surprise. It is a growing realization that one's competitive advantage is slipping away—the plant has been operating for too long above optimal capacity, or the level of customer complaints is rising. This pain can be the hardest to deal with. Initiating sponsors of change campaigns hope that with a modification here and a twist there, problems will subside.

Sometimes, a growing realization not dealt with at the appropriate time turns into full-fledged frustration or dissatisfaction, and in some cases, even into shock. However, it could be argued that the situation should never have been allowed to progress that far.

If a company is going to lose major market share or profitability, or otherwise bid farewell to what it regards as vital, then the pain level is sufficiently high. If failing to change will result in a situation in which a company will not be able to survive, surely the pain level is sufficient.

Be Wary

No one likes to be caught flat-footed, but even with the best of ongoing intelligence reporting, sometimes it happens. Such situations call for measured response, not knee-jerk reaction. Often, the reaction further exacerbates the problem.

Proceed

It is the job of top managers, the sponsors, to initiate change campaigns as soon as they feel, or even anticipate, sufficient pain.

Avoiding the Pain of Failing Spectacularly

It's one thing to fail on a project, but it's quite another to fail spectacularly, lose lives, and have the whole world seemingly come down on you. This is what happened to project teams at NASA. In 1986, when the *Challenger* shuttle exploded barely a minute after launch, the agency was at a low point. Internal investigators, congressional reviewers, newspaper reporters, and legions of bystanders all wanted to know what went wrong.

A few years later, when the *Hubble* space telescope was launched and proved to have serious, if fixable, refraction problems, the entire agency was again under intense scrutiny.

Overlooking Simple Solutions

In both instances, NASA engineers overlooked relatively simple technological solutions to potential problems. If pain is the mother of change, then NASA had plenty of it. Criticism of the agency was widespread. A new management team was assembled to refocus the agency and individual departments on the need for total quality.

An office of continual improvement was created for the sole purpose of educating NASA teams, well, continually. Following the *Challenger* explosion and the technical problems of the *Hubble* space telescope, a dramatic shift in attitude developed among the remaining workforce throughout the agency.

Be Wary

Waiting too long to initiate change can be fatal. If a company decides to make a 180-degree turn, after the competition has a tremendous lead, the marketplace has shifted, and technology has been upgraded, the pain may be extraordinary and felt all the way down to the lowest levels of an organization. Yet no magnitude of change campaign may be sufficient to salvage the situation.

Forsaking Power Plays

People were far less interested in maintaining group or social identity, or individual agendas or power plays. They were also engaging in other behavior that didn't add to the agency's overall mission. The energy and intensity that fueled the Apollo Project in the 1960s and '70s started to become evident. Maintaining the status quo and the accompanying paralysis that emerged were regarded for what they were: barriers to the agency's continued existence, let alone to the accomplishments of its missions.

"I Feel Your Pain"

As a change manager, you're called on by a sponsor who is in a position to either feel or anticipate pain that necessitates change. From that standpoint, your immediate quest is to understand the pain, real or anticipated, on the level that your sponsor experiences it. That gives you the best chance of having sufficient motivation for seeing the project through to completion, not withstanding your own professionalism, which would prompt you to strive for success simply as a function of the change campaign being assigned to you!

Change Master

You know you're in deep trouble when you're part of Jay Leno's nightly opening monologue.

The change campaign to which you have been assigned is hopefully one that will not only alleviate the pain for now, but will also result in a solution or solutions that keep pain from recurring in the foreseeable future.

Dispensing Pain in Measured Intervals

Often, a sponsor needs to develop pain management techniques to ensure that those involved in the change campaign will stay sufficiently motivated. As a change manager, you may find yourself practicing some of the same pain management measures as a sponsor.

For example, the sponsor may issue proclamations, memos, and reports that indicate potential doom "unless ...." The sponsor may also make personal appearances at timed intervals to keep the troops on high alert.

Here are some phenomena that are likely to arise and you have to be ready for:

> ➤ **Anticipate predictable slumps.** There are intervals within a change campaign when some of the troops drop back a little, proceeding at three-quarters speed. This can be acceptable at the outset of a project (as discussed in Chapter 15, "Scheduling Days of Grace"), when you have a slower pace in mind for project participants as part of your overall project plan. Beware, however, that a slower pace when you weren't planning on it spells trouble.

> ➤ **Count on mysterious forces.** The universe works in mysterious ways. When the pain of remaining where you are is sufficiently high to set in motion a change campaign, counterforces seem to arise. A few days after the start of a glorious change campaign, a setback will inevitably occur. Some new equipment doesn't arrive, someone is pulled off the team, the desired budget for the campaign is

Change Master

An organization-wide or team-level setback can prove to be fatal, or it can be a rallying point from which people decide to aspire to the heights they know they have the ability to reach. In NASA's case, the setbacks proved to be catalysts for the agency's transformation.

Proceed

Not all change campaigns are so vital to an organization that failure to achieve the desired outcome would likely result in the decline of the organization. Nevertheless, that is the attitude with which you want to proceed—that successful resolution of the challenge at hand is vital to the continuing viability of your organization.

reduced, and so on. It's almost as if you are being asked to fight a battle, and soon after you get started, you're asked to fight with one hand tied behind your back. The enthusiasm at the start of the campaign wanes, and now the desired end result seems quite distant.

Change Master

Timing the release of pain-inducing tools is less manipulation and more an indication of a profound understanding of human nature. The practitioner indicates that he has what it takes to keep a campaign in high gear as the energy and interest of the campaign staff wane, and while distractions and competing elements within the workplace increase.

Be Wary

Don't assume that simply presenting the facts in a logical way will be enough to win people over. Paradoxically, most people need to be emotionally affected before they engage in logical behavior.

➤ **Stock your arsenal.** To combat the problems of uneven performance by staff during a change campaign, some change managers maintain an arsenal of pain management tools to be used at appropriate intervals. Rather than announcing all at once the potential consequences of not proceeding from Point A to Point B, sometimes it makes sense to dispense a few of them here, a few later, and a few more later still.

➤ **Get a clear view of your pain.** In *The Path of Least Resistance*, Robert Fritz says that you can create a split-screen image of where you are and where you want to be that creates what he calls structural tension. Visualize the movie screen of your life and then split the screen into a top half and bottom half. The bottom of the screen is how things are now—stressful, anxiety-provoking, or undesirable. At the top of the screen, envision how you would like the situation to be. Get a clear view of this. By envisioning both your current state and your desired state, the inherent structural tension of having these competing visualizations "on screen" at the same time helps to move you in the direction of your desired state.

The Need for Pain Management

Do you really need to resort to pain management? After all, if your team has the facts laid out for them, won't that be sufficient for them to take action, stay on course, and see the project to its completion? No, no, a thousand times no.

President Jimmy Carter would often analyze an issue at length and, when he was ready to make a presentation to Congress or the American people, he was highly prepared. He carefully presented facts and figures. The strategies that he offered for overcoming a particular problem were presented with the skill of a mathematician or a logician. Perhaps a few highly intellectual types responded to such presentations, but most people did not.

Head Follows Heart

People want to be reached emotionally. Then they are more amenable to respond to a rational argument. Head follows heart, not the other way around. If you don't appeal to people's hearts, you are not likely to get to their heads, and thus, you are not likely to have an impact.

As you'll see in Chapter 6, "The Rational-Empirical Approach," only a small portion of the population ever takes action based on the sheer logic of the situation. It seems a little convoluted, but that is human nature. It is also an ironic aspect of our evolution. Do we need to be in a crisis situation before we take action?

What if the crisis is so bad that by the time we take action it is already too late? Could the hole in the ozone, the greenhouse effect, and global warming already be progressing at rates that have sealed our fate? We won't know for another couple of years, although big oil interests will ensure that between now and when we truly know, a ton of verbiage is printed that says "there is no problem with the environment."

Err on the Side of Caution

While there is "genius in boldness" (as you'll see in Chapter 19, "Staying Flexible in Your Plans"), in this case, the prudent manager would err on the side of caution. If there is even a chance that we could be irreparably damaging the environment and putting future generations in peril, let's take action now. Once again, this is not the way that human nature works.

Sufficient numbers of people would have to be experiencing considerable pain now before swift, massive, and effective action would ever be taken. This is why the process of voting in a free society is so important. Hopefully, we elect leaders who have the vision and foresight to rally the populace years in advance of when a situation would become dire.

Calling the turns is always a critical capability (as discussed in Chapter 27, "Tomorrow Will Be

Change Master

In your own organization, if you never become a sponsor, your ability to appropriately induce sufficient levels of pain will help ensure your viability and promotability within your organization.

Different"). Anybody can make linear projections, that is, predict more of the same, and often be right. The rare professional who can accurately call the turns, who can say the market or the perceived value of the product or service is changing, is the person whose services will continue to be in high demand.

The Least You Need to Know

➤ Keeping a change campaign moving forward "is only possible when the pain of the present state exceeds the cost of the transition state."

➤ Even when people fully, intellectually embrace the need to change, the tendency to slip back to what they were previously doing is powerful.

➤ Your quest is to understand the pain, real or anticipated, on the level that your sponsor experiences it.

➤ To combat uneven performance, maintain an arsenal of pain management tools to be used at appropriate intervals.

➤ Most people need to be impacted emotionally before they engage in logical behavior.

Part 2

The Four Approaches to Change Management

Every organizational culture is different, but by classifying change environments into categories, you have a better chance of devising an appropriate change management plan. In this part, I will discuss four basic notions of how people behave. Each chapter offers a singular view of how people interact and proceed in this world.

In everyday life, people tend to embrace portions of each of the four behavioral styles discussed in this part. However, it's still highly useful to understand the behavioral styles in their pure forms—as you manage a change campaign and interact with sponsors, advocates, targets, bystanders, and well-wishers, you have a mental template for assessing where people are coming from.

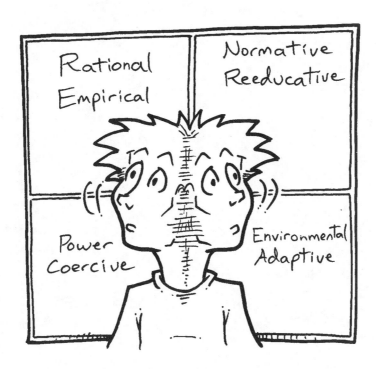

That's "Empirical", not "Imperial"...

Chapter 6

The Rational–Empirical Approach

> ## In This Chapter
>
> ➤ Becoming a master of persuasion
>
> ➤ The two primary tasks of the change manager
>
> ➤ Communicating with your staff
>
> ➤ The art of listening
>
> ➤ Establishing incentives that prompt action

Do you feel that people are rational and have the capability, intelligence, and where-withal to enhance their own self-interests? The rational-empirical approach to change management—don't let the high-minded term scare you—is based on the belief that there are predictable behaviors of people, and that they pay particular attention to their own self-interests. Understanding this type of behavior gives the change manager a workable strategy for proceeding.

Some proponents of this approach believe that change targets are wrapped up in superstitions, half-truths, and ignorance, while nevertheless maintaining rationality. Change targets will follow their self-interest if it is revealed to them—which means, of course, that often they don't know what's best for them.

Whether or not you take this more cynical view, the fundamentals of the rational-empirical approach remain the same. People will change when they receive effective, informative communication and when the incentives for change are sufficient.

Becoming a Master of Persuasion

A change manager who wants to effectively use the rational-empirical approach to change needs to become a master of persuasion, honing the ability to convince people that a change is good for them. If someone was using a particular type of software, for example, and was now asked to upgrade to an objectively faster, more powerful software that would *engender* higher profitability for the organization, the ever-present tendency to resist still needs to be dealt with!

Word Power

To **engender** something is to help produce, bring about, or make it so.

Change Master

Overall, the rational–empirical approach might require a little more planning and effort compared to, say, the power-coercive approach (which is discussed in Chapter 8, "The Power-Coercive Approach"). The effects, however, are likely to be more pronounced, long-lasting, and internalized, as the targets of change are able to ultimately conclude on their own that adopting the new software made sense.

Explain, Demonstrate, and Train

Explaining how the new software would handle current challenges more quickly and easily, allow for greater flexibility, and accommodate anticipated changes in operations would be the first order of business.

Then, you would give such workers a hands-on opportunity to work with the software, ask questions, get immediate feedback, and gain a level of comfortable familiarity.

You might devise comprehensive training sessions, secure a mentor or coach for one-on-one counseling, and hold a team-wide forum. You might take such a person to view the software in use someplace else in the organization, talk to people who have used it and swear by it, or read testimonials that attest to its great value.

The Great Persuader

In *How to Have a Good Year Every Year,* author Dave Yoho explains that how you use language determines your ability to persuade. "Many words and phrases, because of misuse and overuse, are not persuasive; instead they tend to neutralize otherwise effective interaction," says Yoho. "Overused words, such as personal references (I, me, my) and meaningless adjectives (fantastic, fabulous), are often neutralizers or turn-offs."

Yoho writes, "Persuasion is how you use language to ensure that someone's experience is pleasant and comfortable enough that he will be willing to accept what you would like him to do within your environment." He emphasizes that to persuade someone to do something requires finding out what he likes to do and showing him a way in which he receives what he wants through your medium.

"This is true whether you are selling steamships or ideas," Yoho says. "If I can learn enough about you, where you're headed and what your needs are, then I can show you ways to get what you want, and if it's through my medium, fine."

The Power of Expertise

As a change manager employing the rational-empirical approach, you also need to harness the power of expertise. If you are already a master of using the new software or can call in others who are, you help accelerate the staff's potential to embrace the new software.

People have a natural inclination to respond favorably when they perceive they are interacting with an expert. Resistance levels drop. The potential for participation and even enthusiasm increases. Hey, it's a confusing, over-communicated world out there, and the opportunity to work with and benefit from an expert is often regarded as a welcome experience.

Change Master

Expertise in a given discipline is often underrated in terms of its ability to impact others. If you are an expert on the topic at hand and you can convey your know-how, you are primed to being more persuasive to those who could learn from you than someone who is just getting up to speed himself.

Leading a Two-Headed Mission

While the rational-empirical approach holds that people will pay homage to their own self-interests, two primary tasks emerge for the change manager who wants to embark on this approach:

1. Effectively communicating why the change at hand will be in the target's best interest. The next few pages will focus on that particular issue.

2. Establishing incentives to hasten the target's pace at incorporating the new change. I'll tackle establishing incentives later in this chapter.

It's for Your Own Good

In all communications to your staff, particularly at the outset of a change campaign, strive for concreteness and specificity. Avoid buzzwords and jargon. Your staff is already overloaded by more information and communication coming at them on a daily basis than they ever presumed they'd face.

Catch phrases can be effective once a campaign is in full swing and staff has been fully indoctrinated. At the outset and periodically throughout a campaign, the most effective means of communicating what needs changed and why it's in the best interest of those participating is done through specific words and phrases. When you say such statements as:

➤ We need to improve relations.

➤ We need to become more responsive.

➤ We need to focus more on the customer …

… and so on, such statements have little power. What do such statements actually mean? How do they translate into action to be taken on the part of your staff and benefits that they will derive as a result of participating on this campaign?

Your task is to offer concrete, action-based, quantifiable goals that lead to the desired end result. Each task and subtask needs to relate to the larger good that you're seeking to create. Likewise, each of the assignments that your staff is to handle needs to be presented so the staff person understands:

➤ Why it is in his or her best interest to complete a given subtask.

➤ What needs to be done to complete the task.

➤ How the subtask leads to one or more of the major steps.

➤ How the tasks lead to the completion of the change campaign.

➤ What he or she must do to guarantee that the subtask yields the desired end result.

Be Wary

When adhering to the rational-empirical approach, lingering on critical issues that your staff needs to hear is a form of gambling that you don't want to undertake.

Paint the Picture for Them

Show your staff how what they do fits into the overall picture. Convey to them how it is going to be when you've moved from Point A to Point B. Offer rational explanations while being cognizant of the need to also appeal to their emotions (as discussed in Chapter 7, "The Normative-Reeducative Approach.")

Bring in the Heavy Artillery

Perhaps you need to bring in others, particularly at the outset of a campaign, to communicate the larger vision. This may involve summoning an initiating or sustaining sponsor, someone else within the organization who has knowledge of the mission, or even an outside consultant or expert.

For example, sometimes professional speakers are brought in to motivate the troops at sales rallies or new product launches, during a merger or acquisition, or at other critical junctures. Such speakers are actually serving as adjunct change agents supporting your overall efforts and giving you a third-party communication boost that often can't otherwise be duplicated.

No Time to Linger

Since time is of the essence for many change campaigns, your communication strategy needs to be in place at the outset. Particularly for high-resistance campaigns, the more information you can impart and the sooner, the greater the odds that you will gain the support, commitment, and possibly enthusiasm of your staff.

No change manager is a perfect communicator. The timing, frequency, scope, and impact of your messages may be flawed based on the real needs of your staff. Keep at it just the same. Do your best, and by and by, most if not all of the staff is likely to come around.

Using a Mixed Bag of Communication Tools

Is it okay to use a variety of communication tools in conveying the self-interest benefits to your staff? Yes. In-person, face-to-face communication is best and provides the most immediate feedback, but memos either in hard copy or via e-mail, and campaign charts, graphs, and other reports can be effective as supporting communication tools.

Instead of sending 10 e-mails in two weeks, why not record your message on cassette or burn it on a CD-ROM, and circulate a copy to each of your staff members? Another time, you could employ a short video. Yet another time, you could send each person a snail-mail letter.

Even the best-written, most effective e-mails can seem sterile to those who have received too many e-mails, many of which don't seem to be that different from one another.

Be Wary

If you find yourself relying exclusively on circulated memos or e-mail, you might want to re-think your strategy. People grow tired of too many communiqués via the same channel.

Change Master

Each form of communication provides another way of reaching staff members who may have temporarily become distracted or tuned out.

Leaving the Door Wide Open

Embarking on the rational-empirical approach necessitates that you give staff-wide leeway in the ability to share their concerns. By maintaining an open-door policy, or at least as "open a door" as you can, encouraging questions, and inviting your staff to be candid with you, you increase the rate at which they buy into the changes while decreasing resistance.

Be Wary

Many managers believe themselves to be open and approachable. If you were to survey their staffs you'd learn otherwise.

Mark Henderson is the president of a small company that produces educational CD-ROMs. He proclaims an open-door policy, encouraging his staff to come see him "any time you want." Although Henderson professes an open-door policy, he creates an atmosphere in company staff meetings indicating that he loathes all intrusions.

When Katie, a new employee, knocks on his door with a suggestion that could accelerate progress on a change campaign, Henderson thanks her and quickly ushers her out of his office. She waits long to hear any word about her suggestion.

Henderson figuratively slammed his open door in Katie's face by not showing interest and not providing any feedback, good or bad.

Poor Results Among Themselves

Top managers often rate communication among themselves as their principal area of difficulty—more problematic than handling conflicts among staff, holding better meetings, or making decisions. If managers find it difficult to have probing, problem-solving conversations among themselves, imagine how much more difficult it is for them to communicate effectively with team members on a change campaign.

Word Power

De facto means how something is, independent of laws, formal rules, or written guidelines.

Open communication, the kind that helps maintain committed staff and probably helps the profit sheet as well, is the kind that makes workers feel they have a stake. Face-to-face meetings are the best, since they allow the most possibilities for dialogue.

Open or Closed Communication?

To determine if your *de facto* communication style is open- or closed-door, ask yourself the following questions:

➤ Do I encourage my team to make suggestions?

➤ Do I give feedback when I get a suggestion? Immediate feedback as well as long-term feedback?

➤ Do I show a genuine interest in my staff or do I simply tolerate them?

➤ Do I provide a clear picture of where the campaign is heading and how each team member fits into the picture?

If your organization has a pattern of open communication, take advantage of every opportunity to learn from others who are adept at it. If the pattern is closed, do your best to be an island of enlightenment.

Practicing the Art of Good Listening

Some managers regard themselves as effective listeners, yet most people throughout society, managers included, are not good listeners.

"Active listening carries a strong element of personal risk," says psychologist and author Carl Rogers. "To sense deeply the feeling of another person, to understand the meaning that certain experiences have for him or her, to see the world as he or she sees it, we risk being changed ourselves."

"It is threatening to give up, even momentarily, what we believe and start thinking in someone else's terms," say the authors. "It takes a great deal of inner security and courage to be able to risk one's self in understanding another."

Listening Is a Big Part of Our Lives

Although we learn how to read, speak, and write as children, and are encouraged to hone these skills throughout our lives, we rarely, if ever, receive any formal training in listening nor do we pay attention to its importance in our lives. Yet, people spend nearly half of their communication time listening.

One of the greatest courtesies you can give to a team member is to be a better listener. In working with others, listening takes on an added measure of importance. After all, to meet tough challenges and critical deadlines, and stay within budget, you need to work as effectively and efficiently as possible much of the time. Being a good listener is effective and efficient.

Proceed

Good listening is an active, complex process that takes knowledge of a few basic tenets and lots of practice. In a professional or personal relationship, it pays to sharpen your listening skills.

Openness Yields Openness

Active listening involves taking in the words of the speaker and seeking to grasp the facts and feeling behind them. Active listeners respond in a conversation by stating their impression of what the other person is saying. Psychotherapists have long used this technique because it reassures the patient that the therapist understands, and it encourages the person to open up.

Here's a long list of actions, not just words, to encourage your staff to open up to you fully—because you're open to them!

➤ Welcome their suggestions even if you don't like the suggestions.

➤ Occasionally have lunch together, as equals.

➤ Help them to be their best, but don't expect them to be perfect.

➤ Take what they say at face value—believe them.

➤ Trust in them, and demonstrate your trust.

➤ Acknowledge them when they've accepted a tough challenge.

➤ Strive to be as fair and consistent with them as you possibly can be.

➤ Show enthusiasm when you see them.

➤ Maintain any promises you make, however big, however small.

➤ Answer their questions as completely as you can.

➤ Let them take the lead in areas where they have the most competence.

➤ Offer praise, recognition, and reward immediately following a good performance.

➤ Now and then, ask them about themselves.

Establishing Incentives That Prompt Action

Should you chose to embark on the rational-empirical approach, following effective communications, a major responsibility is to establish incentives among your staff that prompt action.

People tend to follow their self-interest once it is revealed to them but as Professor Warren Bennis has observed, deep-seated change is based on the communication of information and "the proffering of incentives." Stated bluntly, people want to know what is in it for them—what are the tangible and intangible rewards of embarking on the path that they have been asked to take.

The Stake in My Heart

In recent years the concept of stakeholder has gained popularity. A stakeholder is a person or party who has a stake in an organization. Something is at risk and hence there is something to be gained or lost. Stakeholders of a corporation encompass investors, the board of directors, top managers, middle managers, and employees. Others may include suppliers, creditors, advisors, partners, and joint ventures.

Your team members need to regard the success of a project as inextricably linked to their own success. You want the goals and objectives as you have outlined them to be understood by the staff, embraced, and ultimately internalized—that is, regarded as if they created them themselves.

Goals from External Sources

There's a common misperception that a goal you undertake has to be your own, devised by you, set by you, and pursued by you. This is untrue. Studies have shown that it's entirely possible for one person to set goals for another and to have the entire process work. In fact, in sales organizations, every day sales managers develop quotas for the sales staff.

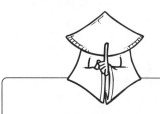

Change Master

Your quest as a change manager working with a team is to involve each team member in the change campaign in such a way that each regards him- or herself as stakeholders.

The key element here is to have the person for whom the goal is set adopt the goals as his or her own. This is welcome news for parents, managers, or anyone else who has the inherent or mandated responsibility for the performance of others!

Incentives That Tap Internal Wants

The issue of what incentives to offer and when to offer them is poorly dealt with in management texts. One of the best sources of information on how to identify and employ incentives is *Bringing Out the Best in People* by Dr. Aubrey Daniels.

Daniels's main thesis is rooted in the fundamentals of behavioral psychology— behavior that is rewarded, especially directly following performance, is repeated. The rewards need to be related to the interests of the individual being rewarded. This is where the challenge comes in.

No two people are "turned on" by exactly the same set of rewards. Among the many possible incentives you can offer project staff, these may be popular:

➤ Flexible hours

➤ Company-wide recognition for tasks performed well

➤ Preference in task assignments

➤ Tickets to cultural or sporting events

➤ Letters of praise or commendation

➤ Time off with pay

➤ Preference regarding equipment

➤ Elevated job title

Dr. Daniels's approach makes sense because the stakeholders of any entity, particularly of your change management team, differ widely in their skills, background, training viewpoints, and dispositions. To employ a cookie-cutter approach to incentives is analogous to believing that everyone likes the same foods, the same movies, the same books, or the same pastimes.

Depending on the size and diversity of the members of your team, the approach you take could vary widely between one participant and the next!

The Least You Need to Know

➤ People will change when they receive effective, informative communication, and when the incentives for change are sufficient.

➤ How you use language determines your ability to persuade. In all communications to your staff, particularly at the outset of a change campaign, strive for concreteness and specificity.

➤ Show your staff how what they do fits into the overall picture. Convey to them how it is going to be when you've moved from Point A to Point B.

➤ Good listening is an active, complex process that takes knowledge of a few basic tenets and lots of practice.

➤ Behavior that is rewarded, especially directly following performance, is repeated.

The Normative-Reeducative Approach

If you're a change manager working with staff members and you need them to behave in certain ways, how exactly do you get them to do so? Do you explain to them what they need to be doing? Do you punish them if they can't respond appropriately?

This chapter gets a little heady, but stay with it! Throughout much of the twentieth century, a variety of theories were proposed on how to get people to change. One of the most popular was championed by Kurt Lewin, who is regarded today as a pioneer in what is called *reeducation*.

Lewin was a German Jew who had to flee from Germany before World War II. Both his parents were executed in concentration camps. Lewin's education and training as a philosopher of science, combined with his horrendous experiences as a young man in Nazi Germany, gave him a perspective that few others had. Lewin was a strong advocate for employing the scientific method when it came to any investigation of human endeavor.

The Granddaddy of Problem-Solving

The six steps of the scientific method represent the essence of effective problem-solving. What more methodical, objective procedure could one use to obtain an answer to a nagging question?

1. **Step 1 is observation.** Here, you use all of your five senses. You observe the situation or problem at hand and begin to formulate certain questions.

2. **Step 2 is asking questions.** Specifically, you want to know how and why things occur. The scientist keeps a record of his questions and takes notes as he seeks to answer them. Soon enough, he has enough observations to state a problem in specific terms. This step also involves conducting research. Here, you learn what others have discovered in relation to your problem.

3. **Step 3 is formulation of a hypothesis.** You make an educated guess about the solution to the problem you have identified. Many scientists and researchers keep a journal in both formulating problem statements and formulating hypotheses. In its simplest form, formulating a hypothesis is ruminating on the answer to a question.

4. **Step 4 is experimentation.** This step includes visualizing different ways you could test your hypothesis. Sketch out procedures or possible experiments that will help you to test your hypothesis. You may have to run the procedure several times to ensure that you have accounted for possible variables.

5. **Step 5 is gathering and recording results and compiling data.** All the while, you want to make precise measurements and accurately record them. Later, you are going to analyze your data and attempt to come up with conclusions. Seek to remain as unbiased as possible. Simply record what you see; don't try to interpret or shade the results so that the results "work out" the way you want them to.

6. **Step 6 is the conclusion.** Here, you use the data and analysis to either prove or disprove your original hypothesis. Maybe you can't make a conclusion. The true scientist notes any complications that occurred during the experiment and any possible improvements that could be made if others want to experiment further.

Proceed

In scientific inquiry, disproving your hypothesis is not failure. In change management, not arriving at a solution for a problem likely represents failure. Nevertheless, by undertaking a systematic approach to creative problem-solving such as the scientific method, you have a far better chance of reaching the desired objective.

Reeducation Works Wonders

With his training and experience, Kurt Lewin developed a (behavioral) scientist's understanding of what will and will not induce people to change. He found that people will not change merely because they are asked to, even if the need for change is explained to them and there is consensus that the proposed change represents a wonderful turn of events.

People will change when they have a distinct feeling that the change will be in their own best interest. Reeducation supported the idea that to change human behavior patterns, you need to work on the core values, beliefs, relationships, and connections that people have in order to better understand them before you can design a program that will be effective.

The Group Is the Thing

One of the many principles Lewin devised for an effective reeducation process cannot be brought about item by item. According to Lewin, an individual will change—adopt a new system of values and beliefs—when he or she accepts belonging to a group. True change occurs when a person adopts the values and beliefs of the group. A change agent who understands this necessity can be highly effective in inducing change.

"The acceptance of a new system (the change) is linked," Lewin said, "with the acceptance of a specific group, a particular role, and a particular source of authority as new points of reference."

People Who Need People

An easy way to think of people who change based on normative-reeducative principles is to paraphrase the line from the Barbra Streisand song in which she says, "people who need people are the luckiest people of all." When it comes to change based on normative-reeducative theory, people who need people are the most predictable people of all.

Factoid

The normative-reeducative approach holds that people will follow social norms and commitments and that change happens as a result of identifying with a group and sharing the values of that group.

The Key Principles of Reeducation

In Lewin's view, reeducation as a change strategy was based on a series of principles, each of which gave added insight to a change manager attempting to affect change with and among targets of change. The following list briefly describes some of Lewin's key principles:

➤ **Processes are alike.** "The processes governing the acquisition of the normal and abnormal are fundamentally alike," Lewin said. In other words, people could be reeducated to exhibit abnormal behavior just as well as normal behavior. This means the change manager who wants to be effective first needs to understand the beliefs and behaviors of the targets of change.

➤ **Reeducation must fulfill a task.** For reeducation to work, it has to fulfill a task that basically is equal to a change in the target's culture. What this means is that for an individual to change his or her ideas about something, the reeducation requires a change in the individual's culture as well. Lewin felt strongly that mere education would not change a person if that person's culture was unaffected. If you're managing a change team, to get the participants to change, you have to also change something about the culture of the team and the culture within which it operates.

➤ **Experiences alone cannot help to foster knowledge.** Targets of change—that is, members of your staff—have a better chance of embracing a new change if they're able to participate in the design and execution of the discovery process.

A staff member is not simply a passenger in the vehicle of change; in a sense, he or she is a conductor or driver as well. This means that he or she is allowed to make mistakes, experiment, veer to the left and right occasionally, and, ultimately, help plot the course that will prove to be effective.

➤ **Social action is steered by one's perceptions.** For individuals to change, they have to perceive that their relationships to the immediate environment is changing. This could be the group or the entire organization. It helps if the staff members believe that what they are doing makes or will make a difference.

➤ **Correct knowledge doesn't overcome false perceptions.** We are all products of what we believe to justify our place in the world and how we interact with it. The normative-reeducative approach contends that only when individuals feel they are in a highly supportive, even loving environment will they be prompted to relinquish their prior worldviews. Then, they will allow new data and information to steer them, rather than their long-held perceptions.

➤ **Incorrect stereotypes originate from incorrect concepts.** Lewin maintained that a prejudice would diminish one's ability to think rationally and lead one astray. Unfortunately, people often ignore a valid theory to accommodate their own unrecognized biases. He felt that prejudice was the equivalent of a bad theory, and a bad theory is never likely to result in effective change. Since truth supposedly can't dislodge erroneousness and stereotypes, the effective change manager has to help people recognize their predispositions.

➤ **Changes of heart don't flow from changes of head.** You've encountered situations many times which demonstrate that although somebody has the facts, that doesn't mean he's going to act upon them. Pure logic is not much of a motivator (as discussed in Chapter 5, "Stay Sane, Manage the Pain"). People often proceed the other way around.

➤ **Individuals' changes are linked to group membership.** As mentioned, Lewin said that the development of an individual's value system—and hence, capacity for change—is directly related to the individual's participation in a group. When we feel that we are part of a community, the community's views and inclination to change are inextricably interfused with our own. Lewin went a step further and said they are actually the same process.

In terms of managing your change team, this means that as the group changes so do the individuals within it. Concurrently, as the individuals within a group change so does the group. The chicken and egg question is moot. They move in unison!

Change Master

People are first swayed emotionally and then they form the logic that supports their sentiments. A change in organizational values rarely results in automatic change of individuals' feelings. The wise change manager never loses sight of this truth.

People Are Social Beings

Following the establishment of these principles, Lewin concluded that an individual's acceptance of a new system (that is, a change) is directly linked with the acceptance of a specific group and the continued reaffirmation of that group by its members. Others outside the group conceivably could affirm and reaffirm as well.

In your own situation, when contemplating the normative-reeducative approach to change management, all you need to remember is that people are basically social beings. They will adopt new cultural norms and values in block steps with the group that they identify with. Your job is to effect change by helping them redefine and reinterpret their existing norms, biases, and values, and helping them adhere to new norms and values.

The merging of group norms, personal values, and common goals can result in long-lasting internalizing changes. At the organizational level, a normative-reeducative approach to change can actually shift an entire organization. The change solidifies and takes hold when it becomes "the way that we do business around here."

Advocates of the normative-reeducative approach contend that it's more effective than the other three approaches, discussed in Chapters 6, 8, and 9, because the change becomes part of the culture.

➤ Social forces, individual values, and group dynamics keep the change in place.

➤ There is less friction in the system.

➤ People are less resistant.

➤ Forces of opposition, at least in the short run, are minimal.

Unfreeze Your Target of Change and Win

Reeducation occurs most readily when targets of change can become unfrozen, and hence more receptive to new information, viewpoints, and methods. Surprisingly, reeducation strategies can be simple to implement. For example, people can be dramatically influenced by role models or mentors.

The strong influence of families, schools, organizations, institutions, and religious movements often have leaders who profoundly influence followers. People mostly model their behaviors after these leaders, but often they act merely as mentors, providing a sense of psychological safety.

Behavior That Influences

The targets of change, like all human beings, are routinely resistant to new ideas and new ways of doing things (for details, see Chapter 4, "Dealing with Resistance"). The mentor or role model who already exhibits the desired behavior and incorporates the associated beliefs that support the desired change essentially "tells" the protégé that it's okay to follow.

If the sole information that the targets of change are exposed to is disseminated by powerful mentors and role models, then learning, understandably, tends to follow in that direction.

Proceed

As a change manager, when you sense that the targets of change have become "unfrozen," it becomes critical to ensure that they are influenced by appropriate mentors and role models. They then will be the most receptive and most heavily impacted.

Reeducation Through Trial and Error

In the absence of mentors and role models, a highly motivated target of change can still be an effective learner. In this case, the individual could engage in one or more activities:

➤ Tap into his or her personal network.

➤ Make Web searches on key words and topics.

➤ Read articles and books that further his or her understanding of the issue.

➤ Talk to new people who may have new insights to impart to him or her.

➤ Take a course.

➤ Simply reflect.

The Power and Danger of Self-Learners

History is replete with highly motivated learners who, in the absence of direct guidance, lifted themselves up by their own bootstraps, made dramatic changes in their lives, and became resourceful members of society. Abraham Lincoln was primarily a self-taught lawyer. The general education of many American pioneers was self-taught. Stories also abound of the incarcerated who, over the long years, used their time for self-education and emerged as totally remade individuals with new eyes with which to view the world.

Effective solutions to challenging problems often come from those self-learners who have devised and share their insights with the group.

Change Master

In the course of a change campaign, you can't necessarily count on having a staff of highly motivated self-learners. However, if you detect some people among your troops who are in this category, it is largely to your benefit.

The self-learner who is allowed to devise his or her own effective solutions to change campaign challenges has the best chance of success. Even at the height of self-learning, however, if mentors and role models are readily accessible, the self learner is likely to draw upon them.

Can a mentor or role model unwittingly steer a targeted change in a direction or in a manner that does not truly fit the beliefs and desired methods of the learner? Yes, and that risk is always a possibility.

The New Behavior Must Fit

By whatever method of learning and adoption, to some degree the new behavior of the target of change must conform to the target's personality and general behaviors and then become refrozen.

Be Wary

For refreezing to occur, everyone who holds the same methods and belief systems needs to be trained.

You may witness a situation in which an individual attends some special training program. Perhaps she learns how to become a more participatory supervisor. Then, she returns from the session to her organization where the prevailing environment solidly supports autocratic supervision.

Whatever the individual learned at the training session is now in conflict. The training becomes disconfirmed. Any changes she exhibited in her supervisory style do not refreeze. The net result of the training is that it's a waste or, worse, the individual is more confused than when she first attended the training!

All in Unison

An educational institution was confronting significant internal and external changes. Key staff was in a quandary regarding the organization's new strategic focus and felt as if the organization was more often adrift than not. A change campaign was initiated to more directly include all managers and key staff in issues related to programs offered, quality of service, and community liaisons.

The change management team decided to conduct a retreat for managers and key staff to further clarify where the organization was heading, get consensus, and enable people to air their views. At the retreat, subgoals were established in support of the organization's overall goals and objectives. With participation of all managers and key staff, the shift in the organization's strategic focus benefited from a power surge that helped the organization meet its objective and supply synergy for what was next.

Strive for Understanding

Change managers commonly find themselves confronting a pervasive problem. Employees within organizations are subject to unspoken messages and expectations that sometimes contradict or undermine established written policies and procedures.

When this is the case, the change manager needs to comprehend this unspoken lingo to gain an accurate understanding of a company's underlying messages and the forces at play that maintain the status quo. The change manager also needs to succinctly determine what behaviors result.

High Ambition, Limited Resources

In *The Unwritten Rules of the Game,* Peter Scott-Morgan contends that it's appropriate and desirable to focus on the most pressing business issues facing a firm. If you try to deal with all issues, you end up potentially giving short shrift to those that were critical. Hence, you put the firm's future in jeopardy.

The source of critical issues facing a firm often are derived by the relevant, unspoken messages and unwritten rules that inhibit progress. As such, the change manager can only progress by identifying and understanding the unwritten rules and then offering appropriate incentives to staff that lead to new behavior (see Chapter 6, "The Rational-Empirical Approach").

Understand the Basics

As a change manager leading a change campaign often with limited funds, limited staff support, and limited time, you'll likely be unable to incorporate sufficient training into your plans to take full advantage of the normative-reeducative approach to change management.

By understanding the basics, however, and that, to one degree or another, people most readily change when they see they are a part of something larger than themselves, you have valuable insights. You will be better prepared for understanding individual members of your team, conducting team meetings, and helping the group progress through various stages of the change campaign.

The Least You Need to Know

➤ People change when they have a distinct feeling that the change will be in their own best interest.

➤ Change most readily occurs when an individual accepts belonging to a group and adopts the group's system of values and beliefs.

➤ Targets of change have a better chance of embracing a new change if they're able to participate in the design and execution of the discovery process.

➤ Reeducation can occur when targets of change can become unfrozen and hence more receptive to new information, viewpoints, and methods.

➤ When you sense that the targets of change have become "unfrozen," ensure that they are influenced by appropriate mentors and role models—they will be the most receptive and most heavily impacted.

Nothing like coercing a little power to help work through a change!!

Chapter 8

The Power-Coercive Approach

In This Chapter:

➤ Recognizing that people are basically compliant

➤ Exercising power as a speedy change-inducer

➤ Exercising power appropriately

➤ Resorting to sanctions and dependency

The power-coercive approach to change management is wantonly used by some, naively used by others, and all too often the default form of change management. The underlying premise is that people are basically compliant and will do what they are told with little or no convincing.

Getting people to change is based on the exercise of authority and the threat or actual imposition of sanctions for nonperformance. This approach has also been called the force-coercion approach. Regardless of what you call it, its employment carries great risks and potentially great rewards.

The Premise: People Are Compliant

When wielded appropriately, power can be one of the fastest, and surprisingly one of the most effective approaches to inducing change. The great danger, however, is that when people respond based on the imposition of authority, fear of punishment, or the

Change Master

There are many instances in society, organizations, and specifically within change campaigns where compliancy is appropriate, necessary, and the most effective approach to change management. Examples include acute or short-term situations in which there is little time for bonding, building commitment, or team member self-appraisals.

lure of rewards, they tend to be responsive only when the change manager is present, visible, and in full throttle of the exercise of his or her power.

Critics of the power-coercive approach contend that it …

➤ Cannot bring about lasting change.

➤ Holds high potential for antagonizing targets of change.

➤ Ultimately can breed deep-seated resistance.

Each of these concerns will be addressed throughout the chapter. For now, let's focus on the notion that people are basically compliant.

Being in Compliance with the Powers That Be

The presumption that people are compliant is not a value judgment. Some people are compliant most of the time and virtually all people can be compliant some of the time. Being compliant is not necessarily synonymous with being docile, wimpish, or lethargic. It is simply a state wherein one or more persons accedes to the demands or wishes of another.

A new product launch under severe deadlines, an emergency rescue squad racing to save someone's life, and various military operations are all examples of time-constrained tasks for which the power-coercive approach might be appropriate. However, not all such uses of the power-coercive approach need to be acute or emergency-type situations.

Give Me My Marching Orders

Use of the power-coercive approach can be effective when targets of change recognize the expertise and authenticity of the change manager, sponsor, or whomever is wielding the power. If I am 150 pounds overweight and I sign up for your weight-loss program, become part of a team, and attend sessions on a regular basis, I want to be told what to do. Here, rewards for appropriate behavior and punishment for inappropriate behavior may be entirely suitable.

In this situation, I am the initiating sponsor who has yielded power to the change manager, that is, the weight-loss center director or team leader who then wields power over me, now serving as the target of change. If I have been sent to the weight-loss center by my spouse, however, then I am not the initiator. Even if I was highly resistant at first, I may yield to the directives of the change manager if I see progress. After all, my own weight-loss methods had obviously not worked.

Even if I initially didn't see the need to lose weight, if I start to have more energy, and I feel that I sleep, breathe, and look better, I may quickly buy into the entire campaign regardless of the approach taken by the change managers.

Being Compliant by Default

At work, I may find myself reporting to a change manager whose operating style is that of a puppeteer. I may resent his heavy-handed approach to management, or even lament having to work with such an individual. Nevertheless, the odds are that I will be compliant for several reasons:

➤ This is my job, and it is often a hassle to find another one. The path of least resistance is for me to stay where I am in the short run even if the operating environment is somewhat unpleasant.

➤ I may have experience working under such conditions and know how to weather the storm. The days will pass, the project will be done, and I can move on to something else.

➤ I may actually be able to learn new skills and gain valuable experience as a result of participating in the project.

Be Wary

In a power-coercive setting, behavior such as abrasiveness or disrespect will potentially dissuade a change target from being compliant.

In fact, there are many potential benefits even when working with an objectively bad boss:

➤ Working for a boss who you don't respect may strengthen your ability to deal with people—including good and bad future bosses—and it may help you hone your diplomatic skills.

➤ Learn from your boss's mistakes. Instead of wasting mental energy grousing about the things your boss is doing wrong, contemplate how they could be done right in the future.

➤ Having a pressure cooker for a boss can be a nightmare and is the cause of many an ulcer. You're not likely to be the only one who notices your manager's volatile behavior. Strive to be a model of calm level-headedness.

Proceed

Your ability to stay cool and perform well, contrasted with your boss's temper tantrums, may eventually win you kudos from colleagues and top management.

Power As a Fitting Alternative

In some settings, the power-coercive approach may be the change manager's only practical alternative. If you're working with novice or undereducated staff, particularly undisciplined or at-risk employees, giving orders may ultimately prove to be the most viable alternative to reach the desired outcome.

Carrying the Big Stick

When I was 22 years old, before I entered graduate school, I worked one summer for a moving and storage company in Bloomfield, Connecticut. Each day the drivers (who showed up on time) and helpers (I was a helper) left the company parking lot at 6:30 A.M.

The drivers, or "lifers" as they were called, came from all kinds of backgrounds, but mainly they consisted of high school dropouts. It was a demanding, exhausting, and unrelenting line of work. Most of the lifers were visibly aging faster than normal.

In reflecting upon my days with the moving company, it became clear to me that while management wielded a heavy stick, resorted to authority, and frequently yelled at the staff, other approaches, particularly for handling short-term critical jobs, may have been less effective. The drivers were part of a union, and if they felt sore enough about the treatment they received, they could always initiate a grievance through their representative. Curiously, they hardly ever did.

Bonded by Resentment

Getting chewed out by the big boss was a weekly ritual for most and nearly a daily ritual for some. At the least, that gave them something to gripe about with one another. *Social psychology* holds that if A and B are at odds with each other, such as two drivers working for the moving company, and C comes along who represents an enemy to both, then A and B can form a bond of sorts in their disdain for C. This is exactly what happened at the moving company.

Word Power

Social psychology is the study of how individuals act in relation to others.

While most tasks that the drivers faced didn't represent change management projects, on special occasions such as handling a first-time assignment, working for a new client, or moving delicate instruments, clearly the company and its drivers engaged in varieties of change campaigns.

In each instance, the power-coercive approach was the underlying method that management employed. It is questionable whether they even had an inkling that the rational-empirical approach, normative-reeducative approach, or environmental-adaptive approach were possibilities.

Good Job, Bad Job

The rewards and punishments at the moving company were clear. If you did a respectable job, delivered the goods on time, didn't break anything, treated the client with respect, turned in the appropriate paperwork, and kept your truck in top condition, you were likely to receive a plum assignment or two over the next couple of weeks. A bonus might be in order for you. Your request for specific days off might be honored.

If you didn't do any of the above, or worse, flagrantly fouled up in some way, you could count on a tongue lashing the moment management found out. A smaller bonus or no bonus would be forthcoming. You would get the worst assignments. You would be in the manager's doghouse.

The drivers all knew and understood these operating guidelines. They didn't resort to voluminous policies and procedure manuals. By the second day on the job, as a result of *banter* with the rest of the guys, they ascertained the operating environment in which they had been hired. By the first week, they comprehended what types of behavior were rewarded and what types were lambasted. By the second week, at the latest, they surmised what form of rewards were possible, and what sanctions were likely.

Word Power

Banter is loose talk, gossip, and wise-talking.

Freedom As an Abstract

"Most of us believe that the love of freedom is inherent in human nature, and that our natural tendency is toward democracy," says James Q. Wilson, professor of strategy and organization at UCLA. "But history suggests that human autonomy will usually be subordinated to political control. If that is true, our effort to increase individual freedom is an oddity, a weak effort to equip people with an opportunity some do not want and many will avoid," says Wilson.

The author of many books, including *The Moral Sense,* Wilson observes that human nature is no accurate guide in how to design organizations or teams. Human nature allows for many arrangements, he says, "some good, some bad and some completely atrocious." Freedom is an ideal worth striving for; however, it can offer us both that which we want and that which we don't want.

Wilson says, "The legacy of freedom has supplied us not only with prosperity, but with attacks on

Be Wary

Freedom among team members in change campaigns, if not managed properly, can yield disastrous results.

87

the origins of prosperity. Not only with a society that respects rights, but with one that litigates illusory claims in the name of rights; not only with great universities that foster research, but with ones that indulge nonsense; not only with a culture that accepts inquiry and openness, but with one that patronizes familial decline and moral relativeness."

The previous discussion is not a broad, sweeping justification for blanket use of the power-coercive approach to change management. Rather, it is an acknowledgment that more liberal approaches to change management, such as the rational-empirical, the normative-reeducative, and the environmental-adaptive, are capable of yielding less-than-desirable results.

In some circumstances (usually short term), these approaches run a distant second to the power-coercive approach in terms of the predictability of success.

The Appropriate Exercise of Authority

An underlying assumption of the power-coercive approach to change management is that targets of change, who are part of a hierarchical, formal structure, are compliant with the instructions, plans, and leadership of those in power. The primary objective of a change manager or sponsor is to modify the behavior of change targets so that their behavior supports the given instructions or plans.

Heed These "Don'ts"

What, then, constitutes appropriate exercise of authority? The question is most easily answered by addressing what is *inappropriate* exercise of authority. Certainly, you never want to ask people to engage in behavior that threatens life or limb, or has long-term negative impacts on their mental or emotional beings. Other don'ts include the following:

➤ Don't ask that people operate contrary to the strict dictates of their faith.

➤ Don't ask them to engage in illegal, immoral, or unethical practices.

➤ Don't put yourself in a situation in which you are inducing staff to put themselves in financial risk.

➤ Don't ask your staff to risk any more than you're risking, and usually less than that.

➤ Don't use privileged information about an individual in an injudicious manner, or for even the most limited interpretation of mental or emotional extortion.

➤ Don't ask targets of change to betray the larger organization.

➤ Don't ask them to operate outside the bounds of the organization's culture and climate unless the change campaign itself is specifically designed to modify the culture or climate and everyone understands this to be the case.

➤ Don't allow your exercise of authority to seem capricious or vindictive.

There are standards to maintain, protocols to follow, and decorum to uphold. Even in the military, the quintessential power-coercive model for change management, everyone from a drill sergeant to a four-star general is held personally responsible for how he or she dispenses authority. He or she can even be court-martialed and sentenced for transgressions and injudicious use of authority.

Be Wary

If you make any type of error in communication, it is your responsibility to attempt to rectify the situation as soon as possible.

Become an Effective Power-Coercive Manager

As a change manager who has chosen, or is forced to apply, the power-coercive approach to handling your change campaign, you want to uphold the credibility and dignity of your position. While the directives you issue to staff may not be subject to debate, you want to ensure that they are clear, on target, and delivered in a timely manner so that those charged with acting upon them can have the highest probability of succeeding.

Even *martinets,* whether or not they know it, need critical feedback from their staffs. It is one thing to be an autocratic leader; it is another to doggedly proceed down a path when one of your scouts tells you that the bridge ahead has washed out.

Word Power

A **martinet** is a dictatorial, autocratic type of person, sometimes found in the military or government as well as other organizations.

Be Tough but Fair

You can be a tough leader, but to be effective, you must also be fair. People have an ingrained sense of what is fair within group dynamics. If you are unfair to one member of the group, others readily contemplate that it's only a matter of time until you're unfair to them.

On the heels of fairness comes the need to avoid playing favorites. If your staff has ceded to taking strict marching orders, they prefer everyone to be marching in unison.

Proceed

Often the gripes and resistance that a change manager can encounter in a power-coercive situation springs more from issues of unfairness and favoritism in and among staff as opposed to the stringency of the assignments.

Be a Straight Shooter

As with the other change management approaches, you want to strive to be accurate and honest with your staff. Avoid misleading them or making promises you can't keep. Have the strength to offer realistic portrayals of …

➤ What is being asked of the staff.

➤ How they will be supported.

➤ What hardships they are likely to endure.

➤ What deadlines are crucial.

➤ What is expected of each individual.

Walk That Fine Line

To provide your staff with the push they need to accomplish near-miraculous results in record time, carefully straddle the line without crossing it. Abandon hold on unrealistic expectations.

In the military, leaders who push too hard and too fast encounter low morale and accompanying lethargy, and in worse cases, desertion or sabotage. If you cross that line, the campaign may be lost. Some people will never return to a state of appropriate compliance. Your power will be undermined. To compensate, you may feel the need to ratchet up the level of sanctions, but resist. That will only breed greater resentment and resistance, thus further undermining your effective use of power.

Proceed

As any good manager and leader should, you should constantly acknowledge your staff for their participation and accomplishments.

Resorting to Sanctions

Management theory holds that the stronger the resistance to a change campaign, the greater the need for a power-coercive approach. Likewise, if the time frame for accomplishment is short or if the resources available to support the campaign are limited, resorting to a power-coercive approach may be desirable.

Word Power

Sanctions are also known as penalties or punishments.

Sanctions and Dependency

People's dependency on an organization largely dictates how effective the power-coercive approach and the use of *sanctions* can be. If people are highly dependent on an organization; live paycheck to paycheck; have few job alternatives; and are not financially, mentally, or emotionally prepared to walk, you are on relatively safe ground using the power-coercive approach judiciously. You can employ sanctions designed to elicit suitable performance as long as you do not burden the staff beyond an acceptable threshold.

Limited, Individual Application

Effective use of sanctions varies widely depending on ...

➤ The nature of your change campaign.

➤ Your staff.

➤ The duration of the campaign.

➤ Your prior history with each individual.

➤ Pressures from the sponsor.

➤ Other external factors.

Sanctions need to be imposed on an individual basis. Making entire groups suffer for the lapses of one individual may work for a limited time in a controlled environment, such as with a sports team or in the military. However, it can backfire in major, disruptive ways in a work environment.

Poor workers are replaceable. You are better off having too few staff members than a staff that continually consumes your time and energy, not to mention budget, while delivering little in the way of performance.

Sanctions with Bite

To determine the most effective sanctions on an individual basis, you have to know with whom you're working. What do they value? What do they most dread losing? For some, it's no bonus; for others, it's lack of vacation time; and for others it's no time off.

For some people, a verbal or written reprimand is earth shaking. For nearly all, having to put in overtime or work weekends is a drag beyond description. The hint of demotion or transfer to a less desirable post can be compelling negative inducements.

Change Master

When you're working with a highly mobile staff, perhaps composed of knowledgeable workers who potentially have other career options and income-producing opportunities, neither the power-coercive approach nor the use of sanctions are likely to be effective in most circumstances.

Be Wary

You can always escalate the sanctions as the situation merits. However, if you impose sanctions in a descending manner, already stung by earlier penalties, some people may be immune to lesser impositions.

For some, a *decoupling* of carefully accrued perks can work wonders such as …

➤ Relocation from the corner or otherwise desirable office.

➤ A change in parking space.

➤ Withdrawal of a club or pass card.

➤ Cessation of communication privileges such as specialized e-mail accounts, Internet access, fax machine privileges, or even calling card access.

The list of what you can dangle in front of people can be long indeed. The key in each instance is to …

1. Never issue a warning that you do not fully intend to back up with action. Bluffing can cost you credibility.

2. Arrange the sanctions in ascending order to the degree practical—that is, you want to make penalties small at the outset to demonstrate your point and to keep the per-staff losses at a minimum.

3. The sanctions need to be imposed in ways that do not seem vindictive or cruel. They are simply measures installed to induce certain types of behavior or levels of performance.

4. Part and parcel with sanctions comes redress for appropriate performance or behavior. How and when do people regain what you have taken or withheld from them? Spell this out clearly so that staff doesn't remain in limbo status.

Word Power

Decoupling means detaching or removing something.

Proceed

It's better to determine at the outset what infractions merit what level of sanction in order to apply sanctions as uniformly as possible.

Watch the Knee Jerk

A change manager inexperienced in resorting to sanctions often imposes them based on knee-jerk reactions to upsets and breakdowns during the campaign. This results in an unfair and uneven application of sanctions.

Regardless of the extent of sanctions you have at your disposal, remember that people can deal with only so much change in a given time period. If you find yourself spending more and more time resorting to sanctions, the problem may well lie with you or your plan of action as opposed to your targets of change.

When the Cat's Away

In a power-coercive environment, if you ease up too soon or too often, the staff will invariably seek out ways to revert to more comfortable and familiar patterns and behaviors. They will do this in ways that aren't readily apparent—that is, when the cat is away the mice will play. Sometimes, they will even do it right in front of your face.

Managing a change campaign using the power-coercive approach has been likened to keeping a candle lit in a rainstorm. Some days it feels as if everything around you is in a state of chaos. Your responsibility may be that of change management but you need to call upon leadership skills as often as anything else.

The Least You Need to Know

➤ The power-coercive approach to change management presumes that people are compliant and will do what they are told with little or no convincing.

➤ Getting your staff to act compliantly is presumably based on the exercise of authority and the threat or imposition of sanctions for nonperformance.

➤ The power-coercive approach can be effective when targets of change recognize the expertise and authenticity of whoever is wielding the power.

➤ You can be a tough leader, but to be an effective leader, you must also be fair.

➤ The directives you issue to your staff need to be clear, on target, and timely to ensure they have the highest probability of succeeding.

➤ When applying sanctions, determine at the outset what infractions merit what level of sanction, and then apply sanctions as uniformly as possible.

Chapter 9

The Environmental-Adaptive Approach

In This Chapter

➤ Laying down the law

➤ How and when to make changes

➤ Overcoming attachment to existing norms

➤ Exploiting your company's strengths

The underlying premise of the environmental-adaptive approach to change management is that while people instinctively attempt to avoid disruption or loss, they do have the ability to adjust to new situations. The change manager's quest here is to erect some new type of operating structure and incrementally shift targets of change from the old structure to the new one.

Letting Them Do What *They* Want, on *Your* Terms

The environmental-adaptive approach is championed by Fred Nickols, a veteran management consultant and author, based in Robbinsville, New Jersey. As an example, Nickols refers to media magnate, Rupert Murdock who owned a printing operation on Fleet Street in Boston. Without informing anyone at his facility, Murdock began constructing an entirely new operation several miles away.

Orchestrating Announcements

When construction was complete and the building was ready to be occupied, Murdock assembled all his employees at the original location for an announcement. He proclaimed that he had some unfortunate news and some good news as well.

Change Master

To induce people to conform, create a situation in which conforming is the most tempting of their options.

First he delivered the unfortunate news: The existing facility was being shut down and the entire staff was being terminated. Naturally, this was an unwelcome and shocking surprise to everyone. Murdock, who many regard as having always operated in a crafty and sometimes unscrupulous manner, then made a second announcement.

A new facility was commencing operations a few miles away and there was a position available for every single member of the staff. The hitch was that it would be on completely different terms. Murdock's strategy actually contained elements of the three other change approaches: the rational-empirical approach, the normative-reeducative approach, and, most notably, the power-coercive approach.

Leaving No Choice but to Adapt

An ideal arena in which to create a new structure in place of the old is on the Web. Launching a new Web site in place of an old one is a relatively minor example of a situation in which people lose the familiarity and functionality of the old site. While they feel somewhat disrupted as a result of the change, they are forced to adapt to the new site and what it has to offer.

If your company is planning to launch an entirely new Web site in place of the old, progress can continue on a daily basis unabated without informing the employees until need be. When the new site is perfected and ready to be unveiled, the CEO can simply e-mail everyone in the organization, perhaps early in the morning of one workday, presenting the URL within the e-mail message.

Employees can simply click on the URL and behold, what used to be no longer is, and what was slated to be, now is. The new or revamped site is now the official site, full of new screens, new information, and different layouts. No time for transition. Assimilation has to come quickly. Does everyone adapt? Yes. What choice do they have?

Mixing Is the Best Strategy

Fortunately, your application of the environmental-adaptive approach to change management need not be radical, nor incorporate the heavy-handed tactics of the power-coercive approach. Nickols believes that applying a single change approach cannot work effectively. Essentially, you must create what he terms *a grand strategy* that involves a mix of the four approaches.

Hey, I Had No Choice

You rely on the environmental-adaptive approach when you have little choice but to do so. When people are forced to make a change, the best thing that you can do is help them to see the potential benefits of making the change efficiently and effectively.

Niccolò Machiavelli in his classic book *The Prince,* said that, "In order to retain a newly acquired state, regard must be had for two things":

Word Power

A **grand strategy,** as used here, is a plan that incorporates the relevant aspects of the rational–empirical approach, the normative–reeducative approach, the power-coercive approach, and the environmental-adaptive approach to best tackle the matter at hand.

1. That the line of the ancient sovereign be entirely extinguished; and

2. The laws be not changed or the taxes increased so that the new may in the least possible time be thoroughly incorporated in the ancient state.

Out with the Old, In with the New

In modern vernacular, to make a change permanent, the previously existing establishment must be abolished, and a new structure must be created to which the people may be able to quickly become adapted. This necessitates not making unnecessary changes when asking people to swiftly move from A to B. Ask your team to adapt in ways that you deem critical, but let more trivial matters slide for the time being.

One Step at a Time

The best of companies, nevertheless, acknowledge the importance of integrating change into the workplace before events force those changes to occur. Machiavelli said, "No one should ever submit to an evil for the sake of avoiding a war. For wars are never avoided, but are only deferred to one's own disadvantage."

Be Wary

Ask too much of your staff, and you run the risk of the change process proceeding poorly.

This translates to: No matter how difficult a change may be, delaying it only increases the number of obstacles that you and the targets of change will face further down the road.

Small Changes, Dramatic Differences

Occasionally, the most modest of changes, made as soon as a need arises, are enough to result in dramatic, positive differences. According to Andrew Hendry, Ph.D., of the University of Massachusetts, in nature, animals of the same species, "can quickly develop new traits under the pressure of a new environment and rapidly begin diverging into different species as a direct result of the ecological pressures."

Factoid

Even small changes in adaptation can result in dramatic differences in terms of the ability of a species to survive and adapt.

Factoid

To be effective on a continual basis, human beings need to adapt to their dynamic work environments just as animals must adapt to their own environments.

In his world-changing book, *The Origin of Species*, Charles Darwin in 1859 explained that the law of natural selection governs the divergence of species:

> It may metaphorically be said that natural selection is daily and hourly scrutinizing throughout the world, the slightest variations, rejecting those that are bad, preserving and adding up those that are good; silently and sensibly working, whenever and wherever opportunity offers at the improvement of each organic being in relation to its organic and inorganic conditions of life. We see nothing of these slow changes in progress, until the hand of time has marked the lapse of ages.

As accurate and brilliant as Darwin's observation was more than 140 years ago, through the work of Hendry and other scientists, we now have the opportunity to witness first hand the result of evolutionary changes in species. For example, the socci salmon who dwell in Lake Washington near Seattle, a near perfect living laboratory, have fueled scientific understanding of evolution since the 1930s.

These findings represent positive news for change managers all over the world because they confirm the viability of the environmental-adaptive approach to change management. Within limits, people can change, and, in certain circumstances, they can change effectively in a hurry.

Attachment Reins Supreme

Much of the problem in getting people to move quickly beyond their reflexive resistance to change is their attachment to existing establishments. Attachment is a strange but universal phenomenon among human beings.

Years ago, we purchased a piano for my daughter, Valerie, from a music store. It was about $600, not a grand piano. It was a little old and a little beat-up; it didn't quite have 88 keys, but for a four-year-old it was just fine! My little girl learned to play very well.

When Valerie reached eight years old, it became apparent that she needed a full 88-key piano. We visited a piano store and ended up buying her a grand piano and trading in the old one. Two days before the grand piano was to be shipped to us, when Valerie realized that we would be saying good-bye to the first piano, she broke down and started crying. This was strange to me because the piano was an inanimate object.

I asked her what was the matter and she said, "I've had this piano all my life; I don't want it to go." I said, "But Val, we're going to get a new, big piano that's much better."

She said, "I know, but this is the only piano I've ever known." I tried to be a good father. I said, "Well, maybe we could take a lot of pictures of you and the piano so we'll always remember it." Still mournfully sobbing, she said, "I've already taken some pictures, but we could take more."

Searching for a way to ease her pain, I said to her, "Val, think of it this way. The piano's going to go back to the store but some other parents are going to come in and buy the piano for their little girl, who's just starting, and she's going to learn how to play piano."

I knew Valerie was going to get past her attachment when, still sobbing, she said, "Or maybe it will be a little boy."

Hooked on a Feeling

Attachment in the workplace is common when people rely on familiar age-old equipment and are hesitant to convert to new, technologically advanced equipment, even though they offer the potential for extreme increases in productivity. It is also seen when employees become hooked on particular processes, policies, chains of command, communication patterns, or even pervasive office rituals.

Like a pair of old comfortable shoes, attachment in the business environment blinds us to the realities of the ever-changing world. It fools us into believing that existing customs or procedures cannot be improved without risking a negative effect on cost, time, communication, or productivity. It prevents us from seeing opportunities that practically smack us in the face. Our attachments enable competitors to leapfrog ahead of us and leave us wondering how and why.

Say "Yes" to Change

Government bureaucracies, populated with career civil servants—particularly the federal agencies housed in Washington—have the strongest and longest-term reputations for attachment. Employees tend to carve out their tiny fiefdoms, give sharp focus to their benefits, hunker down for the long decades, and retire early, basking in the security of generous government retirement packages.

Be Wary

The larger and the more bureaucratic the organization, the more attachment reins supreme. Attachment to a particular product or service may be your biggest weakness in the business world. Be prepared to let go and refocus your energy elsewhere.

Obviously, that situation is changing and certainly there are elements of it in other sectors of the economy. As Scott Adams illustrates in his widely read *Dilbert* comic strips, attachment in the corporate world is alive and well. Some corporations are attached to making profits even when long-term analysis reveals that their products irrefutably are harmful to people—yes, I am talking about the tobacco industry.

Rationalizing for a Lifetime

Tens of thousands of employees, managers, top executives, and boards of directors are all attached to producing tobacco products under the guise of "free choice" for consumers. The rationalization process of these vendors to justify producing products that are so destructive to the human body is one for the ages.

The best companies seem to be able to focus on both short-term profits, social contributions, and long-term successes. The most successful companies are those that are able to recognize that the products, services, and marketing distribution systems that proved effective and profitable in the past are not necessarily the same as those that will thrive in the future.

Word Power

Creative sabotage is the process in which an organization discontinues popular products or services in swift recognition of the need to meet the ever-changing and ever-more-demanding needs of the marketplace.

Overcoming Attachment

If you're a change manager in a progressive organization, you have a higher probability of managing change campaigns with the requisite sponsorship needed to achieve the desired end result. Such sponsors realize, either intuitively or through learning, that abandoning ship and engaging in *creative sabotage* is the best path to follow in some circumstances.

Building New Structures

An ideal environmental-adaptive approach would be to take care of all possible contingencies in moving targets of change from Point A to Point B. As a result, the collective level of stress, anxiety, and negative anticipation would be at a minimum, and assimilation, adaptation, and comfort levels would be at optimal levels.

When people are forced to adopt new technology or new processes, it is helpful to design training programs that enable them to bridge the gap with a minimal amount of disorientation and discomfort.

When asking your employees to learn new software, for example, rather than simply forcing them to abandon the old system for the new, develop simple corollaries that illustrate the similarities and differences between the old and new techniques.

Form Follows Function

Building new structures is not limited to the physical aspects. Structure also encompasses roles and responsibilities, relationships and interpersonal networks, and information and communication flow. Changing the physical structure, such as relocating from one building to another, may or may not impact the human aspects of structure.

A new phone system, new Web server, and even the physical layout of the premises themselves may necessitate a change in the way that people operate. As a change manager, your quest is to have form-follows-function—you design how you want things to be and appropriate forms are established that support the intended function.

Be on Guard

The reality in many work environments is that function follows form. Suppose you want to encourage ad-hoc employee discussion because it seems to foster high creativity. The only place where employees can congregate, however, is in narrow, unattractive hallways that are anything but soundproof.

Be Wary

Even companies that don't sell harmful products or services are prone to the trap of falling in love with what they presently offer without adapting to the ever-changing marketplace.

Proceed

Moving into a new environment doesn't need to be scary. If you can show targets of change how what they already know and do relates to what they need to know and do in the future, the transition is likely to run more smoothly.

By default, the frequency of ad-hoc conversations will be minuscule. Creating small, ad-hoc areas for employees to congregate is likely to encourage such behavior.

Exploit Your Company's Strengths

When he played shortstop for the Los Angeles Dodgers in the 1960s, Maury Wills was renowned as the base-stealing leader. Top management at Dodger Stadium in Los Angeles directed the grounds crew to bank the ground along the foul lines, from home plate to first base and third base respectively, so that bunted balls would tend to stay in fair territory.

Wills was an expert bunter, and the ability to get him on first base gave the team opportunities to take advantage of his base-stealing talent. Likewise, other batters on the Dodgers followed suit, laying down bunts at appropriate junctures in the game. The Dodgers even traded for players and developed players in their farm system who were fast on the base paths and expert base stealers, who could bunt their way onto first.

Throughout the decade, the Dodgers employed a form-follows-function approach to competing that proved to be quite successful. The bunting and base-stealing skills, in addition to the talented pitching staff, gave their team a blend of talents who responded to the dynamics of the field itself.

Be Wary

Relocating can have drastic effects on your employees. Changes such as the size of an office or the layout of the premises can influence an employee's view of his or her position or rank in the company. Pay attention to logistical modifications that may have impact.

Few Runs, Many Victories

The otherwise anemic-hitting Dodgers could single, walk, or bunt their way onto base, steal second, be driven over to third by an infield out or sacrifice fly, and score in the same manner. For many years, the Dodgers were among the lowest scoring teams in baseball, yet won three national league championships and two World Series between 1963 and 1966.

After their best pitcher, Sandy Koufax, retired at the age of 30 due to an arthritic elbow, the plan fell apart. The pitching staff was not strong enough to support a team of bunters and base stealers. It would be many more years before the Dodgers would reemerge as the National League and World Series champions.

The grounds crew was directed to relevel the playing field along the third baseline and first baseline to reflect the management's new approach to the game: trying to *procure* long-ball hitters who could help the team score runs.

Gradual Transference

People oppose and loathe disruption but will readily adapt to new circumstances when the need arises. Still, it's best, if you can, to make the leap a small one. Too much change too fast is going to throw anybody out of kilter.

A Russian proverb states that you can't cross a chasm in two leaps. However, you may not be able to cross the chasm in *one leap* if you haven't been practicing your long jump lately. Anyone can improve his or her performance, literally in the long jump and figuratively in terms of adapting to new circumstances, given that he or she has sufficient time for training or preparation.

If your organization has the time and resources to support a change campaign that allows for moderation in adapting to new circumstances, consider yourself fortunate. Under such conditions, you could design a program to help targets of change understand the new circumstances, and learn specifically what will change, how it will change, and how it will impact them.

Word Power

To **procure** something is to buy, acquire, or otherwise get possession or hold of it.

Proceed

If you can't confine the magnitude of the change, then perhaps you could lengthen the time that people have to adapt to the new circumstances.

Perhaps you could spend time identifying the benefits of the change, the specific challenges each person would likely face, and the resulting opportunities. You might have time to communicate this information in person, via memo, via e-mail, in small group settings, or through any other mode that might be helpful.

You could offer timely support to staff immersed in the adaptation process.

You could review results, gather feedback, make refinements to your plan, and help ensure that more people would be successful with fewer breakdowns.

A change campaign predicated on transference from the old to the new in moderation is wonderful when it happens. It may not happen often, so savor it.

The Least You Need to Know

➤ Although people resist change, they have the ability to adjust to new situations.

➤ With the environmental-adaptive approach, to make a change permanent, abolish the previously existing establishment, and create a new structure that people quickly adapt to.

➤ Pay more attention to the needs and opportunities of your own company rather than constantly comparing yourself to others.

➤ Don't let attachment prevent you from abandoning old ideas and pursuing new ones when the market demands change.

➤ Show targets of change how what they already know and do relates to what they need to know and do in the future to make their transition smoother and less scary.

➤ Staff will be less resistant to change if you make the transition as easy as possible.

Part 3
Leading Through Organizational Change

So far you've been exposed to the basics of change management as outlined in Part 1 and the four approaches to change management as elaborated in Part 2. You're now ready to turn your attention to bringing targets of change through a change campaign and surviving potentially disruptive, challenging issues.

Some of what you'll learn in Part 3—such as abruptly abandoning a change campaign to which you've been heavily committed—may seem as if it's beyond your ability. However, when you see why it may be necessary to cultivate such talents, you begin to realize that you can *do it.*

Chapter 10

Preparing Your Team for Change

In This Chapter

➤ Defining and forming your team

➤ Starting off your change campaign

➤ Charting your progress

➤ Directing your team

➤ Keeping everyone motivated

The Human Resources Planning Society annually undertakes a survey and report, conducted by the State of the Art Council, to determine what the most important responsibilities of its members should be. Recently, the findings suggested that, among other things, human resource professionals need to develop global human resource management, build management depth, and add value to organizations.

Organizations are recognizing that their abilities to respond, adapt, and innovate don't start with any particular change campaign. Instead, they rely on *the quality of people brought into the organization* and the continued commitment to developing human resources.

High-quality people make for high-quality teams, but a change management team is more than simply an aggregation of individuals that happen to be assembled to execute a specific change campaign. It is a unique unit that requires supervision, understanding, autonomy, and responsibility. This chapter focuses on the fundamentals of assembling an effective change campaign team.

What Is a Team?

A team is a gathering of individuals who assemble to accomplish a purpose. These individuals collaboratively achieve a greater result than any single individual could, while respecting and appreciating their differences and collectively learning from the experience.

In their book *The Wisdom of Teams,* authors Jon Katzenbach and Douglas Smith offer the following key distinctions between different types of teams:

1. **Work group:** This is a group for which there is no significant incremental performance need. The members interact primarily to share information, practices, or perspectives and to make decisions to help each individual perform within his or her area of responsibility. Beyond that, there is no realistic or truly desired common purpose, incremental performance goals, or joint work products that call for a team approach or mutual accountability.

Be Wary

All the planning in the world won't make up for a staff that has too many other assignments and responsibilities, or lacks the requisite motivation.

2. **Real team:** This is a small number of people with complementary skills who are equally committed to a common purpose, goal, and working approach for which they hold themselves mutually accountable.

3. **High-performance team:** Ideally made up of 6 to 12 people, this team is similar to a real team. Its members, however, are also deeply committed to one another's personal growth and success.

It is important to recognize the varieties of working group relationships. Based on the type of organization you lead, the type of change that you spearhead, and the size and nature of your staff, there are seemingly endless variations as to what kind of team you manage. To keep things simple, this text will continue to use the term *team* to represent two or more people engaged in a change campaign.

Change Master

The high-performance team significantly outperforms all other teams. It is a powerful option and an excellent model for all real and potential teams.

Striving for the Highest Good

In preparing your team for a change campaign, your goal at all times is to understand the background and skills of each of your staff members. You want to be able to deploy them for the highest good—in a way that is worthy of them, supportive of you, and most importantly, highly effective toward the achievement of the desired change.

Is Your Organization Supportive?

All other things being equal, if you work within a nurturing organization your probability of success is enhanced. If not, you will have to work much harder.

How do you know if you're in such a supportive organization?

➤ Look at the organization's track record for implementing change.

➤ Determine if new products and services are developed and made available on a regular basis.

➤ Notice if internal processes and systems have undergone modification and upgrading on a continuing basis.

➤ Observe whether managers who undertake appropriate risks are rewarded and even promoted, or if they get ignored, passed over, or, worse, let go.

Installing a Team-Based Culture

Moving from a nonteam environment to a team environment is not a light undertaking. You may also need to implement team-building sessions, assessing the effectiveness and quality assurance of such sessions.

Forming a Team

If you are in the fortunate position to be able to choose your team members, then you have the opportunity to assemble staff members who will complement each other's backgrounds, skills, strengths, and weaknesses. The longer you have known members of the team prior to selecting them, the greater the degree of certainty as to how they will perform, and what they are possible of achieving.

One could make the argument that selecting your own staff is inherently risky because of the preconceived notions you have regarding staff capabilities and how they will work with one another. As many teams discover, only when you initiate tasks, log long hours in cooperation and coordination

Change Master

Line supervisors and managers brought up in traditional management environments may be reluctant to surrender some of their power as the organization converts to a team-based environment. Hence, you may need to design a program that works directly with such individuals, assuring them of the importance of their places in the organization.

Proceed

Even if your staff, complete and absolute strangers, has been foisted on you, wondrous results can be achieved.

109

Be Wary

Don't overlook the individual staff members' needs to have the opportunity to share their views, lead the discussion, and feel comfortable about being part of the team.

Proceed

It is better to air as many issues at the outset as you can to try to minimize the incidence of hidden agendas and individual power plays.

with each other, and incur frictions, do you begin to understand the emerging group dynamics that your change management team represents.

From that standpoint, staff members assigned to you can end up forming a more effective and cohesive unit than a team composed of all handpicked members!

Bonding Doesn't Hurt

As with any team, all members need to get to know each other at the outset. Initial meetings should focus on cementing relationships, forming bonds, getting to know each other as individuals, establishing communication patterns, identifying and clarifying roles, and mapping out a schedule that everyone understands and adheres to.

Establishing a Campaign Orientation

If team members already know one another, the time you need to invest in establishing relationships, forming bonds, and developing a feeling of cohesiveness may not have to be much. With any staff, however, it pays to review the fundamentals.

Who reports to whom? What are the protocols regarding getting something copied, faxed, downloaded, converted to slide show, and so on?

Set Them on the Right Road

Orientation is an excellent time to let every member stand in front of the group and say a little about him- or herself, even if everyone already knows him or her, and what his or her concerns are in relation to this campaign. It is also the ideal time to discuss the ground rules, much as it is done in baseball. What is out of bounds—absolutely forbidden? These are usually time and money issues, such as a staff member authorizing payment for something that only the change manager can authorize.

➤ If the campaign requires an internal hierarchy, then who reports to whom?

➤ Can change managers turn to people outside the campaign, and what are the guidelines involved?

➤ How can the staff members be of particular benefit to one another?

➤ How can they help each other to avoid duplicating efforts?

➤ Are they willing to share private phone lines, pagers, and other means of personal access, if necessary?

➤ If your team is lacking in particular expertise, how will the team cover the shortfall?

➤ Can someone get up to speed in a hurry?

➤ Will you have to turn to added staff resources or to subcontractors?

➤ Can you borrow staff on an interim basis?

Regardless of what team you assemble, or what team is assembled for you, there are bound to be shortfalls, especially on first-time or challenging assignments, in terms of the skills needed to ensure a successful campaign. For example, career professionals today may prefer to be coached rather than managed ....

Proceed

While these are issues readily identified and resolved by the change manager, the team as a whole also can be adept at getting to the heart of the issue and finding effective resolutions.

Everyone in Unison

The most effective way to ensure that staff members make their contributions in a timely manner is to share information freely. Even in small teams, however, the roles and responsibilities of the members often vary widely. Some people may have a large share of the work assigned to them while others only have tiny portions.

Change Master

Responsible team members can handle and, increasingly, want to have the access to the "sacred" change management documents and reports that you as change manager refer to daily to keep on track.

Charting Your Progress

Change management tools should be shared with team members to ensure that everyone is playing the same game, for the same team, with the same final objective in mind. Everyone should have some access to and familiarity with the software programs, work breakdown structure, details of events or task areas, *Gantt* or *PERT/CPM charts,* or other specifics of the campaign.

Word Power

Gantt or **PERT/CPM charts** are traditional project planning and management tools that are useful for a wide variety of applications.

Charts offer a literal depiction of how team members' contributions fit into the overall campaign in a way that discussions, meetings, and endless e-mails never quite approach.

While it is beyond the scope of this book, *The Complete Idiot's Guide to Project Management,* as well as host of other fine books, provide the details of working with project management tools. (For more details, see Appendix A, "Further Reading.")

When one team member looks on a Gantt chart or critical path chart and sees that his or her input is vital to what another member needs, and vice versa, there is an immediate increase in probability that both will perform as indicated.

In chart form, you can succinctly capture the essence of a change campaign in a way that your staff and others can readily understand. For example, by using a grid or matrix, available with most word processing software, you can depict before and after situations for various components of your change campaign.

Using a simple example, suppose your team needs to shift from using manual charts or project management software to an online shared software program that performs all the same functions of the old. The new system, however, also allows anyone to log on at any time to make modifications or gain immediate updates. The skill levels required of targets of change in the "before" situation versus those in the "after" situation can be deftly portrayed in a two-column grid such as the one below.

	Initial Skill Level	New Skill Level
Skill Area 1	40%	60%
Skill Area 2	35%	75%
Skill Area 3	10%	30%

Directing a Winning Team

Change managers are similar to film producers who have to worry about big picture issues such as worldwide distribution, assignments of licenses and rights, marketing, advertising, and promotion. The camera crew, actors, and stagehands are the team members. On any given day, if somebody doesn't show up, the entire production schedule is at risk of falling behind.

The Movie Analogy

In the movie industry, the script is distributed to all those who have a vested interest in ensuring that the production goes according to schedule. Individual lines of each actor are documented in the script. Camera angles, scenes, and settings are written out in black and white. The production schedule is posted far in advance.

Agents, managers, handlers, schedulers, assistants, runners, caterers, coaches, and all supporting characters play important roles at various times throughout the production to ensure that everything stays on schedule.

Think of assembling, managing, communicating, and motivating a winning change team as analogous to directing a movie. You, as change manager, are on the "set" every morning, ready to shoot that day's scene.

Staying on Track

More than anything, what keeps a movie production on schedule is the realization among all players involved of the importance of staying on track. The same is true with a change team.

When all players have a vivid understanding of their roles and how they are interrelated, then group cohesiveness, uniformity, and peer pressure can generate significant input.

Be Wary

Don't "over chart." With your ability to generate and print program data with a single mouse click, it's easy to inundate your change team with a blizzard of downloads, papers, and details beyond reason.

Working with Borrowed Staff

The reality for many change managers is that the team they are able to assemble is only available on a part-time basis, is coming from other departments, has divided loyalties, or is working for other managers.

Jack Meredith and Samuel Mantel, in their book *Project Management,* observed that "with few exceptions" most of the people needed for a campaign "are borrowed from the functional departments." To obtain these people, you may have to negotiate (see Chapter 21, "Understanding the Importance of Negotiation") with accounting, production, marketing, and managers throughout the organization.

Be Wary

While the famous outbursts and tardiness of actors and actresses of yesteryear make for interesting reading, today's reality is that the costs of delays are far too great for anyone to start throwing tantrums or not showing up.

You must bargain for the requisite required staff members, and then, if successful, bargain with the staff members themselves as to how much time, energy, and effort they are willing to expend on their temporary assignment. Once again, as change manager, you find yourself in a selling position.

Proceed

You have to sell the challenge of your change campaign and even make it sound exciting.

Factoid

The odds are extraordinarily high that any team you manage today or in the future will be connected by cyberspace rather than geographical proximity.

Rounding Up Your Staff

Although managers of other departments generally comply with requests by managers to borrow staff members, all such requests have limits. Let's face it— you are going to be requesting the most competent individuals, those who have specific skills that mesh with your campaign needs.

In short, you are often attempting to borrow the staff people that other managers would be least likely to want to give up. Why do such managers participate at all? For the good of the organization, because they have to, because they may need to make the same request of you or other change managers at other times, and because they have learned over the years that such requests are inevitable.

Managing the Virtual Team

How do you manage during an era in which your team members may rarely, if ever, see each other and will disband immediately after the completion of the campaign?

Keep in mind that such a team doesn't have to be dispersed throughout the United States or across the globe. In many organizations, virtual teams are formed by people in the same office building, industrial park, or community campus. In such cases, the traditional approach to team management and cohesive development (as discussed earlier) is certainly applied at the outset.

Going for the Early Wins

If members can meet, it pays to expend great time and energy at the initial team meeting. It may be helpful to sequester members for the number of hours or days necessary to form the bonds that will sustain them over the weeks and months that they are not going to be meeting face-to-face on a regular basis.

All for One

In the case of the geographically dispersed team, strive to have all members fly into the headquarters at the outset, and proceed as previously scripted. If an initial face-to-face meeting with all members is not possible, try to have as many members attend as possible.

If that is not to be, spend a pronounced period at the outset establishing cohesiveness via conference calls, video conferencing, and online conferencing. These are potentially viable substitutes for the face-to-face meetings.

Last Laugh with Virtual Staff

Rest assured that great things can be accomplished even with a virtual staff. As more and more people spend more time online, they become more adept, confident, and fluent in their abilities to initiate and maintain relationships and work schedules, and to communicate using such media. Indeed, many team members working for multinational organizations may one day look back and say, "You actually met face to face for these types of campaigns?"

In her book, *Knights of the Tele-Round Table,* Jaclyn Kostner describes the particular issues encountered by managers faced with a virtual team.

Here are some of Dr. Kostner's observations regarding effective management of virtual teams in six basic areas: developing trust, developing group identity, sharing information, developing clear structures, forming informal subgroups, and understanding information. These observations are followed by potential problems and their solutions.

Change Master

As video conferencing, online conferencing, and related technologies continue to offer an ever-increasing array of options, even the globally dispersed virtual team can maintain cohesiveness more easily than one might have supposed a few years ago.

Effective Management of Virtual Teams

Focus Area	Potential Problem(s)	Antidotes
Developing trust	Inconsistent communication, team members not familiar with each other, "us vs. them" mentality.	Use varied methods of communication. Use e-mail except when signatures are required. Provide access to project-management software for all team members.
Developing group identity	Few shared experiences, lack of unity, little knowledge of each other's responsibilities.	Hold teleconference meetings. Include a variety of team members and involve all in discussion. Use logos, mottos, and humor. Keep in touch between meetings.
Sharing information	Lack of common system for sharing information across distances, lack of formal opportunities for discussion.	Use technology (pager, e-mail, Internet) for added information-sharing. Give all reports to members. Put information at one location, such as a program Web page.
Developing clear structures	Uncertain responsibilities of members, different expectations from clashing cultures, few clear decision-making processes.	Use consistent meeting formats. Define goals, problems, and concerns at first meeting, and repeat often. Have members describe concerns and evaluate as a group.
Formation of subgroups	Tend to create antagonism between team and manager, between team members, or among subgroups themselves.	Identify and track cliques Look for ways to mix members from different groups, and initiate or create them. For example, create subcommittees for dealing with problems.
Understanding information	Team members have incomplete or inconsistent information, and each member has a different perspective on the information.	Ask for explanations of viewpoints. Ask members to describe planned actions and solicit possible impacts on others. Give each a different level of information.

The Least You Need to Know

➤ The skills, interests, and aspirations of your team members will have a dramatic impact on the overall success of the change campaign.

➤ Borrowing staff members from other departments tends to be the rule rather than the exception. Surprisingly, most managers tend to be cooperative.

➤ If you haven't done so already, managing a virtual team will be on the short-term horizon for you.

➤ As career professionals become more adept at virtual team membership, managing at a distance doesn't have to be an arduous struggle.

➤ Keeping team members focused is an ongoing task that requires paying close attention to motivators and learning the needs of individual staff members.

Leading Your Team Through Change

Creative leadership strategies are crucial for leading your team through change. Leadership is more than calling meetings, speaking with staff members, and circulating memos. It requires a hands-on approach to addressing the personal issues of change.

The tips in this chapter will enable you to lead your group through change and survive the onslaught. Unfortunately, casualties of change are sometimes unavoidable; when they occur, these strategies will help minimize any accompanying damage.

Avoiding Rigid and Brutish Approaches to Change

Some organizations take rigid approaches to change management. Their change management philosophies can be summed up as "Here's the new situation. Deal with it!" While such a hard-line stance may be easy to articulate—as well as being personally

Proceed

You can't simply tell people how to change. You have to actively lead them through change.

Be Wary

While the use of management force may be an effective way to minimize short-term disruptions, it will only make your long-term problems worse.

Change Master

Each person maintains a constant equilibrium between his or her internal driving and restraining forces. When change is introduced in the form of a driving force (directives from management), employees will muster a compensatory restraining force (resistance to change) in an effort to maintain equilibrium.

appealing to the more authoritarian managers (as discussed in Chapter 8, "The Power-Coercive Approach")—it's far from the best way to lead through times of change.

Such managers present an impenetrable facade as a way of forestalling any resistance to change. They seem to think that if they can be tough enough to insist on unwavering compliance, their employees will be scared enough into submission.

Don't Intimidate Your Staff

When you intimidate people into toeing a new line, you've only effected an outward (and temporary) change in their behavior. Inwardly, that inevitable resistance to change will still be present until it is addressed on a psychological level. The employees' resistance will simmer beneath the surface, generating a conflict between thought and behavior, until one of two things happens:

1. Unresolved resistance begins to affect employees' behavior, and their performance begins to deteriorate.

2. They overcome their resistance, buy into the change, and resolve the conflict.

Chances are greater that the first of the two possibilities will occur.

Take Innate Resistance into Account

Kurt Lewin, first cited in Chapter 7, "The Normative-Reeducative Approach," mapped out the dynamics of normal resistance to change in his "force field analysis" theory (see Chapter 24, "Change Strategies from the Gurus," for details). Simply put, in every change situation, there are driving forces that push for change, and restraining forces that resist it. These forces exist on individual and group levels.

Managers need to take this resistance into account when attempting to lead an organization through change.

120

Work Against Resistance

The unfreezing/refreezing model of change works with resistance instead of against it. This model views an organization as an ice cube: relatively static in form and structure. To reshape the ice cube, you have to first unfreeze it, pour the water into the new shape, and then refreeze it. On a personal level, this means you have to understand and acknowledge the difference between change and *transition*.

Change in the context above is external and represents the new policy, structure, or practice the manager is trying to implement. Transition, however, represents the internal reorientation that people have to undergo before they can become effective change agents.

A person has to go through the transition process to unfreeze old, preexisting patterns. He or she can then change over to new modes of behavior and refreeze into the new paradigm.

Factoid

Transition is the process of an individual deciding to accept change, buy into its necessity, and work on its behalf.

Proceed

Prudent top executives in companies understand that adapting to new management is not something that can be left to chance.

Leading Troops in Transition

The rumor mill in any organization is ripe with half-truths and false leads the moment it becomes known that a company is going to merge or become acquired by another company.

➤ What will new management bring?

➤ Will there be expansion, growth, and new opportunities for all?

➤ Will there be blood letting—a hunt for excess layers of fat in the old company?

There's a Place for Us

Even after new management assumes power and two entities merge, those from the acquired half of the company still feel uncertain of their place and longevity in the newly formed organization.

The Wells Fargo Home Mortgage division faced such a situation when it acquired the Country Mortgage Company. The national sales manager handled the assignment of fully integrating the new staff (a change campaign, to be sure) so that they not only felt welcome in their new organization, but were fully comfortable being a part of it.

A three-day orientation session was held in the Midwest which included both old division and new division employees so that everybody would be marching from the same literal playbook (a two-inch-thick three-ring binder), as well as forming interpersonal connections. They also received a roster of key contacts including complete address, phone, and e-mail information of people to call when they felt the slightest bit uneasy.

Beyond the Orientation

The sales manager continued to direct and monitor the integration of the acquired company's employees over the next nine months. On anonymous survey forms, acquired staff reported that they did indeed feel as if the acquiring company had fully embraced them and was desirous of maintaining a long-term relationship. And, the sales manager was greatly successful—the attrition rate was exceedingly low.

Many organizations do not welcome new employees as effectively as Wells Fargo. Often these employees leave, because there is …

➤ No one to call.

➤ No one to provide a simple answer at a critical moment.

➤ No one to turn to in general.

If you're tasked to handle such a change campaign, undoubtedly you'll want to ensure that both upper management and existing staff members play vibrant roles in the acquired staff's success at adapting to the new management regime.

Be Wary

The cost of turnover among acquired staff can be crippling to the acquiring company.

Change Master

Whether it was long or short, you took some time to come to grips with the change at hand. By the time you present it to your employees, you've already begun, or perhaps even completed, your own transition. Your staff members, however, are still at square one. They will need time, just as you did, to process this change.

A Little Help Is Appreciated

You can help people manage their personal transitions by giving them plenty of time in which to process the transition mentally before they're expected to be 100 percent enthusiastic about supporting change (see Chapter 15, "Scheduling Days of Grace," for details). Time often seems like the commodity in shortest supply, but many organizations would have more time to implement changes if executives acted with enough foresight to allow leeway in the beginning of the change process.

The higher a manager is situated within an organization, the less time it takes to make his or her transition. He or she can see down the road to where the company is heading. Staffers usually have a more narrowly focused view. Give them time to understand the change, and don't expect them to complete the process as quickly as you did. It takes time for ice to melt and more time for it to refreeze.

Progressive, Adaptive Organizations

In contrast to the less caring organization, some organizations have a more progressive component. John Kotter and James Heskett examined more than 200 top corporations and determined that "adaptive" corporate cultures have a pronounced impact on long-run economic performance. They chronicled their findings in *Corporate Culture and Performance* (Free Press, 1992).

Adaptive organizations, the authors found, had visionary leaders who "walked the talk," and were more responsive to organization stakeholders. They tried to empower employees, and were committed to continuous improvement in operations. Curiously, such visionary leaders were more concerned with improving their own corporations than worrying about competition.

Proceed

To help your company reach its full, unique potential, pay closer attention to your own strategies, employees, and techniques. Concentrating on the tactics of other businesses, however enlightening, sometimes can be a distraction.

Word Power

Adaptive organizations are those led by insightful top management who are committed constantly to improving operations, empowering the staff, and increasing shareholder value.

Creating a More Flexible Staff

You can do all the right things on your end and still wind up with a staff that doesn't want to sign on to any change, regardless of how good (or unavoidable) it might be. How does this happen? The culprits are often inflexible organizations and their inherent intolerance for change. Such organizations also display a marked lack of openness to innovation and new ideas.

Let 'Em Learn from Their Mistakes

How can you stay loose so that your staff is more flexible and open to change?

Adopt the attitude that mistakes are an inevitable part of life and that they provide valuable opportunities for learning and growth.

Instead, cultivate the attitude that sometimes mistakes are unavoidable. If you do so, team members will be more likely to develop the flexibility you need them to have. Once your staff knows that you don't hold an unrealistic expectation of perfection, staff members will be more willing to accept responsibility for the mistakes they do make.

Provide Support for the Weary

When people learn from their mistakes, they tend to share that wisdom within the company so that the group as a whole will benefit from the process. The following poem succinctly conveys that learning from one's mistakes does have real-world application. Also, when people get support for taking responsibility for their mistakes, it's easier for them to criticize themselves constructively rather than negatively or destructively.

Be Wary

Convey that mistakes are unacceptable, and you're bound to see a high degree of cautiousness and conservatism on the part of your staff. This fear of making mistakes only makes your job even harder.

Change Master

Since mistakes are both inevitable and undesirable, the only rational attitude is to completely acknowledge them so they can be minimized in the future.

Autobiography in Five Short Chapters

Portia Nelson

I

I walk down the street.
>There is a deep hole in the sidewalk.
>I fall in
>I am lost …
>I am helpless
>It isn't my fault.
It takes forever to find a way out.

II

I walk down the same street.
>There is a deep hole in the sidewalk.
>I pretend I don't see it.
>I fall in again.
I can't believe I am in the same place.
>But, it isn't my fault.
It still takes a long time to get out.

III

I walk down the same street.
>There is a deep hole in the sidewalk.
>I see it is there.
>I still fall in … it's a habit.
My eyes are open. I know where I am. It is my fault.
I get out immediately.

IV

I walk down the same street.
> There is a deep hole in the sidewalk
> I walk around it.

V

I walk down another street.

(From *There's a Hole in My Sidewalk,* Beyond
Words Publishing, 1993)

It's good for your staff members to be demanding
of themselves and adhere to high performance and
behavior standards. However, when an unhealthy
attitude toward mistakes is prevalent in an organization, that drive toward excellence can become
harsh and unproductive.

The bigger the mistake, the more important the
lessons it contains. This could be difficult to swal-
low when it seems like disaster is staring you in the face, but if you can find a way to
focus on the positive aspects hidden in them, the information you reap could be
worth the pain involved.

Change Master

A change manager, or any effective leader for that matter, needs
to stress that when things go
wrong, employees should calmly
and objectively assess the situation. Then they can truly learn
from mistakes.

Developing Adept Change Artists

The ideal staff for any change manager would go beyond simply being flexible and
open; it would be adept at instigating, responding to, and managing change. Sound
like a tall order? It is for most organizations, but not for the reasons they think. Many
organizations make one fundamental mistake that is guaranteed to prevent staffers
from becoming adept at change, and that mistake is giving people accountability
without authority.

Graded but Not Empowered

Have you seen this scenario before? A change campaign is initiated, teams are created,
agendas are brainstormed, and timelines are developed. A collegial, enthusiastic feeling pervades the meeting room, at least until the meeting ends and people get back
to their desks.

All too often, they come to the realization that they're going to be held accountable
for the results of the new initiative, but management hasn't given them the requisite

Proceed

Ensure that your team members know they have authority in your change campaign so they don't feel inferior to you and become afraid to implement changes.

Factoid

Virtually everyone has an innate desire to wield some amount of authority in the world, and most people understand that accountability goes along with it.

authority to make sure the initiative is implemented properly. People in this situation are hamstrung before they ever get off the starting line.

People who find themselves in this unfortunate situation are likely to believe that they'll get the blame for any failures, but not the credit for any successes. How enthusiastically do you think they'll support your change efforts once they reach this conclusion? Instead of helping them to become change agents, you've turned them into the opposite: change opponents.

Hand Over the Authority

Employees can't be change agents if they have no agency. It may be difficult for you to do, but the more authority you can give people, the more accountability you can expect them to take on.

As authority and accountability increase together, people will transform into energetic change agents who are personally invested in helping you manage change as productively as possible.

Give Me Feedback, Please

People want to be held accountable. They want to invest themselves in a change campaign. If you give them tasks and make them accountable without the commensurate authority, you can bet they won't be personally invested in it.

"What happens if I give them the authority, and they mess up?" Think back to your own development as a leader. Was it a completely mistake-free process? Did you ever encounter or cause bumps in the road? Of course, you did. Why should the people under you now be held to a different standard?

This process is where grooming of future leaders begins, a process that some organizations simply leave to chance. It benefits the individual, as well as the organization, to delegate as much authority and accountability as possible.

Helping Your Team Succeed

Many change managers approach their change campaigns as one giant effort to get people to do something. Instead, why not look at your job as an effort to help the members in your group succeed? The difference is not merely *semantic*. When your goal is success instead of the fulfillment of a given task, your horizons expand to make room for a wider variety of achievements and accomplishments.

Resources Make the Difference

The reason most individuals and groups fail is that higher-ups—which could be change managers or sponsors—have not made available the necessary resources to get the job done. Don't let that happen to your team.

When you give someone a task or responsibility, think all the way through the finest details of implementation. If you can't answer a question, they probably won't be able to either. Help your team succeed by connecting employees with the vital resources they need.

Information is perhaps the most important resource of all. Paradoxically, it's the one that management often chokes off to a trickle. This tendency looks particularly perverse when you consider that your staff always wants as much information about a task as possible.

As your change campaign gets into full swing, you can observe your staff becoming more desirous of timely, crucial information. Unfortunately, that's when change managers are sometimes least prepared to *capitulate*.

Communication Is Key

Help your team succeed by establishing two-way lines of communication. Don't sequester yourself in long closed meetings from which little information is transmitted to others who could use it.

Sometimes, change managers who want to put the best face on a situation will leave out important facts or embellish them to give the best impression possible (see Chapter 13, "Managing Up, Managing Down"). Often, you're hurting the campaign by preventing employees from seeing reality.

Word Power

Semantic means of or relating to words or word choices, as in "the matter is not simply semantic."

Word Power

To **capitulate** is to relent, succumb, or surrender, but, in this context, it means to cooperate. Remember also, there's never a good time to give your staff the silent treatment.

Change Master

Don't be an information miser, hoarding each fact like it was your last stock option. Give the people in your group the information they need to chart their own respective courses.

127

Be Wary

It may seem as if change man-agement is a never-ending process and no matter what you accomplish, it will never be enough.

How can they succeed at their jobs when they don't know their true situations? During change campaigns, telling the truth often is more important than relating good news.

Is That Your Final Answer?

When it comes to change management or manage-ment in general, in the long term, there are no final answers. Realistically, every change campaign leads to another. Effective resolution, not so paradoxically, generates new problems. Ineffective solutions generate new problems or exacerbate existing ones. In either case, new types of campaigns need to be initiated.

The rewards and kudos for effective leadership toward the successful completion of a change campaign are often considerable. Even if you are reassigned to a new task the next day, there are always a few moments to bask in the glory of what you have achieved.

The Least You Need to Know

➤ Try to view mistakes as opportunities, not disasters.

➤ People become adept change agents when they have authority to match their accountability.

➤ Change campaigns are more successful in organizations that help employees succeed rather than in those that view changes as individual problems to over-come.

➤ Change managers can help staff members succeed by connecting them with the resources they need to do their jobs.

Chapter 12

Marshaling Group Resources

In This Chapter

➤ Priming the idea pump

➤ Facing conflict

➤ Achieving the synergy of teams

➤ Recognizing the value of coaching

➤ Emphasizing continuity amid changing times

➤ Taking advantage of outside resources

The inventor Alex Osborne assembled a roster of questions that would prompt him or any other user to more regularly attain conceptual breakthroughs when seeking to derive new product and service ideas. His list contained such questions as ...

➤ Can the item be made smaller?

➤ Can it be condensed?

➤ Can it be shortened?

➤ Can it be made lighter?

➤ What can be subtracted?

➤ What can be separated?

➤ What can be streamlined?

➤ What can be understated?

Such insightful questions helped redesign the traditional cassette tape recorder into Sony's creation of the miniaturized, lighter, streamlined tape recorder now universally known as the Discman.

You can use the same types of questions when leading your team through a change campaign. You're working with people, of course, not machines. By having your team members examine the situation in different ways, new ideas and creativity will be generated.

Be Wary

In retaining the same staff members over and over again for change campaigns, even when they have proven to be highly effective in working together, you risk applying staid approaches to varying challenges.

Factoid

Conflict within a change campaign team, like resistance to change itself, is a predictable component of human behavior. While some see conflict as destructive or debilitating, this need not be the case.

Prime the Idea Pump

One study concluded that the typical investment in new computer systems does not pay off—most investments failed to achieve the sponsor's desired outcome. Surprisingly, the failures were rarely due to the hardware or software itself. In most cases, the ventures failed due to human and organizational factors. Somebody within the organization failed to pay attention to some critical component of deploying human resources.

Every component of a change campaign ultimately is assigned to someone. A growing body of evidence indicates that comprehending these individual players is paramount to the success of the effort.

When you have the opportunity, work with a variety of team members and constantly rotate people on and off your staff. This may sound like extra work, but it is one of the best ways to ensure that your team and your change campaigns benefit from alternative ideas and fresh perspectives.

New staff people offer the potential of adding new ideas, knowledge that perhaps your group may not already possess, and innovative ways of tackling problems.

Don't Run from Conflict

With the addition of new faces and opinions, some conflict between people usually is unavoidable.

It is best to identify conflict as quickly as possible. Left untouched, it will grow, fester, and thwart a team's progress in ways that could put the entire change campaign in jeopardy.

Two Types of Conflict

To harness conflict for the value that it can provide to the change team you need to understand two basic categories of conflict.

➤ One is the type that focuses on the self. This focus occurs when one person has trouble relating to another on the team, or the team itself. This type of conflict can result in *mistrust, lack of unity, hostility, jealously, or even withdrawal.* Such conflict is based on relationships with other team members or others within the organization.

➤ The second type of conflict has to do with a particular task, how the group is expending its resources, or the appropriateness of certain procedures. It is not based on the personalities of team members or interpersonal interaction. The conflict would exist ideally, independent of who is on the team.

Team-building exercises help diminish conflict related to personal power plays and disunity among team members. Team members who recognize that they share some deep-rooted values and aspirations are often amazed at how easy they can come together in an atmosphere of cooperation and trust.

Change Master

Conflict related to tasks and with the change campaign itself can be constructive, motivating, and even energizing. Some management theorists hold that there is an optimal level of this type of conflict.

The Benefits of Conflict

Benefits may be derived from conflict. Publicly aired within a group, brought under the microscope, and intensely examined, team conflict can help surface issues early in a campaign. There may be time and resources for effective resolution, as opposed to late in the campaign when there may be nothing anybody can do.

Some organizations and change managers actively exploit conflict for its social and psychological benefits in helping the team move forward. Conflict between specific team members often generates both the motivation and energy to address underlying problems within the entire group. Certainly, conflict helps different people achieve a mutual understanding in ways that *passivity* simply doesn't engender.

Word Power

Passivity is the same as listlessness or lethargy and sometimes conveys a lack of energy.

Not Fatal, Often Synergistic

When team members understand that conflict need not be fatal, and that withholding true feelings or otherwise engaging in avoidance behavior actually diminishes the effectiveness of the team, they are more encouraged to be up front with team members more of the time. Conflict can help stimulate a sense of urgency within a group and sharpen team members' comprehension of the true objectives of a change campaign.

Social psychology theory holds that effective conflict resolution between two warring parties can result in *synergy* that was not otherwise available.

By bringing underlying issues to the surface, a team potentially clears out some of the barriers early in the campaign on the path to achieving the desired outcome.

Strive for Synergy

Once you add a second person to a change initiative, and certainly a third or fourth, the dynamics of the campaign change profoundly. The most effective teams, according to Daryl Conner, are those in which one and one equals "more than two." In other words, two people working together achieve more than the sum of the results of each of them working independently.

Undefined Partnerships Peter Out

Even in the smallest of groups, the two-person group, it is often best to have one person who is clearly in charge and designated as the change manager. Fifty-fifty partnerships are fine in theory but potentially can lead to far more squabbles than when there is a clear leader.

Looking back in show business, for example, whether it was Rogers and Hammerstein, Gilbert and Sullivan, Martin and Lewis, Stiller and Meara, or Sonny and Cher, many 50-50 partnerships ran into trouble as each partner jockeyed for control.

In firms organized as partnerships, problems linger because the term itself suggests that somehow tasks will be apportioned with equanimity. Often, one or both of the partners has no intention of matching the other task for task. Also, one partner may prove to be more effective at overall operations, while the other proves to be more effective at some functional discipline.

In a corporate setting, a change team that is part of a division, department, or group may wish in spirit to operate like a partnership, but it is probably best to avoid that form of organization.

Friends Beware

The saddest situation can occur when two friends form a partnership. Because their friendship is strong and they've gotten along well for years, they assume that the same relationship can be maintained in a business setting. Husband-and-wife teams in business can run into similar problems.

Partnerships can sometimes be effective as business entities and in managing change. The odds are that with one person in charge, the other member, or members, have a clearer understanding of their roles and responsibilities. Still, it is important to consider the consequences before forming such a team.

Factoid

In the professional services arena, accountants, attorneys, dentists, doctors, engineers, and real estate agents traditionally initiated firms as business partnerships. Changes in tax, liability, and estate planning combined to make the corporate form of organization far more viable for professional service firms.

Recognize the Value of Getting Coached

Although it is important that each member of your team have his or her own role and duty in the campaign, all members can act as coaches to each other.

"As we age, men belong to fewer and fewer teams. We become proud, solitary beings who think independence is the mark of maturity," Joe Kita said in the April 1998 issue of *Men's Health*. (Kita's observations are no less applicable to women.)

"Being a member of a real organization means setting definitive goals, making definable progress, and, most importantly, having comrades with whom to share defeats and victories. It surprises me how much I missed this, how much I need this," he noted.

"There's a similar satisfaction in being coached by team members. Even though my coach, Pat Boyle, is 12 years younger than me, I look to him for advice," Kita observed. "It's reassuring to see him every afternoon. He represents a very defined and focused part of my day. All I'm expected to do is follow orders and respond to the best of my ability. The only reward is his positive acknowledgment. But, that's enough."

Change Master

There's something so enjoyably mechanical about being coached that it becomes almost relaxing.

Proceed

Convince your team members to coach each other through your change campaign. By doing so, they provide support for the campaign as a whole. The productivity that results from working together will produce far greater results.

Word Power

Adaptable teams are groups of people in a purposeful state of flux to meet the ever-changing requirements with which they are tasked.

While there may be many people at work giving orders, there's a critical shortage of people acting as coaches. A true coach wants you to improve and succeed, as much for yourself as for the team. He or she is an objective taskmaster, the "field psychologist" who understands what drives you. That's why it's important to have coaches on your team. They keep you and your team members humble and on course.

Changing Times, Adaptable Teams

Robert Bookman, president of Bookman Resources in Chevy Chase, Maryland, helps organizations meet the challenges posed by work groups that take on new roles and forms. "*Adaptable teams,* as we refer to this new category of work group," says Bookman, "are currently forming in almost every sector of our economy."

Bookman noted that among adaptable team members, some people are assigned to work on common short-term problems. "Even as the group expands and contracts, each member is required to know what the others are working on. If some team members don't carry their own weight, everyone knows it.

"If people excel by superior knowledge, ideas, or natural leadership, the group will defer to them for guidance, regardless of whether they're seasoned veterans or new engineers just out of college," he adds. "Perhaps most daunting of all, everyone is held mutually responsible for the final products."

Twenty-First Century Team Challenges

In this team environment, Bookman observed that colleagues no longer ask, "What is your position on the corporate ladder?" Instead they ask, "What can you contribute?" Because of knowledge relevant to the tasks at hand, a person with high responsibility on one campaign may only have a tangential role on the next, or participate in several projects at a time.

"Teams in the future may last for years," Bookman says, "but more often we'll see teams disbanded and regrouped anew with high frequency. It will all depend on what is needed at the time."

Heliotropic Teams

The pinnacle of team harmony is making your team *heliotropic* so that each member is intensely devoted to the success of your campaign. Heliotropic-type teams involve people in what they find meaningful and life-giving in their work. Bookman says, "It is a search for 'what we're doing right.'"

Heliotropic teams do not deny problems. On the contrary, they make strategic decisions to focus on and move toward a desired future in such a way that the difficulties are more easily resolved. In heliotropic teams:

Word Power

Heliotropic means growing in the direction of the sun; as used here, it refers to teams that stimulate learning, innovation, and enthusiasm.

➤ People are in a habit of catching each other doing things right.

➤ People feel free to try experiments, take risks, and openly assess results. No one is seriously punished for making a mistake.

➤ People feel they're doing something that matters to them personally.

➤ People treat each other as colleagues.

In addition, people enjoy and practice the wisdom of philosopher and author Eric Hoffer who reportedly said, "in times of change, learners shall inherit the earth, while the learned are beautifully equipped for a world that no longer exists."

Change Master

In heliotropic teams and heliotropic organizations there's a mutual respect and trust in the way people talk to each other and work together, no matter what their positions may be.

Emphasize Continuity Amid Change

People have an inherent need to know where they stand within an organization, that their contributions are appreciated, and that there are certain prevailing guidelines and protocols. In addition to having your team work together, a good ways to produce positive results is by giving your staff members a sense of balance while they're being asked to change some aspect of the organization or themselves.

A Sense of Stability

Even the most innovative organizations, constantly engaged in change campaigns, need to give their workforces some sense of continuity.

Factoid

In the midst of tumultuous change, people want to know that the values of an organization remain stable.

People prefer to work with people who they already know and like. They will seek continuity in terms of who they work with, what is expected of them, what kind of information they receive, and how they are to impart information. Failing that, they at least prefer to work with people with whom they can cooperate.

Peter F. Drucker, in his book *Management Challenges for the 21st Century,* observes that information is particularly important to maintaining balance (see Chapter 25, "Gurus with Academic Ties," for more details). "Balancing change and continuity requires continual work on information flow. Nothing disrupts continuity and corrupts relationships more than poor or unreliable information … except deliberate misinformation." Drucker says, "It has become routine for any enterprise to ask at any change, even the most minor ones, 'Who needs to be informed of this?'"

Minor Updates, Major Relief

When I worked for a small management consultant firm in Vernon, Connecticut, in the mid 1970s, we had a weekly staff meeting that I found most comforting. While many people report that they loathe having to sit in staff meetings, for me, it was a weekly opportunity to reestablish a sense of equilibrium in a constantly changing environment.

Each of our three consultants, as well as the president of the company, reported on the consulting projects he or she was handling. Going down the list, reviewing what success or failures we encountered, we also solicited one another's help and advice. In routine fashion, we discussed all of the firm's active clients, updated our respective rosters, and returned to our offices.

Each consultant knew where he or she stood. Each consultant knew what else was occurring in the firm. Each of us could call on another for information advice or other kinds of support at any time.

Comfort in Reporting

Reporting on a regular basis served many functions. We knew exactly when we would receive updates from one another, and that eliminated unnecessary interoffice communication. The reporting of our progress was itself an incentive to be productive.

Publicly announcing the status of each project helped each staff consultant to articulate in his or her own mind what had transpired, what would be done next, and what might be needed from other staff consultants. Everyone received weekly a typed updated report (this was when dinosaurs roamed the earth and we didn't have computers yet).

Mutual Support

If you knew that John was working on a project that required a critical reference source, a vital phone number, or a key calculation, and you could supply it, you were only happy to do so. When he recognized his capability to support your efforts, John would do the same for you.

These cross linkages and cross support structures enabled us to have a broader view of projects outside our immediate sphere, even when working on projects alone, which was usually the case.

We didn't regard ourselves as change managers. Yet, we encompassed many of the effective operating procedures that a change manager needs to employ in today's ultra-hectic environments.

Tap Into Resources Outside Your Team

As I discussed in Chapter 2, "Change Scenarios," involving your customers in a change campaign can prove to be highly rewarding. From the standpoint of using group resources, how often do you consider the knowledge, operating experience, and resources of some of your best customers?

Customers can offer totally fresh perspectives that could spell the difference in the case of developing a new product or service. Customers and clients have policies and procedures in place that may be worth emulating. Using members of your organization, outside of your change campaign, can also be a useful approach to generating ideas and feedback.

Managers and staff people in other departments and other division who have no formal role in your change campaign may nevertheless serve as valuable resources for your group as well. Depending on what types of change campaigns they have worked on previously, and their education, background, and experiences in general, you may find selected individuals who can serve as ad hoc advocates or well-wishers.

A quick phone call to one of these valuable resources, a one-sentence e-mail, or a brief exchange in the hallway may result in you getting just the right input at just the right time to propel your project forward.

By using the ideas of its members, while maintaining a balance between them, your team's best resources will surface. Don't be afraid, however, to use the opinions and input of people outside your team. The combination of these diverse contributions will lead to the best solutions in your change campaign.

The Least You Need to Know

➤ When you have the opportunity, work with a variety of team members and constantly rotate people on and off your staff.

➤ Conflict related to tasks can be constructive, motivating, and even energizing. Some management theorists hold that there is an optimal level of this type of conflict.

➤ The most effective teams are those in which one and one equals "more than two."

➤ The pinnacle of team harmony is making your team heliotropic so that each member is intensely devoted to the success of your campaign.

➤ Even the most innovative organizations, constantly engaged in change campaigns, need to give their workforces some sense of continuity.

Chapter 13

Managing Up, Managing Down

In This Chapter

➤ Buying into what you've been assigned

➤ Gaining a broader perspective of your mission

➤ Transforming yourself on the fly

➤ Selling the news to the troops

➤ Becoming an effective conduit

➤ Inducing miraculous redirections when things look bleak

As the primary change agent, or change manager—the term I prefer—you now understand the roles and some of the responsibilities of the players in a change campaign.

An effective change manager knows the importance of continually dealing with the initiating or sustaining sponsor, targets of change, advocates, well-wishers, and, occasionally, bystanders. In such a capacity, you're the conduit who both reports to the higher-ups and manages key staff.

Buying Into Your Assignment

One of the fundamental issues inherent for any change manager is buying into what has been assigned. All would be well if each time you were assigned to a change campaign you fully supported it and fully embraced the desired end result without any prodding. In reality, there may be many situations you are asked to manage about which you have mixed feelings.

Suppose you're involved in some type of reorganization that will ultimately mean the loss of jobs in your organization. Perhaps you are asked to manage staff, some of whom won't be retained by your organization. This could put you in a bind, even a moral dilemma. What do you do?

Word Power

To **rationalize** a situation is to mentally minimize or play down its negative aspects and justify it.

Proceed

The change manager who understands that sometimes laying off staff is an unavoidable (if highly disruptive) reality of operating a business is likely to have an "easier" time of engaging in such a reorganization project. He recognizes that it would help preserve the organization as well as solidify the employment prospects for those slated to be retained.

Perspective, Not Rationalization

With the types of change impacting organizations (as discussed in Chapter 2, "Change Scenarios"), it's likely that many of the change campaigns you're asked to manage, and a variety of tasks within those campaigns, are not to your favor. This is where it becomes important to find a way to buy into what you have been assigned.

I am not suggesting that you *rationalize* your behavior in the face of something you are vehemently opposed to doing. I'm talking about gaining a fuller perspective of your organization's, department's, or division's needs; what is to be accomplished; and how that fits into the overall vitality and longevity of your organization.

Downsizing Isn't Pretty

Many change managers have had to "downsize" a department or division. Surveys show that having to terminate employees is the least enjoyable task of managers. Yet, often it can be soundly demonstrated that people must be let go for the viability and profitability of an organization. The calculations for a company that has shown losses for the last several quarters may indicate that unless expenses are reduced in a dramatic way, everyone's jobs may be lost, not merely those who've been targeted for termination.

Similar situations may occur when a product or service line is going to be dramatically altered. Products may be dropped, combined, merged, or sold off. Services could be expanded, upgraded, diminished, or dropped entirely.

Whether or not such moves have an impact on employee longevity, people who have invested long hours in the development of a product or service only to see it dropped from the lineup often feel let down.

Gaining a Broader Perspective

As you can quickly surmise, a potpourri of change campaigns and change scenarios exists that you might be asked to lead. Many such campaigns may necessitate having to buy into what you've been assigned when you don't necessarily agree with the changes handed to you from above.

Here are a variety of measures to help you gain a broader perspective and appreciation for the purposes and activities of your organization, department, or division:

➤ If you haven't done so lately, read your organization's mission statement, any statement of values, the founder's message, and any mottos, slogans, or "sacred words" that propel your organization.

➤ Read your organization's annual report, quarterly reports, and any 10K or 10Q statements that may be available. Such documents contain letters from the CEO, the president, and, often, division presidents and vice presidents. These letters were prepared for shareholders of all stripes—including other corporate officers, those who may have purchased the organization's publicly traded stock, employees, and retirees with vested pension plans. They often succinctly encapsulate the perspective, direction, and plans of the top organization officials who wrote them.

➤ If the opportunity presents itself, attend your organization's annual stockholder meeting. This may seem like dramatic overkill in terms of sharpening your ability to buy into what you have been assigned. However, if the stockholder meeting is conveniently located near your base of operations and you can make the event, you will gain an education that few other managers ever receive.

➤ Visit your organization's library. There, you will be privy to past annual reports, public announcements, advertisements, promotional literature, and a vast array of other printed documents that can put you on solid footing when it comes to understanding the overall mission and direction of your organization.

Factoid

The prerequisite for attending a shareholder meeting is simply to own one share of stock. If you don't own one, you can buy one online today.

History in the Making

All organizations, even those chartered in recent years, have history. It's your responsibility to understand that history. Fortunately, you have many sources to which to turn, such as those cited above. The longer your organization has existed, the more history there is to review. Offsetting that is the realization that more resources are often uncovered.

Conversely, you may encounter information about programs or plans that didn't work, and hence save yourself time and trouble, especially if it appears that the climate and circumstances haven't changed.

Founding Patrons and Matrons

Every organization has a founding member or group of members, a first president, a first board, and so on. Many of these patron and matron saints are still either actively involved with the organization or mentally and emotionally involved behind the scenes.

Find out about the goals and aspirations of your founding fathers and mothers. Perhaps in the course of your campaign you can even call on these knowledgeable elders. They will be amazed, pleased, and enthusiastic sages. With everyone on e-mail, it's easy to include them when you have questions.

Transforming Yourself on the Fly

Suppose the change campaign you've been asked to manage needs to begin immediately. There is little time for reflection or background research. Because of changes in the marketplace, competition practices, or an opportunity that simply can't wait, you've got to get started tomorrow, or this afternoon!

Proceed

Tactfully and skillfully find out as much as you can as quickly as possible about initiating sponsors with whom you are unfamiliar.

How do you transform yourself on the fly? How do you buy into something that you would be predisposed to shun if you had the opportunity? This is not an easy issue to tackle, but there are some exercises and insights you can draw on to increase your capability for transforming your perceptions about a change campaign in a short amount of time.

Know Thy Sponsor

Your relationship with the initiating sponsor may be sufficient for you to get started. If you already know and respect the sponsor, and have been through a similar situation with the sponsor before, then your loyalty and trust in him or her may carry the day for you.

If not, perhaps you are privy to the sponsor's track record. What has this person initiated previously that you thought was questionable at the time, but turned out to be for the good of everyone involved? Can you compare notes with other change managers who have been assigned change campaigns by this sponsor before?

Borrow Some Moccasins

Recalling the Native American saying "Walk a mile in another person's moccasins" can work well here. Regardless of your relationship and knowledge of the sponsor, can you fully embrace what it must be like for him or her to arrive at the conclusion that a change campaign needs to begin?

➤ What pressures might the sponsor be facing?

➤ What constituents might be influencing the sponsor's quest?

➤ What do you know about external pressures on your organization, internal pressures, and other prevailing factors that might be at play?

Change Master

To the degree that you can arrive at some level of understanding as to why the sponsor is initiating a change, you are in a far better position to initiate any change campaign on the fly, regardless of your initial perceptions of it.

Call All Corollaries

Can you find corollaries within your own organization? If so, you gain perspective in a hurry:

➤ Have other projects, similar to what you have been assigned, been initiated?

➤ How did they turn out?

➤ What were the pitfalls along the way, and how did the change manager handle them?

➤ How did the staff and targets respond to the projects?

Use Your Wits

Beyond the suggestions above, draw on whatever else you possibly can to prime yourself for the task at hand. The more transformations you can quickly handle, the more valuable an employee, manager, or executive you can be in the future.

Change Master

Because the ability to adapt and embrace situations quickly is so contrary to human psychology, those who do display this ability automatically become regarded as someone special within their respective organizations.

The odds are that you're going to face this situation more frequently throughout your career. The changes that your organization, department, or division has to fathom are only going to come more often, and with less notice. The change manager who develops a solid reputation for being able to start and stop on a dime will increasingly become the type of person with whom others want to work (see Chapter 14, "Managing Inside and Outside Your Head," for details).

Selling the News to the Troops

Whatever issues you have with embracing a change campaign, rest assured that your staff will have the same reservations and probably others, because they are privy to less information than you. To them, the reasoning behind what they are assigned to do is often mysterious. Somebody wrote a memo. Somebody sent an e-mail. They have been reassigned.

Since you're a conduit between a sponsor and the targets, your role requires more finesse, tact, and delicacy than either of the other two parties.

Whom Do You Trust?

Suppose one way or another you've bought into what you have been assigned but you don't have trust in those above you. Is it fair that you communicate your lack of trust to your staff? Most management texts say "no." Conversely, if you are completely open and forthright with your staff, airing all notions of doubt that you harbor, can your staff possibly be as effective in pursuit of the change initiative?

You have to walk a fine line here. You don't want to mislead your staff and you don't want to cause them to lose motivation. What is the best course of action? I wish there were an easy answer. It changes based on the situation.

Here are some of the common denominators you can count on from one change campaign to another, given that you find yourself in a conduit bind:

Change Master

Your ability to be open and forthright with your staff can be the crucial element in the success of a change campaign.

➤ Keep focusing on the greater good that's behind the project initiated. Is the desired result something that everyone can learn to embrace?

➤ Iron out with your sponsor as many of your misgivings as is practical. Maybe some of the doubts and concerns that you have can be alleviated before you end up conveying them to your staff.

➤ It is okay to appear human to your staff. If you are heading down a path that is new to you or you are assigning something that you believe has significant risk, by all means, let them in on it. Candidness here and there, without going overboard, can go a long way in shoring up your relationship with your staff.

Secrets of the Crypt

Suppose you're working with a sponsor or boss who you trust implicitly. He or she comes to you and says, "Here is the situation. I would like you to keep it under wraps and not share this with your team." What would you do?

The best approach would be to proceed based on your boss's wishes because of the relationship and trust already built up. In that case, you turn around and give the company line to your troops, because, essentially, that's what is called for.

How Little We Know

Suppose you face a situation in which, regardless of your relationship with the sponsor, you have strong reason to believe that you haven't been given the whole story. In that case, you can still level with your employees using language such as:

➤ It is my understanding that …

➤ As far as I know, …

➤ Given what I have been told, …

➤ My take on the situation is …

Lie for Me

Suppose your boss asks you to lie to your staff. Are you okay with that? Sometimes, in a change situation, it's going to happen. You have to consider the sponsor, your responsibilities, and your staff. You must also maintain perspective as to where the organization is heading and the external factors that might be causing your boss to make such a request of you.

Is there a universal solution on how to handle a request for you to lie? There should be! It's paramount that you understand your responsibility and when your boss tells you to do something, you have to separate yourself from the people who report to you.

Be Wary

There are such things as benevolent lies. Still, a lie is a lie. If the people who report to you find out that you haven't been totally square with them, it could have downstream repercussions even though you are following orders.

You have to make some conclusions in a hurry:

➤ Do you trust the people above you?

➤ Do they have a reputation for doing the right thing?

➤ Do they have the capability to guide you in the right direction?

➤ Ultimately, is it all for the best?

Be Wary

People are generally regarded as the most important assets in an organization today. If you continually push people in situations that require them to compromise personal values, it's only a matter of time before the best people depart.

Change Master

The people who report to you have a way of hanging on to your every word and retaining far more of what you say than you retain yourself. They match what you have said with your actions, and judge you accordingly.

The Binds That Tie

Double-bind situations are not pretty, and you don't want to encounter one after another. Unfortunately, in some organizations, particularly those not adept at managing change, double-bind situations become a way of life.

In the extreme, this can result in double-bind organizations. These represent businesses and other groups whose survival seems to be tied to asking managers to operate on the edge of their ethics. Perhaps this is a viable survival strategy in the short run, but I can't see it being a viable long-run strategy.

Becoming an Effective Conduit

Since you are the conduit to your staff, what can you do to increase the probability of success independent of your relationship with the sponsor? Here are some suggestions:

➤ Prepare your staff by having preliminary meetings, perhaps one-on-one with each member, before meeting as a group. After meeting as a group, meet one-on-one once again.

➤ Share your vision of what it will be like once the change campaign is successfully completed. Do what you can to get them to latch on to that vision.

➤ Be open to new ideas, as long as they don't interfere with or circumvent your understanding of what the most appropriate path is in achieving the desired result.

➤ Offer late-breaking news, as soon as you get it, so that there is very little gap between what you have learned and what your staff needs to know. People appreciate being in the loop, and can sense when they are not.

➤ Seek and maintain consistency between what you say and what you do.

The Reframe Game

Based on what you know about human resistance to change, much of your task in serving as a conduit consists of framing situations so that corresponding parties can latch on to your views. When dealing with your sponsor, for example, at certain times and in certain circumstances, it may seem as if both command and control flow in one basic direction. Actually, you have more leeway over the situation than you might suppose.

If your sponsor is new to sponsorship, or is in a new arena altogether, your experience and your views may weigh heavily on what he or she decides to do as a change campaign unfolds. Since change management can be regarded as progress-

Proceed

You may find yourself being called in at the outset of a change campaign—asked to be part of an original task force or team that supports the sponsor in identifying, establishing, and authorizing the change.

ing from one state to another, how you define or describe where you are and where you want to be can have a significant impact on how you will proceed.

Diagnose Well, Benefit Quickly

The best theoreticians generally believe that a well-defined problem is a problem on its way to being solved. When you are fortunate enough to be in a position where you can influence the sponsor as to how to proceed, how you frame, or, in the case in which a problem has initially been handed to you, reframing the problem may ultimately dictate how you proceed in the change campaign. Toward that end, you get to manage your own destiny!

Reframing with Your Staff

When working with your staff, reframing takes on a different nature. Here, you are selling them on an action plan that essentially has been mapped out prior to their inclusion on the team. Normally you'll meet with pockets of resistance here and there, some of which won't immediately surface.

Your job in managing down consists of reframing as you proceed. Each time you hit a pocket of resistance or something that your staff doesn't understand, your job is to coach the challenge in terms that they can buy into, relate to, comprehend, and initiate. (See Chapter 10, "Preparing Your Team for Change," and Chapter 11, "Leading Your Team Through Change," for more details.)

Inducing a Miracle Redirection

If you've ever seen the movie of William Shakespeare's *Henry V* produced by and staring Kenneth Branagh, you may recall his enactment of a miraculous redirection in military history. Greatly outnumbered by the French at the Battle of Agincourt, Henry offered a speech so stirring and inspiring that his troops fought with a vigor transcending that of which soldiers were known to be capable. So, too, we hear of coaches who give half-time pep talks that turn their teams around and enable them to achieve victory.

Leadership Makes a Difference

Unquestionably, people respond to effective leadership. When Colin Powell took over the U.S. State Department in January 2001, newspaper reports that his closed-door, 90-minute speech to top agency officials was supposedly the stuff of which legends are made. Powell didn't allow a recording of it, but, allegedly, lifelong State Department employees were motivated in a manner that they had not encountered in decades, if ever.

Drawing on his talents and techniques refined from six years on the lecture circuit, speaking at some of the largest conferences and conventions throughout North America, General Powell changed minds at the State Department with a single presentation. He shared his vision, his personal philosophies about work and life, and what he thought was possible for the agency, the United States, and the world.

Draw On the Best of You

You may not be a sparkling orator. Still, there are elements in your personality and communication style that undoubtedly can be used to win people over, help them be their best, and promote overall excellence.

In the movie *Jerry Maguire*, Renée Zellweger's character says to Maguire, played by Tom Cruise, "Basically, I'm looking for some inspiration." Aren't we all? Whether or not they ever admit it, the people you manage are looking to be inspired. When you can fulfill that need, miraculous redirections are indeed possible!

The Least You Need to Know

➤ Buying into what you have been assigned might be a challenge for you. Draw on many information sources to gain a fuller understanding of the underlying need.

➤ Managers who are able to undertake transformations on the fly are increasingly in demand.

➤ Double-bind situations such as being asked to retain certain types of information and not sharing it with your staff merit your careful thought and independent analysis.

➤ Selling your staff on the tasks required to successfully complete a change campaign and keeping them informed are never-ending tasks of a change manager.

➤ How a problem is defined largely influences how it is to be solved. If you have input into this process, consider yourself lucky.

➤ People are looking to be inspired.

Chapter 14

Managing Inside and Outside Your Head

In This Chapter

➤ Change is the only constant

➤ Affirmations can work wonders

➤ Committing yourself to a change campaign and letting go

➤ Achieving closure after a change campaign

➤ Getting ready for the next challenge

As you learned in the last chapter, the role that you're likely to play, change manager, requires you to be a conduit, continually dealing with staff members you manage and higher-ups to whom you report. To properly handle the position, you have to learn about managing inside and outside your head. What does this mean? You have to develop and improve your own mental processes for dealing with new direction, which could include making a 180-degree reversal in plans or walking away from a project.

Change—The Only Business Constant

Each year it seems that there are few things one can safely predict in terms of the direction of an organization or an entire industry, due in part to the constant improvements in technology. As the following timeline emphasizes, you *can* count on change as your constant companion nearly every step of the way for the duration of your career.

Technology Rules

1440	Movable type (Johannes Gutenberg of Mainz)
1502	Wristwatch (Peter Henlein of Nuremberg)
1642	Mechanical adding machine (Plaise Bascal)
1793	Cotton gin (Eli Whitney)
1801	Weaving machine (Joseph-Marie Jaquard)
1803	Steam engine (Robert Fulton)
1834	Analytical engine (early computer) (Charles Babbage)
1844	Telegraph system (Samuel Morse)
1866	Transatlantic cable
1876	Telephone (Alexander Graham Bell)
1903	Powered flight (Wilbur and Orville Wright)
1911	Automobile electric ignition system (Charles Kettering)
1942	Automated computer ENIAC (U.S. Army)
1969	World Wide Web (Tim Berners-Lee)
1975	Personal computer (IBM and other vendors)
1981	User-friendly Apple computer (Steven Jobs and Stephen Wozniak)
1993	Mosaic, Netscape Internet browsers (Marc Andreessen)

Coming to prominence:

1995–2005	Web TV, palm top, cell phone, pager, intranets, RealAudio, RealVideo, RealPlayer, MP3, HDTV, satellite radio, broadband, optical readers

Harking back to Chapter 1, "No More Standing Still," increasingly the term *management* will mean "change management," and the natural human response to change is resistance.

Managing Your Own Perceptions

An effective change manager remains on constant alert, particularly during a change campaign in which he or she may be experiencing resistance.

Being an effective change manager means managing your own perceptions about change. I spoke at a conference in Paris on the topic of my book *Creating Breathing*

Space. Afterward, at a reception, one of the participants asked me if I am always encouraging, energetic, and productive. I answered, "Of course not. I get into ruts as much as anyone." The participant said, "What do you do to get out of a rut?"

The query stopped me cold. By some small miracle, I had never given the matter any extended thought. Then, semi-miraculously, the answer came to me. I said, "I fight for *objectivity*."

When I find myself in a situation in which I feel blocked, I attempt to recall similar situations and what I did to blast through the bottleneck.

If the challenge before me is unlike anything I have previously experienced, I then think of a solution that helped in a different situation that might be applicable in the current one. If I'm still drawing blanks, I scan my memory bank for something somebody else did that might work for me.

Practicing "Head-Changing" Behavior

Suppose you're only 28 years old or have recently been promoted to a career-stretching change management position. Are there behaviors you can continually practice that will enhance your flexibility and resourcefulness in the face of a highly significant, disruptive event? Is there anything you can do in advance to diminish the inherent human tendency to be resistant to change?

Fortunately, there are, and they're not arduous.

On a fundamental level, these "head changing" types of activities may include any of the following:

➤ **Reading case histories about change**, particularly in your industry or market. After doing so, ask yourself the following questions:

What confronted the players?

How did they respond?

What was the result?

Be Wary

It is relatively easy to observe other's resistance to change. For many people, it is exceedingly difficult to detect their own resistance.

Word Power

To have **objectivity** is to have a clear, impartial, and neutral focus.

Change Master

The longer you live, the more problems you will face for which, given that you maintain mental sharpness, you may be able to draw upon previous observations and experiences to help resolve them.

➤ **Finding effective sounding boards** that will help you discover more about yourself. Then, critique and assess your own resistance. Other people can readily see things about you that you don't easily see in yourself (and thus help you explore your own pockets of resistance).

➤ **Remaining abreast of developments** in your industry or market, even those you dislike. Similarly, it is important to stay aware of developments in industries or professions that impact yours (see Chapter 23, "Keeping a Keen Eye on the Competition," for details).

➤ **Being willing to commit extra hours**, on a campaign basis and not as a long-term method of doing business, to help ensure that a particular change campaign is successful.

Simply being open to explore new subjects and new lines of inquiry in your personal life can aid in embracing change at work.

➤ Peruse different magazines, newspapers, journals, articles, and books.

➤ Watch different movies.

➤ Take courses other than those you would normally be inclined to take.

➤ Visit Web sites that lie outside of your immediate interest area.

➤ Strike up conversations with individuals to whom you're not usually attracted and see what you can learn from them.

➤ Visit antique shops, variety stores, and gift shops even if you're not eager to do so. Notice new creations, games, gifts, toys, and knickknacks that strike your fancy.

➤ Take vacations in areas you haven't visited before. Take tours that normally wouldn't be attractive to you.

➤ Use different types of transportation.

➤ For a limited time, try a hobby that is vastly different from other hobbies you have tried.

➤ Complete crossword puzzles, cryptograms, and other types of word and numerical games. Allow yourself to simply play.

➤ Rearrange your physical surroundings. Try new colors, shapes, textures, and anything else that contributes to a new perspective both literally and figuratively.

Change Master

Recognize that the disruption change represents often translates into some extra hours on the job addressing what has happened or simply trying to understand it.

Directing Yourself Through Affirmations

Affirmations are beneficial for increasing your receptivity to and effectiveness in managing change while vanquishing your own resistance. By making positive affirmations daily, which are nothing more than deeply felt choices, you actually enable yourself to move closer to obtaining them. It may sound simplistic, but the only skeptics are those who haven't tried.

Make such choices regularly regardless of how you feel at any given moment. Your quest is to keep making affirmations and allow them to sink in to all levels of your consciousness.

The following list provides specific affirmations you can use to increase the probability of becoming an effective change manager. Note: All of these statements are worded in their most positive form because the goal is to move toward your choice rather than away from something that you are attempting to avoid.

➤ I choose to easily accept this change with high energy and enthusiasm.

➤ I choose to readily take action in support of this change.

➤ I choose to be effective in motivating others in support of this change.

➤ I choose to easily identify associated problems and resolve them.

➤ I choose to remain optimistic in my ability to handle broad sweeping change.

➤ I choose to accept all the new opportunities that this change represents.

➤ I choose to be open to other people's points of view.

➤ I choose to creatively approach adversity.

➤ I choose to easily incorporate this change into my daily activities.

➤ I choose to have clarity and focus.

➤ I choose to follow my own inner wisdom.

➤ I choose to easily convey to others my willingness to accept this change.

➤ I choose to easily become an effective change manager.

Be Wary

Don't confuse this with "positive thinking," which focuses more on your attitude than your decisions.

Committing and Letting Go

"Managing a successful organization in today's fast-moving world economy is like flying a jet fighter," says William A. Schiemann of the Metrus Group based in Somerville, New Jersey. "Minimum time to react; environmental forces fluctuating between extremes; stress on the machinery."

Suppose you have accepted the challenge of tackling a change campaign. You have a comprehensive understanding of what you are up against. You have charted the players and taken steps to serve as an effective conduit to those above and below you in the organization.

One morning you walk into work and find that practically everything related to your project has been modified (that is, the change has occured), a major resource has been withdrawn, the time frame has been altered, the objectives themselves have undergone a dramatic redirection, or, worse from the standpoint of your own psyche, the project is terminated at what seems a moment's notice. You poured your heart and soul, your energy and your expertise, and, figuratively, every fiber of your being into the campaign—and it's gone.

Change Master

As it is human nature to naturally resist change, once someone embraces a change and launches a full-scale campaign, the opposite may occur—one resists giving it up.

Not Once in a Lifetime

If this phenomenon happened to you only once in your career, or once within each organization or at each post, you might simply write it off as "one of those things." Increasingly, however, change managers of all stripes often find themselves in situations in which they are wholeheartedly committed to a change campaign, only to be told, often without warning, that the campaign has to be abandoned because of new plans.

The unprepared change manager, who is suddenly introduced to 180-degree reversals or abandoned plans, can experience protracted bouts of mourning and even a form of shellshock.

The Entrapment of Attachment

It's easy to become fixated on your efforts—your progress in pursuit of a change campaign. The phenomenon is called attachment. Curiously, attachment helps to both explain why you might initially be resistant to change, and, after embracing a change, why it's hard to abandon a change campaign. In both instances, there is impetus. In the case of the first, it is a challenge to move. In the case of the latter, it is a challenge to stop moving. Maintaining the status quo, or doing what you have been doing, is also a variety of impetus.

Getting in motion, following a plan, making progress, and revving up your energy level and commitment are other forms of impetus.

A Moment's Notice

An effective change manager recognizes the dynamics of her environment and is able to nurture the ability to commit to a change campaign. At the same time, she cultivates the capability to let it go at a moment's notice.

Everyone has seen this phenomenon. In book publishing, for example, an editor may spend hours day after day, week after week, copyediting a manuscript that, for one reason or another, the publishing house doesn't publish. Or, the editor is simply reassigned to a more pressing project and has to abandon the heavy mental investment in the earlier manuscript.

Perhaps he is moved to a new division, or the publishing house itself merges with another business entity and must reorganize. Maybe the line of books the editor has been working on has been reconfigured or scrapped. In any event, the editor needs to let go of the current manuscript and let go quickly while keeping the residual psychological baggage to a minimum.

Change Master

A vital characteristic and operating dynamic of effective change managers in today's often volatile, routinely unpredictable, and sometimes chaotic business environment is to nurture the capability to commit. At the same time, they must be able to let go. It is a paradoxical set of traits, but they are irrefutably necessary.

Software, Hard Turn

Software developers face the same situations and may find themselves having to turn corners even faster. If the competition comes out with some vastly superior types of software, projects need to be upgraded or scrapped immediately. Perhaps there is market resistance or breakthroughs in hardware technology that render the current change campaign all but obsolete.

Identifying Your Erroneous Zones

A useful exercise for any change manager to engage in before initiating a change campaign is to identify areas where he or she may be predisposed to limiting beliefs or behaviors. For example:

➤ Do you have a tendency toward over-filing, over-organizing, over-collecting, or other ritual behavior that ends up impeding rather than enhancing your overall progress?

➤ Do you have a high need to be accepted? If so, how might this affect your actions in the campaign that you are about to tackle?

➤ Are you the type of person who waits for explicit permission? If so, will that hamper your progress, potentially causing you to miss opportunities with short time frames?

➤ Do you repeatedly push yourself to your productive limit, hence becoming a drag and drain on those you work with? Or, do you know how to maintain high productivity even in the face of strenuous projects that potentially may take a heavy toll on your physical and mental well-being?

➤ In your personal life, are you predisposed to spending money as soon as it comes, and how may this manifest itself in your professional life?

➤ Do you regard the budget for your change campaign as arbitrary, not to be heeded?

➤ Have you "learned" to become easily intimidated by the experience or status of others?

➤ Do you believe yourself to be too old, too young, the wrong gender, or the wrong ethnic background to be effective in this change campaign?

➤ Do you feel that you don't have the right education, background or training?

➤ Do you lack the confidence to take charge in the manner you are capable of doing?

These "inside-your-head" issues can be as significant as any tangible, external barriers that you may face in implementing your change campaign. The sooner you are able to surface such issues, the greater the potential for you to get beyond them.

Achieving Closure—A Many-Splendored Thing

Change managers who thrive in a frequently shifting environment have invariably mastered the ability to achieve closure following the completion of a change campaign, whether they achieve or abandon the desired objective.

Change Master

If you get nothing else from this book but guidance on using completions, you will benefit.

Completions can be acknowledged when merely finishing a subtask. They are analogous to driving along a scenic mountain highway and stopping periodically at overlooks to get breaths of fresh air, stretch out, and acknowledge how far you have come.

You Are a Master of Completions

Seeking completions is a powerful way to perpetually gain closure. You are already a master of many aspects of completion. When you awake each morning, you have completed sleep for the previous night. When you turn in a big report at work, and you know it's ready, that is a completion.

Large or small, completions provide a mental and emotional break.

Walk-Away Strategies

Acknowledging your completions is a type of ritual, and rituals certainly can serve important functions. Rituals at the end of a change campaign help cement the realization that it's time to move on. Some walk-away strategies are already familiar to you, such as:

➤ Literally taking a walk, the duration and length of which depend on how long you feel you need to feel refreshed, both mentally and emotionally. Some people do so over the course of an entire weekend. Others can do it during one day's lunchtime.

➤ Talking with others. This has been one of the time-honored techniques for achieving closure of all types. Other parties can include friends, relatives, peers, bosses, coaches, and anyone who is a good listener and can help you work through perceptions and feelings about issues.

➤ Clearing your desk, which is both symbolic and practical. Removing the paperwork, files, and documents related to the previous change campaign enables you to both mentally and physically clear away space for future tasks.

The same procedures occur in terms of managing your computer's hard drive. Some files get redirected, new folders are created, and other files are deleted, and so on. As I discuss in my book *The Joy of Simple Living,* taking control of your space and your immediate environment goes a long way toward enabling you to have energy, focus, and direction for what is next.

Make a List, Check It Twice

Drawing up lists of pluses and minuses to achieve closure on decisions was mastered 200 years ago by Benjamin Franklin. List-making works well for many of the challenges that you face today.

Proceed

Pros-and-cons lists help to achieve a sense of closure on par with that of acknowledging your completions.

Suppose you're abruptly yanked from a change campaign and have little time before starting on the next one. In the interim, or at the end of the day, if that's the only time you have, draw up a list of what was good and bad about the project you were working on. Address the following questions:

➤ What did you like about it?

➤ What challenged you?

➤ What motivated you to do your best?

➤ What were the tangential benefits?

➤ How did it add to your overall career experience?

In a second column, jot down what wasn't so great about the project.

➤ What was tedious or repetitious about it?

➤ What kind of anxiety did you experience?

➤ Were there components that you would have preferred to skip all together?

➤ What was wasteful, off-center, or unnecessary about the project?

By compiling such lists, you find yourself more able to move on.

Turning on a Dime and Feeling Fine

It may be hard for you to accept that you could become quite adept at turning on a dime (abandoning change campaigns on a moment's notice). Certainly, after you have had the rug pulled out from under you a couple of times you are likely to be better at cushioning your fall.

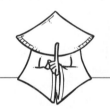

Change Master

Your poise and demeanor during the close or abandonment of a campaign may speak as loudly as your efforts during the campaign.

In nearly every instance in which you faced a change, when you were objective about it, there were still many lessons that you learned, skills and experiences that could be transferred to other campaigns and used throughout your career, and valuable insights gained. From that standpoint, you may find yourself feeling good about abandoned projects. (After all, it's not as if incompetence on your part was the basis for abandoning the change campaign.)

The ability to maintain composure after an abrupt change conveys a powerful message to a sponsor who may have reluctantly been forced to abandon the project. The political candidate who doesn't do so well in the early primaries, for example, may have to tell his top campaign worker to pull up the stakes. That doesn't mean the candidate wouldn't want to work with him again on another campaign if the opportunity presented itself.

Cranking Up the Engine

Suppose you're forced to abandon one change campaign and later that day, or the next day, you find yourself on a new one. You've turned on a dime. Now how do you crank up the engine in record time, and keep your mind sublime? The answer is total immersion, as discussed in Chapter 16, "Jump Starting to Total Immersion."

I've always felt lucky in my career. Each of the more than 600 conferences and conventions at which I have spoken represents personal, intellectual challenges. After studying the needs of the audiences in advance and understanding the objectives of the meeting planners, I made presentations that addressed the current, prevailing issues in a way that was informative, entertaining, and memorable.

Likewise, my other career role—that of an author— compels me to have to "get up to speed" in a hurry on each of the chapters that will comprise my latest book. In both professions, I find myself "cranking up the engine" on a regular basis.

Like anyone else, I am subject to bouts of procrastination and resistance. I know from experience, however, that when I totally immerse myself in the topic at hand for only a few hours or a few days, the barriers fall away and my impetus propels me along further and faster.

Proceed

Surround yourself with the artifacts of what you will need for the next campaign—books, articles, documents, files, you name it. Accept the new campaign as a personal and professional challenge.

The Least You Need to Know

➤ One can withstand major redirection, such as 180-degree reversals or abandonment of change campaigns, without protracted bouts of attachment and mourning.

➤ In many industries and professions, people are routinely pulled off projects abruptly. An effective change manager makes the transition with as little upset as possible.

➤ Simultaneously cultivate your ability to commit to a change campaign and to let go of it if need be.

➤ Closure or completion enables you to acknowledge where you have been and to have more energy, focus, and direction on what is next.

➤ Generating a list of pros and cons about an abandoned project is an effective tool for obtaining closure.

➤ To crank up the engine or to get started quickly on your next change campaign, surround yourself with the artifacts of the campaign.

Part 4

Ensuring a Successful Campaign

Sometimes you have to take the bull by the horns and proceed down a path that may seem bold to some, rash to others, and downright foolhardy to still others. Yet, overcoming potential encumbrances to a successful change sometimes commands cries for novel ways of initiating a campaign and executing tasks.

Intrigued? Then turn the page and read on. The following chapter will ease you into the oh-so-important notion of giving yourself some slack in embracing a specific change.

Chapter 15

Scheduling Days of Grace

In This Chapter

➤ Proceeding at half-speed

➤ Putting the odds of success in your favor

➤ Assimilation versus disruption

➤ Being gentle with yourself

➤ Concluding the grace period

"You can't hurry love," or so the lyrics go of the Supremes' 1960s hit song of the same title. No less true, in a manner of speaking, is that you can't hurry change. This chapter is the first of four that explores innovative ways to ensure a successful change campaign. Here, we'll examine a kinder, gentler approach to change, one that acknowledges that you and your staff need precious time to assimilate what is required to make a lasting and effective change.

Proceeding at Half-Speed

Days of Grace is an autobiographical work by the late Arthur Ashe, a tennis player, sports commentator, and historian. Ashe died at 47 from AIDS, which he contracted as a result of a blood-supply mix-up at a hospital lab. He had finished writing a huge three-volume set on the history of the African American athlete starting from the 1650s.

While working to complete *Days of Grace* and spending time with his wife and daughter, he was able to reflect upon the last few months of his life in a way that most people never do. These were his days of grace, when time slowed down, and when each day was precious. Ashe said that he became profoundly thankful for each month, then each week, and then each day that he had left.

A Better Chance

Scheduling days of grace in the context of a change campaign is not nearly as poignant, but it does serve a real purpose. By slowing down, clearing out the extraneous, sharpening your focus, and becoming more in tune, on a higher level, as to what changes need to be instituted, you have a better chance of succeeding than you would otherwise.

Proceed

Give yourself the opportunity to work without disruption. Assemble the resources you need. For the time being, let other pressing issues fall by the wayside. Give the task at hand sharp focus.

Contemplate the last time you were asked to tackle any project, on your own or within a small group. Someone, probably your boss, was waiting for the results, which you needed to turn in on a deadline. What was your immediate reflexive action? For some people it is to clear the deck. They literally create space on their desks, conference tables, or other workplaces.

Slow Down and Win

I suggest that you proceed at half-speed. This may seem paradoxical in the face of an urgent change campaign that you've been asked to manage. Yet, rushing through any plan invariably results in down time, errors, and having to do things over again. The total "rush-through" time ends up equaling what it would have taken if you had proceeded more cautiously.

Word Power

An **old saw** is an old saying, usually conventional wisdom passed on over time.

You've heard the *old saw* about not having enough time to do a job right the first time, yet having to make the time later to fix it. As I discuss in my book *Breathing Space: Living and Working at a Comfortable Pace in a Sped-Up Society,* one of the great paradoxes of our age is that often, to flourish in our sped-up society, sometimes the first and most critical step is to slow down:

➤ To get your bearings,

➤ To read the instructions,

➤ To reflect, or

➤ To rest.

Putting the Odds in Your Favor

What are ways you can effectively slow down on a change campaign to increase the probability of successful execution?

Readers Are Leaders

If you have to, read instruction manuals, books, articles, reports, or data sheets. Allocate twice the time that you instinctively would to the organization, reading, and digestion of such materials.

Before sitting down to read or engage in any other information intake process, surround yourself with the tools that support your ability to capture the essence of what you are reading and apply it in the most judicious manner. For example, you might want sticky notes, paper clips, a pocket recorder, or a bookmark.

Find the Metaphor

Here is an exercise for whatever you've been asked to handle and whatever desired results are to be achieved: Is there something else in your career, your life, or in the world you can identify that is somewhat like what you have been assigned?

Has there been a previous project within your organization that you can examine and learn from? Did you work on something in a previous position, come across an article or case study, or know someone who managed a campaign that has some similarities to yours?

Going a step further, are there any processes in nature, politics, or relationships that have elements that you can draw upon? Looking for a metaphor is not some esoteric, hoity-toity recommendation. After all, people tend to naturally do this anyway. We relate one or more things that we know to what we are presently trying to learn in order to make our learning task easier.

Proceed

In a change campaign, giving yourself time and slack by scheduling days of grace increases the probability of seeing corollaries between what you have been assigned to manage and other things that you have come across in work or in life.

Change Master

In the early days of computers, and then personal computers, manufacturers and developers used a metaphor of the human brain in both the design and explanation of how computers work. It wasn't a perfect match, but it was good enough to give most people an idea as to what computers could do, how they operated, and how to put them to work for you.

167

Pad Your Schedule

To the degree practical, give yourself extra time at the start of a change campaign. This is time not merely for reading, but for thinking, reflecting, scheduling, and anticipating critical junctures in the campaign.

The typical change manager often is thrown into a situation, on short notice, and asked to perform miraculous results. Even in such instances, if you can bargain for some extra time up front, insights, as well as genuine opportunities, emerge that might not have otherwise.

Sharpen the Saw

Stephen Covey, in *The Seven Habits of Highly Successful People,* regards "sharpening the saw" as one of the vital seven habits and devotes considerable discussion to it.

One of the great paradoxes of working in the Western or industrialized world is that sharpening the saw to onlookers appears to be slacking off. You mean you're not going to start cutting the tree right away? How long are you going to be working on that blade anyway?

For a change manager, sharpening the saw may be the metaphor for extensive thinking at the *outset* of a change campaign. There you are, at your desk, staring out the window. People walk by and don't regard you as doing too much. Nevertheless, the time you spent staring out your window may prove to be the most important interval in the future success of the change campaign!

Factoid

Abraham Lincoln once said, "If I had eight hours to chop down a tree, I'd spend six hours sharpening the saw."

Change Master

"Don't just sit there, do something" was a familiar refrain in the second half of the twentieth century. To be an effective change manager often necessitates reversing the slogan. "Don't just do something, sit there."

Doomed to Premature Action

The reflexive decision to take action prematurely dooms many managers. Conversely, taking time to just simply sit and reflect, or sharpen the saw if you will, often results in your ability to proceed at an accelerated pace once you determine the most effective and efficient path toward the desired results.

The chances are considerable, given your upbringing, education, and previous work environments, that you make reflexive decisions to take action as opposed to just sitting and thinking. If you doubt this, consider the last time you bought a new technology item,

168

some software, or even a toy for your child. Did it come with an instruction manual? If not a manual, was there at least a small pamphlet or instruction card?

Read the Instructions

Here's the $64,000 question: Did you read the instruction card, pamphlet, or manual before actually using the item? Or did you dive right in? Probably 95 percent of the population dives right in, never reading the instructions. To this day, people have all types of gadgets, equipment, toys, games, electronic devices, and appliances that they know how to use only partially, because they have never read the instructions.

No, typically there aren't case-specific, printed instructions as to how the project or change campaign ought to proceed. Instructions in this context represent the background materials you can conjure up: The reading materials, reports, data, memos, and anything that is applicable to the campaign at hand. Western literature, television, and movies may glorify the swashbuckler who dives right in, but this is not that type of situation.

Proceed

The best change managers "read the instructions."

Assimilation and Disruption

Okay, you exist in the physical world in a real organization with pressing challenges. No matter how you strive to clear away time and space for yourself, undoubtedly you have other responsibilities, tasks, and demands for your time and attention. Disruption is a regrettable fact of life in every workday.

For some people, constant disruption is the norm. For others, even those assigned to manage very delicate change campaigns, various sponsors, advocates, and well-wishers who ought to know better, are the worst offenders.

Working in the Background

The process of *assimilation* tends to work even in less than ideal circumstances. When you immerse yourself in the intricate details of a change campaign and it becomes your major, if not single, focus, miraculously your brain keeps contemplat-

Word Power

Assimilation is the process of adapting a new idea to a process already in progress. Assimilation as used here means directly and indirectly absorbing knowledge near or away from the source.

ing issues and working on problems. Even when you are temporarily distracted from the work at hand or temporarily pulled off a campaign, the knowledge processing can continue.

At the start of a change campaign, when you have a vast array of project materials before you, it may seem overwhelming. Yet, as you pore through them, even large volumes of materials don't seem quite so intimidating. You're beginning to assimilate what you are taking, that is, making a structure and a logical order out of the information.

Much of the information you encounter is duplicative, so that helps to cut down the pile. Some of it doesn't apply at all, and therefore it can easily be recycled. Some of the insights are worth gleaning once, but don't necessarily need to be noted again. Some material clearly relates to the initiation of a project, some to the middle, and some to the end; so, it is easy enough to separate items into piles.

Be Wary

When it comes to managing a change campaign, don't be like the fellow who jumped on his horse and rode off in all directions. Slow down, proceed at "half-speed" for as long as you can, and give the campaign its best chance of succeeding. The pace will start accelerating soon enough.

Word Power

Germination is a growth or sprouting, a budding or blooming that occurs once a plant seed or the seed of an idea is rooted in firm soil.

Working While You Sleep

Over time, you become a master of the information domain you have assembled. You reflect on your assemblage; you talk to others about it; you look up other things on the Internet or in your organization's library and soon you find yourself engaged in the topic material.

When you go home for the evening, whether or not you take work materials with you, your brain keeps working on the project. Even when you are relaxing or engaging in a leisure activity, the process of *germination* is at play. Sometimes called the "eureka effect," germination is the continuing mental activity that your brain undertakes, often in the background to some other present activity, which enables you to gain insights that don't tend to emerge in the office, or when you are focusing directly on the subject matter.

Suddenly, when arising from sleep or taking a shower, seemingly disjointed elements of the project come together. A path emerges or a solution becomes evident.

Get Away, Gain Insight

People report that going away for a weekend, having a short trip, or having an extended vacation often works wonders on their abilities to develop new perspectives on projects back in the office.

Can you rush through assimilation and germination? Perhaps. If time and love cure broken hearts, time and rest yield project breakthroughs.

Reflect and Collect

When once asked his thoughts about a critical foreign policy issue, former Secretary of State Henry Kissinger studiously replied, "I haven't given that measure any consideration. I will have to think about it." A lesser person might have tried to bluff his way out of the situation.

Be Gentle with Yourself

If you're managing a change campaign for the first time or managing a campaign of far greater magnitude than previously, the notion of being gentle with yourself is one worth heeding.

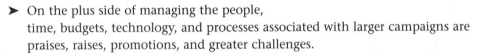

Factoid

Henry Kissinger understood the power of reading and reflection. He knew that to be at his best, he needed time to think, collect his thoughts, and form an opinion.

➤ On the plus side of managing the people, time, budgets, technology, and processes associated with larger campaigns are praises, raises, promotions, and greater challenges.

➤ On the negative side—the part that is rarely reflected in books on change management—is greater potential for mistakes, wasted time, misallocated funds, anger, and frustration.

A World Waiting to Be Discovered

As with so much in life, there are two sides to an experience. Take the case of executives who suddenly have to do more traveling for work. The positive side of business travel is getting to see new places.

Most managers' transportation, food, and accommodations expenses are paid for. They meet new people, have new experiences, and perhaps enjoy benefits they don't have back home. Many of the hotels in which they stay will have ultramodern health clubs and other guest facilities that they enjoy using.

A World of Pitfalls and Perils

What is the down side to business travel? Besides the obvious transportation delays, bumpy plane rides, lost luggage, and inattentive clerks, come less-often cited, but equally frustrating experiences. Travelers tend to lose things more often, such as sunglasses, favorite ties or belts, alarm clocks, and expensive pens. Road food may not agree with you. Your sleeping and waking pattern may be awry.

During these times it's important to be gentle with yourself. You have to realize that the price of affluence, travel, and seeing the world is losing things.

Gentle on the Campaign

There are also prices of change management. They include embarking on the wrong paths, not being able to assemble all the resources you need at the time you need them, and having to "make do" more often than you would prefer. Often these experiences are not necessarily related to your management style, the change campaign, or the particulars of your situation. They occur *because* you are involved in change management!

> **Change Master**
>
> Learning rarely comes in even measure. When you're carving out a plan that no one has embarked upon before, it is difficult to know exactly how long it "ought to take."

Days of Doubt

Whole days will pass when you feel as if you have largely accomplished nothing. Assimilation and germination often work that way. Consider a young musician who is asked to practice a piece that he finds difficult. Before fully mastering that piece, his teacher gives him a more complicated piece to play. Now the young musician is feeling frustrated. He hasn't quite mastered the first piece, and finds himself attempting a more challenging piece.

Out of the blue, his teacher asks him to play the first composition. Bingo! The young musician plays it masterfully. Yet, he hadn't practiced it for at least a week and was fully engaged in attempting to learn the new composition. What happened? Assimilation and germination.

If he is asked to play a third composition more challenging than the second, the same phenomenon is likely to occur. The musician can play the second piece a week later with greater aplomb than if he had simply labored at that piece over and over again.

> **Proceed**
>
> If you are battling self-doubt or are engaged in heavy bouts of second-guessing, remember the importance of being gentle with yourself, particularly in the early stages of a project.

Take It in Stride

In time and with learning, the young musician, as well as a change manager, discovers that "things" are happening and progress is occurring, often when it appears otherwise. Many seasoned change managers, like top executives or politicians, learn to take things in stride. They develop a way of being gentle with themselves, knowing that progress on a change campaign not only is uneven, but often fluctuates widely.

As I've mentioned before, it would be a wonderful world if progress on a change campaign came in predictable, manageable steps. It rarely works that way.

Concluding the Grace Period

After you've done everything that you can to prepare yourself for the challenge at hand, you are ready to jump into the fray. Perhaps you have to fully familiarize yourself with some new software or ensure that your staff is familiar with the campaign. Perhaps you need to become fully familiar with some type of operational procedure out on the factory floor.

For whatever was necessary during the ramp-up period in which you allow yourself some days of grace, such preparations have a way of amply paying for themselves in the days that follow.

The key to knowing when to conclude the grace period is understanding what it takes to master the fundamental skills necessary to propel the project forward. What will it take in terms of hours, days, or weeks for you to acquire the background skills or capabilities that are appropriate prerequisites to …

➤ Launching a project,

➤ Managing it successfully, and

➤ Seeing it to its desired end?

Consider having to learn essential software. You know you've arrived at completion when you're so comfortable with the new software that you wouldn't go back to the old software even if someone paid you. The benefits of using the new software are so obvious that no argument would be sufficient for you to revert to what came before.

With your staff, scheduling days of grace and proceeding at half-speed are no longer necessary when they become impediments. With their newfound understanding or skills, people will become antsy when they can't get on with the project.

This eagerness does not mean that they won't require additional coaching and support as the campaign unfolds. Nevertheless, they've read enough, seen enough, and learned enough to feel comfortable in boldly proceeding where they haven't gone before, in terms of supporting you on this change campaign!

Change Master

Whether it's obtaining a more complete comprehension of the challenge before you, mastering new software, understanding an industrial process, or even learning a new language, the time and energy that you spend on those critical activities is akin to an insurance policy. Your early learning helps you minimize future downtime on the project.

The Least You Need to Know

➤ At the start of any change campaign, fight for the right to proceed slowly.

➤ Disruption is a fact of life for career professionals. Do what you can to give yourself the time, space, and silence you need to assimilate project knowledge.

➤ Through assimilation and germination, you get your best ideas and insights when you are away from the task at hand.

➤ Be gentle with yourself, particularly at the start of a change campaign. There will be delays, frustrations, and things you don't understand.

➤ It's time to conclude the grace period when you and your staff are eager to move on.

Chapter 16

Jump Starting to Total Immersion

In This Chapter

➤ Overcoming procrastination

➤ Gaining familiarity with the issues of your campaign

➤ Recognizing the need for total immersion

➤ Conditioning your environment

Managing the Beforehand is living with the ever-present acknowledgment that change is continually forthcoming and preparing for activities or events in advance. This is aided by constantly establishing relationships with resourceful people who can help. When you fully embrace the notion of managing the Beforehand, there is a potpourri of change initiation techniques you and your team can use to minimize "gearing-up time." For starters, there is the strategy of initiating a small part of the project immediately so that you can get your feet wet, but there are no real consequences as a result of diving in. Let's examine how this works.

Getting a Head Start

Never mind resistance to change—procrastination over handling extremely familiar tasks has been a problem plaguing humanity since people first donned bear skins and loin cloths! One way to burst through procrastination is to begin a small part of the project now. This will let you gain familiarity with the project without having to heavily invest in it mentally.

Tales of Triumph

Here's a quick example followed by one that's a bit more involved. Suppose it's Friday afternoon, and you know you need to begin something challenging on Monday

Proceed

Coincidentally, initiating a small part of a project now to burst through procrastination without incurring too heavy a mental investment works equally well for initiating a change campaign.

morning. Since you don't have to start until Monday, it's okay if you don't do anything about it Friday afternoon. Yet, it is to your extreme advantage if you get started in some way.

So, you make the leap. You decide to open a file folder and merely gaze over the notes in the folder. You look at some of the terminology. You read a key sentence here and there. In a breezy, nonthreatening way, you expose yourself to the issue just a little—not enough to impact the rest of your day or your weekend.

You come back to work on Monday morning and open the folder. You know that you now have to begin in earnest. People are waiting for you, it's your responsibility, and you have no choice. As your eyes peruse the materials in the packet, something wonderful occurs!

Proceed

By gaining some familiarity with the project for Monday, three days prior to the start date, you benefit through the process of germination, discussed in Chapter 15, "Scheduling Days of Grace."

Like an Old Friend

The subject matter doesn't seem so strange. You've seen this before—last Friday. Over the weekend you were not consciously thinking about the project, but nevertheless, your mind was in gear. You now find yourself more ready to get started—all because you simply exposed yourself to the material three days before.

The same process works if you're going on vacation or simply going to lunch. Initiate a small part now. Paperclip something together, highlight something, make a phone call, or copy a page. Do any small task that you would have to do a few days or hours hence, and you will benefit from a slingshot effect.

Testimonials Pouring In

A fellow speaker told me firsthand how effective this technique is. She retired one night with concerns about a project she had to undertake the next morning. At 3 A.M., she awoke. She couldn't get back to sleep, so she took a glance at the materials she knew she would have to tackle headlong at 9 A.M. After reviewing the materials for 10 minutes she did something else, and then felt sleepy and went back to bed.

When she arose in the morning, got dressed, and formally initiated the task, she experienced a personal revelation. The task that she had so dreaded not only seemed nonthreatening, but was quite *palatable*. She was able to finish it far faster than she had anticipated. She was so excited about her discovery she e-mailed me that afternoon and, in vivid detail, described her sensations and her realizations.

Word Power

If something is **palatable,** it is agreeable, enjoyable, or tasty.

Gaining Familiarity

When you and your change management staff give yourselves the opportunity to gain familiarity with the issues of the change campaign prior to the formal launch of the campaign, you can benefit through group synergy.

Manage Your Assets

A bank in Cleveland was growing at a faster rate than any of the top officers presumed that it could. In one year, it acquired several smaller banks. One of the many changes that it needed to put into place was the integration of banking officers and practices from the two latest acquisitions.

The change manager selected to head up the change campaign did something out of the ordinary. Rather than simply provide training to the acquired banks to help them come up to speed with "how we do things around here," he spent more than a week at each facility observing how *they* did things and gaining familiarity with all their processes.

Extended Observation, Smooth Transition

After he learned their standard operating procedures, language, and nonwritten rules of procedure, he designed a course booklet for management staff of the acquired banks that represented a customized plan to facilitate the move from where they were to where they needed to be. He used the appropriate terminology, captured the nuances, and was able to prepare a document that people immediately understood.

As a result of his innovative approach, the assimilation of the two latest acquisitions went more smoothly than previous acquisitions. He was commissioned to handle other change management projects, not simply acquisitions and training—running the entire gamut of change campaigns sponsored by top management at headquarters.

This manager, *willing to immerse himself in operations he was authorized to improve, rose faster and further than many of his counterparts*. At a relatively young age, he had such a wide purview of bank operations that he became indispensable to his organization.

Proceed

Here are eight mini-strategies for jumping in when you're not inclined to:

1. Do the opposite of what you'd normally do.

2. Follow someone else's lead (different than your approach).

3. Forget about looking good.

4. Be honest.

5. Trust your intuition.

6. Focus on originality.

7. Get in motion (that is, start your PC).

8. Make a game of it.

Probe for Understanding

One way to become an effective change manager, as well as indispensable to your organization, is to learn and understand your work environment to a far greater degree than most people ever do. Probe for understanding.

Proceed

Any organization, from the smallest business to the multibillion-dollar corporation, has a mission. If you don't already know your company's mission, learn it.

Your organization's brochure, annual report, promotional literature, or employee handbook will have the mission spelled out. The mission will unify and give meaning to all the division or department goals. Although conflicts among divisions will occur as a result of the nature of different responsibilities, you'll be better prepared to handle change campaigns because of your intimate knowledge of operations.

Your ability to make the correct decisions will be enhanced by greater awareness of your role description, your campaign objectives, and the organization's mission.

Get a Surprise Jump Start

All of your conscious or subconscious mental *cogitation* over change campaign issues adds up to a relative jump start once the project or specific task formally commences. This concept has long been understood by advertisers. Recall the last time you went to the movies and saw a trailer for a movie that wouldn't be playing for many months? Trailers for anticipated blockbusters are always released months before the movies come to the theaters.

Why would somebody pay good money to announce a film so far in advance? The short answer: It gets people thinking about the film. That fleeting memory gets tucked some place in the cranium. Then it is reactivated as the main advertising campaign heats up one to two weeks before the movie is released.

As you're exposed to the latest messages urging you to see this movie, something in your brain connects back to your first exposure—that trailer months ago. If you were at all inclined to see that movie, at this juncture you're as good as hooked.

Check Out the Lozanov Method

The Lozanov Method of learning created by Georgi Lozanov, a professor at the University of Sofia in Bulgaria, holds that your environment has rich potential to influence the rate and depth of your ability to learn. Lozanov is regarded by many as the father of accelerated learning.

Lozanov discovered that the brain has an almost infinite potential for learning if the subconscious mind receives information in the right manner. His techniques have been applied in many corporate training programs both in the United States and abroad. Some companies have been able to decrease training time and budgets dramatically by using his ideas. One computer manufacturer in Germany is planning to convert its entire European training program to this method.

Word Power

Cogitation means the same thing as contemplation or mental reflection.

Factoid

Lozanov introduced a technique called Suggestopedia into his classroom in the 1970s, a technique of implementing positive suggestion in the learning process while eliminating negative suggestion.

Proceed

Rather than approaching learning as a chore, you have the option of approaching learning as a joy.

179

From children to senior citizens, everyone has the opportunity to learn more easily when their respective environment is perceived as safe, fun, challenging, and upbeat.

Total Immersion Takes Guts

Total immersion is a variation of jump starting. Not as brutal as going cold turkey (see Chapter 17, "Going Cold Turkey"), total immersion involves completely surrounding yourself with change campaign–related materials and nothing else. It is having the mental and emotional strength to focus on nothing but the campaign and to give it your complete and undivided attention.

When does it make sense to totally immerse yourself or your team in a change campaign?

➤ When you're up against the wall—there is no time to lose; the pain of staying where you are is much too high.

➤ When only intense focus and concentration will be sufficient to ensure a successful outcome.

➤ When your sponsor presents you with the luxury of doing so.

"Why ever," you may be thinking, "would I consider total immersion to be a luxury of sorts?" The ability to focus and devote your time and attention to a single pursuit in this information-flooded world sometimes can prove highly comforting. Clarity minimizes anxiety. As the German writer and scientist Johann Wolfgang von Goethe put it:

> Until one is committed, there is hesitancy, the chance to draw back, always ineffectiveness, concerning all acts of initiative (and creation). There is one elementary truth the ignorance of which kills countless ideas and splendid plans: that the moment one definitely commits oneself, then Providence moves too. All sorts of things occur to help one that would never otherwise have occurred. A whole stream of event issues from the decision, raising in one's favor all manner of

Proceed

Change managers and change management teams would do well to set up a "command center" to serve as a positive learning environment—with walls adorned with helpful charts, graphs, posters, slogans, and everything else that could have positive impact on the team, their ability to learn, and their performance for the duration of the campaign.

Change Master

Becoming totally immersed is a mental decision first, followed by prompt action and aggressive self-reinforcement.

unforeseen incidents and meetings and material assistance which no man could have dreamed would come his way. Whatever you can do or dream you can, begin it. Boldness has genius, power and magic in it. Begin it now.

Driving the Point Home

A nationally known trucking company faced acute problems of maintaining quality as its employees were confronted by near constant change. The decision was made to identify those people who were most resilient or conducive to deal with change in a way that would benefit the entire home-based operation.

A change manager was installed to identify the 10 to 12 percent of staff from all departments and all divisions that would be part of an intensive total-immersion program to develop mini–change team leaders. The graduates of the program, already in-clined to embrace change with less resistance than their contemporaries, could then be called upon ad hoc to lead change campaigns as the need arose.

Narrowing Down the Crowd

Of more than 5,600 people at the headquarters, 586 were chosen for this special five-day program. The change manager recognized that, at best, the total-immersion five-day program could only be the initiator of a series of programs to ensure that the budding change managers were able to contin-ually refine and *hone* their skills. Still, the company had to start somewhere.

The sponsorship committee decided that after the select group received the week-long training, there would be a three-month observation period to see how often change teams were assembled, who headed them, and what resulted. Following the three-month period, possibly a second program would be initiated, building upon the lessons con-veyed in the first.

Proceed

Your staff may actually be re-lieved to be working on one campaign or one project. It might represent a welcome change from the multitude of directions in which they were being pulled.

Word Power

Hone means to sharpen or file to a fine edge.

Sifting for Change Management Stars

The change manager was also charged with the responsibility of rating the effectiveness of the performances and the solutions of the change groups. The key criteria would be simple. The team would have had to effectively move from Point A to Point B in the time allotted, and with the budget allocated. Essentially, it would close the gap between expectations and results.

By design, most of these total-immersion campaigns would be kept small—nothing extending more than a week or so, and in many cases only days long. By enabling the select group to flex its change management "muscles," it was hoped that ultimately several superstars of change management would emerge. Then, headquarters could call upon a number of experienced change managers and give them progressively more aggressive change campaigns to manage.

Establishing the Corps

As the month passed, 18 of the original 586 proved to have the background, maturity, inclination, and fortitude to move onto the next level. The group of 18 was certainly a larger number change managers than the company had before the initiation of the primary campaign.

As time marches on, the group of 18 will change. Some will leave the company for one reason or another. Some will prove ineffective. Most, however, will probably prove to be highly effective. For all the tumult and toil, total immersion programs can be highly rewarding.

If 10 to 12 veteran change managers emerge as a result of this process, then the trucking company will help position itself to maintain market share and long-term viability in a highly competitive industry.

Finding the Trailblazer

For whatever campaign awaits, remember that if you can find someone who has already blazed that very trail or a similar one, you can immediately gain great jump-start benefits. If someone has learned the

Change Master

Often, your ability to get started quickly on a change campaign is roughly equal to your ability to find a trailblazer, someone who can give you key, vital inputs that will save you hours and days of frustration.

Be Wary

Undoubtedly, you have your own strategy for identifying mentors, experts, and trailblazers. How often do you employ their services to help you become a master of change, particularly at the moments when it's most necessary for you to have someone walking you through the forest?

software you're trying to learn, mastered the intricacies of some new procedure, suck out all they know like a souped-up vacuum cleaner.

Personally, I'm constantly on the lookout for mentors, even of a temporary nature. I want to talk to people who can quickly point me in the right direction. I want people who can impart wisdom and tell me when to turn left or right so that I don't become unnecessarily frustrated, anxious, or bogged down in detail.

I'm also willing to pay for coaches, instructors, and guides as the need becomes apparent. I network heavily, so I'm always in touch with others who have skills and experience of benefit to me and, conversely, whom I am able to benefit as well. Relationships that last, as author Robert Ringer once said, are *value-for-value* relationships—both parties want to keep the connection going!

Immerse Yourself in Change Management

A final thought: How many courses on managing change did you take in high school, college, or graduate school? You may have attended a lecture, a session at a conference, or perhaps a full-day management seminar. You might be the type of person who clips an article or two. It's not likely, however, that you've approached the topic of change with any formality.

Here's a short list of books that people have found to be helpful:

>*Managing at the Speed of Change,* by Darryl Conner

>*Managing in Turbulent Times,* by Dr. Peter Drucker

>*Technotrends,* by Dan Burrus

>*Breathing Space,* by Jeff Davidson

>*Becoming Digital,* by Dr. Nicholas Negroponte

>*The Complete Idiot's Guide to Managing Stress,* by Jeff Davidson

>*The Acorn Principle,* by Jim Cathcart

>*Paulson on Change,* by Dr. Terry Paulson

Simply reading about change on a regular basis helps many people to see it as a less anxiety-laden topic. In addition to the list above, here are some books with new perspectives about work and relationships that will increase your understanding of the changes around you:

>*Bringing the Best Out in People,* by Dr. Aubrey Daniels

Proceed

Take it upon yourself to read one book on change every two months. After all, there are a number of excellent books on the topic. In many respects, change is a process, and many authors have outlined processes that you can understand and apply.

The End of Work, by Jeremy Rifkin

Managing in the "C" Zone, by Dr. Robert Kriegel

The Platinum Rule, by Dr. Tony Alessandra

The Death of Competition, by James F. Moore

Maximum Success, by Brian Tracy

You'll See It When You Believe It, by Dr Wayne Dyer

How to Have a Good Year Every Year, by Dave Yoho and Jeff Davidson

---

The Least You Need to Know

➤ Jump starting is the strategy of initiating a small part of a campaign immediately so that you can get your feet wet when there are no consequences as a result of diving in.

➤ When you and your staff gain familiarity with the issues of the change campaign prior to the formal launch, you can benefit through group synergy.

➤ A change manager willing to become immersed in operations he or she is authorized to improve will tend to rise faster and further others.

➤ Everyone has the opportunity to learn more easily when their respective environments are perceived as safe, fun, challenging, and upbeat.

➤ Often, your ability to get started quickly on a change campaign is roughly equal to your ability to find a trailblazer.

Chapter 17

Going Cold Turkey

In This Chapter

➤ Exploring the skills for successful cold-turkey management

➤ Revamping operations from top to bottom

➤ Considering radical measures and suspending operations

➤ Dealing with all-hands-on-deck situations

➤ Reviewing the four approaches to a successful campaign

Unquestionably the least palatable, most disconcerting approach to change, in complete contrast to the previous three chapters, is going cold turkey. This means jumping entirely into the fray, with no preparation time, and attempting to make it all work.

Going cold turkey sounds utterly dreadful, yet conceivably has its benefits. Kurt Lewin proclaimed that you can't truly understand an organization without trying to change it. By jumping into a change campaign you arrive much sooner at an understanding of the environment in which you are operating.

Even change campaigns that have what appears to be adequate "ramp-up" time sometimes prove to be chaotic, disheveling, uncertain ventures. From that standpoint, jumping into a change campaign, in some instances, may not turn out to be so disconcerting after all.

One time or another, you're going to encounter a cold-turkey change campaign. Here is your playbook.

Not for the Meek

While you may find yourself in such a situation by default, more often the case will be that you're selected to handle such a strenuous and taxing campaign because others in your organization *know* or *believe* that you can.

Be Wary

For everything written about change management, the ever-present reality for many change managers is that "change management" is often too high-minded a concept. You labor over change, you grabble with it, you cope with it, you make an action plan to deal with it, and you hope for the best!

Change Master

Your company may not have the forethought or resources to prepare for such events. If they do have guidelines in place, use them while drawing upon everything that you've ever learned as a change manager up until this point.

Cold-turkey campaigns tend to be emergencies. Think about the emergency room in a hospital, a Navy ship with a fire down below, the *60 Minutes* camera crew knocking at your front door, or flood waters rising at an alarming pace. The change manager needed to handle such situations must be blessed with a variety of skills and characteristics, including …

➤ **A commanding presence.** Maybe you don't have a commanding presence all of the time, but for now, in this situation, you need to be the take-charge leader who will readily mobilize others. There's no time to dwell on the interpersonal dynamics of the situation. Appropriate action is the watchword.

➤ **Instant assembly.** The ability to assemble the team in a hurry is essential. This is not a cherry-picking campaign; often you need to work with whomever is in closest proximity. You may not be able to assemble team members with the skill, background, or temperament suitable for the team to handle such a situation, but you have to go with what you can round up.

➤ **Stay lean and mean.** There is no time to assemble anything but a flat team structure to keep communication direct and informal. Appoint task leaders if you have to, but keep it all as flat as possible.

➤ **Assign and support.** After you dole out assignments to the team that you've assembled (despite your limited time frame, budget, or resources), do everything you can to support them and ensure their success.

➤ **Let go of protocols.** In a cold-turkey situation, the etiquette and niceties that may routinely be part and parcel of change campaigns within your organization may prove to be too costly in terms of time and energy. It may be necessary to temporarily ruffle some feathers, get the job done, and later go on a reconnaissance mission, than to maintain "Dale Carnegie" cordiality, lose the battle, and maybe the war.

➤ **Craft the plan.** Can you craft a plan on the fly? Through training and simulations, the Federal Emergency Management Administration in Washington (FEMA) labors endlessly to prepare its staff to handle emergencies once they actually arise.

➤ **Bend, don't break.** All the while, maintain flexibility. Cold-turkey situations demand the ability to navigate hairpin turns in the road. As you learned in Chapters 13, "Managing Up, Managing Down," and 14, "Managing Inside and Outside Your Head," a good change manager knows how to turn on a dime. He gets as comfortable as he can with having to abandon a project with little or no notice, and can get up to speed in a hurry.

➤ **Push the right buttons.** In a tense situation you are chief conduit, head negotiator (see Chapter 21, "Understanding the Importance of Negotiation"), drill sergeant, and captain of the cheerleaders all rolled into one. You have to be willing and able to push the right buttons in your organization.

➤ **Heed your own lead.** The ability to trust one's instincts is crucial—to move on a moment's notice based on a fleeting feeling that if you don't take bold decisive action, all may be lost. As I detailed in *The Complete Idiot's Guide to Managing Your Time,* when you choose based on intuition, every cell in your body and every shred of intelligence you've ever accumulated is brought to bear. There's a lot behind the solutions you make.

➤ **Maintain a positive mindset.** Despite the obstacles that you face, maintain the mindset that you're going to succeed. In *Apollo 13,* actor Ed Harris portraying NASA control room engineer Gene Kranz quoted that now-famous line, "Failure is not an option." Gene Kranz's crew faced a high-stakes, cold-turkey change-management situation, encountering one obstacle after another in supporting the *Apollo 13* crew. Whether it was air supply, repairs to the outside capsule, power generation, or reentry into the atmosphere, again and again the ground crew devised on-the-fly solutions desperately needed by the crew.

Change Master

Gene Kranz understood that good intentions were not enough. Making a valiant effort did not suffice. Giving it their all would be a letdown if NASA did not get those astronauts home safely.

Revamping Operations from Top to Bottom

Depending on the type of cold-turkey change management you face, you may find it necessary to completely revamp operations. The accident at the Three Mile Island nuclear power plant near Middletown, Pennsylvania, on March 28, 1979, according to the U.S. Nuclear Regulatory Commission, was "the most serious in U.S. commercial nuclear power plant operating history," even though "it led to no deaths or injuries to plant workers or members of the nearby community."

The causes of the accident continue to be debated to this day. However, based on a series of investigations, the main factors appear to have been a combination of personnel error, design deficiencies, and component failures.

The accident apparently began when a malfunctioning valve allowed the pressure to decrease in the system. Another problem appeared elsewhere in the plant that caused the emergency feed-water system to be inactive for a period of time. These malfunctions caused hydrogen to be generated and released into the reactor containment building. By March 30, a "hydrogen bubble" had been created above the reactor core.

Respond Swiftly or Die

The accident caused low levels of radioactive gas to be released to the environment, and there was some fear of an explosion from the buildup of hydrogen. On March 30, Richard Thornburgh, Governor of Pennsylvania, ordered a precautionary evacuation of preschool children and pregnant women from within the 5-mile zone nearest the plant, and suggested that people living within 10 miles of the plant stay inside and keep their windows closed.

Factoid

Response to the accident was swift. The regional office promptly dispatched the first team of inspectors to the site, and helicopters hired by TMI's owner were sampling radioactivity in the atmosphere above the plant by midday.

Off Line for Good

Today, the reactor is permanently shut down and defueled. The facility will remain in long-term storage until the operating license for the entire plant expires in 2014, at which time the facilities will be decommissioned.

The accident at Three Mile Island permanently changed both the nuclear industry and the Nuclear Regulatory Commission. Public fear and distrust increased, NRC's regulations and oversight became broader and more robust, and management of the plants was scrutinized more carefully.

Introducing Radical Measures

In business, totally revamping or suspending operations are largely undesirable alternatives. There is loss of good will among customers and clients, signals to staff that something is vitally wrong, and associated losses in revenues.

Nevertheless, if operations themselves are highly suspect, shutting down may be the best alternative.

Triumphing over Product Tampering

In Autumn 1982, McNeil Consumer Products, a subsidiary of Johnson & Johnson, faced a monumental crisis when seven people in Chicago died from ingesting extra-strength Tylenol capsules laced with cyanide. The incident prompted a nationwide panic.

Johnson & Johnson was faced with quite a dilemma. The company needed to find the best way to deal with the tamperings without destroying the reputation of its most profitable product, Tylenol. It decided to take immediate action and concurrently launched a public relations program, to save its product and the company.

Officials at McNeil Consumer Products made it clear that the tampering had not taken place at either of its plants because of the company's strict quality control, even though cyanide was available on the premises.

What Do We Stand For?

As the Tylenol crisis became more serious, Johnson & Johnson top management turned to their corporate credo, which mandated them to be responsible in working for the public interest. The public and medical community were alerted of the crisis, the Food and Drug Administration was notified, and production of Tylenol was stopped.

Reclaiming Market Share

Tylenol capsules were reintroduced in November with a new triple-seal, tamper-resistant package, positioning McNeil Consumer Products as the first company in the pharmaceutical industry to react to the Food and Drug Administration's new regulations.

Factoid

The company recalled nearly 31 million bottles of Tylenol, with a retail value of more than 100 million dollars. Johnson & Johnson was praised by the media for its socially responsible actions.

To encourage use of Tylenol, McNeil Consumer Products provided millions of discount coupons. Sales people from Johnson & Johnson made more than 2,200 presentations to the medical community during the reintroduction of Tylenol.

No Time to Vacillate

If Johnson & Johnson had not been so direct in protecting the public interest, Tylenol capsules would not have reemerged so easily.

Today, Tylenol is one of the top-selling over-the-counter drugs in the United States.

Johnson & Johnson's handling of the Tylenol tampering crisis is regarded by experts as among the best in the history of public relations.

Suspending Operations

At various times, because of possible food contamination, many fast-food restaurant chains have temporarily suspended operations for a variety of reasons:

➤ To isolate the problem, find its origins, and attempt to be back up and running in record time.

➤ To minimize the possibility of anyone else getting sick in cases where a consumer allegedly had been stricken.

➤ To assure the public that they were doing all they could do and to maintain good will.

Invariably the problem is confined, identified, and rectified. Thereafter, the fast food chain or any other company in such a situation faces the task of restoring the relations with its constituents.

Change Master

The volume of information and communication that any given individual in society faces is so large that the temporary travails of any particular company, given that operations are restored soon, are all but forgotten.

The hungry and the loyal will return the moment that news reports say it's okay or the restaurant itself aptly demonstrates that it is open to business. To woo the more skeptical customer, companies have initiated PR campaigns, run ads, and distributed coupons and discount tickets.

It's Not the Death Knell

In previous years, suspending operations potentially represented a greater setback than it does today. Why? With so many individuals presently operating in a "fast forward" mode, most people simply want to know that a problem has been alleviated. They then readily return to their familiar routines.

Be Inconvenienced and Forget

Consider your own Internet service provider. In the last 8 to 10 weeks, you've had difficulty logging on or getting the full level of service for which you have subscribed. Once the problem is fixed, an hour and certainly a day later, do you give the matter another thought?

If your ISP or broadband carrier causes you to have continuing difficulties, then, of course, you give the matter considerable thought—you may even change vendors. For intermittent problems of a fleeting nature, however, you forgive and forget.

Turning the tables, when you are the product/ service provider, customers are also prone to forgive and forget given that the problems are temporary and fleeting.

Proceed

When briefly suspending operations gives you the upper hand at quickly diagnosing the problem and restoring operations to normal, do it.

All Hands on Deck

Speaking of movies, consider *Top Gun* where Tom Cruise as Lt. Pete "Maverick" Mitchell is flying the friendly skies for the U.S. Navy. When a plane is about to land on an aircraft carrier deck the term "all hands on deck" takes on a special meaning.

Traditionally everyone, including even top officers, would pick up a push broom and sweep that deck as clean and clear as humanly possible. Every pin, every paper clip, every bit of debris that could be cleared is cleared. This is done to ensure the highest probability of a successful landing. Today, there are vacuums and blowers to help clear the deck, but the concept is still the same.

All Staff in Sight

When managing a cold-turkey campaign, you may need to draw upon your hastily assembled staff in a manner that ignores rank, experience, or how long they've currently been on shift.

Cold-turkey change-management campaigns require the time and undivided attention of your staff. They are not situations suited for taking on people part-time or sharing staff with another project.

Miracles Accomplished Here

Staff members who understand that the current situation merits an all-hands-on-deck approach sometimes perform in miraculous ways. Mobilized to accomplish a task with less time and less resources than anyone would normally attempt, sometimes such teams perform exceedingly well.

Emergency situations, where all-hands-on-deck are needed, ultimately can serve several benefits:

➤ You get to discover who is good in an emergency—who keeps their head, who generates creative solutions, and who can be counted on.

➤ You get to see who works well with others during dire situations. If a team can function effectively during emergencies, they have vast potential for operating effectively the rest of the time.

➤ It creates bonding situations that may not otherwise occur during less hectic times.

➤ The experiences gained by staff professionals in emergencies can be invaluable. It can better prepare them for emergencies in the future. It also provides them with a vivid understanding of their own capabilities under dire situations, that they would not otherwise been exposed to—you don't know how good you are until you're put to the test.

➤ It imbues the staff with a "can do" feeling that can have favorable, cascading impact in the days ahead.

Factoid

Henry Kissinger, Secretary of State during the Nixon and Ford Administrations, once said, "The absence of alternatives clears the mind marvelously."

Outside Experts and Other Resources

Having to handle a cold-turkey change-management situation raises the question, should you call in outside experts (as discussed in Chapter 18, "Getting Help from Hired Guns")? The short answer is yes, if avoiding them will have dire consequences.

When you're battling against the clock, you want quick, accurate answers. A testing phase is impractical; trial and error often are out of the question. When the dam is about to burst, you can't convene a group that will sit around and dialog about the issue and then ruminate about solutions. You need to talk to somebody who flat out says "go right," or "go left."

When Saddam Hussein unleashed his ecological warfare against Kuwait and its allies by igniting hundreds of oil wells, taking the time to figure out a plan and how to cost effectively cap them would have been catastrophic.

Instead, Kuwait called in the top wildcat oil-rigging firms in the world, at an understandably high cost, to put out the fires. The cost of not intervening immediately would have been much higher.

Some companies maintain a roster of proven outside consultants and experts who can be called upon a moment's notice to "put out fires." Such relationships make perfect sense. While you don't necessarily want or need to have a high-priced expert on board as a full-time staff person, you certainly want to be able to draw upon this person's expertise in a crisis situation.

You will pay a high premium for the service, but in almost every case, it will be entirely worth it. In the long run, you'll pay far less for consultants and experts, handle more crisis adroitly, and hopefully restore operations to normal as quickly as feasible.

Fortunately there are several association directories available that you can use to quickly identify the consultants and experts who might be most beneficial depending on your industry and market. Key directories include:

➤ National Trade and Professional Associations

➤ State and Regional Associations

➤ Omnigraphic's Directory of Associations

The associations listed will either be staffed by experts or can directly refer you to industry experts. All of these volumes are located in the reference section of any city or academic library. By turning to the indexes of these directories and finding your industry or profession, you can locate several, if not dozens, of potential groups to whom you can turn.

A Quick Review

As a bonus, the following list offers a quick review of the four approaches to ensuring a successful campaign, discussed in Part 4, "Ensuring a Successful Campaign."

➤ **Scheduling days of grace.** After deciding to implement major change, build in "days of grace" to allow yourself to proceed at half- to three-quarters speed. Acknowledge that assimilating the new changes will take time and involve some disruption. Don't *expect* to achieve your normal productivity for now. Be gentle with yourself, recognize that you're doing your best. At the end of the grace period, be it a week or a month, you'll be more than prepared to achieve a higher level of productivity each day. With the changes you're assimilating, you begin operating at a new level. Days of grace taper off as new and unfamiliar tasks become routine for you.

➤ **Jump starting to total immersion.** Initiating a small part of a project or activity in advance (getting a sneak review) so as to gain familiarity for when the project or activity actually begins. Then, surrounding yourself with *everything* you need to fully engage in the change process, which also may involve assembling resources, people, and space, as well as ensuring that you have a quiet environment free of distractions.

➤ **Going cold turkey.** Not recommended for most people! Beyond total immersion, simply suspend operations and engage in whatever it takes to incorporate a new way of doing things. This is enhanced by ensuring that you'll have no disturbances, bringing in outside experts, and assembling any other resources you need to succeed.

The Least You Need to Know

➤ Even change campaigns that have what appears to be adequate "ramp-up" time sometimes prove to be chaotic, disheveling, uncertain ventures.

➤ The etiquette of change campaigns within your organization, in a cold-turkey situation, may prove to be too costly in terms of time and energy.

➤ When gut instincts warn that without bold and decisive action all will be lost, the ability to act on a moment's notice is crucial.

➤ Briefly suspend operations when it gives you the upper hand at quickly diagnosing the problem and quickly restoring operations to normal.

➤ Mobilized to accomplish a task with less time and less resources than anyone would normally attempt, change teams sometimes perform exceedingly well.

Chapter 18

Getting Help from Hired Guns

In This Chapter

➤ Defining the current problem

➤ Determining the readiness for change

➤ Identifying the pitfalls of using hired guns

➤ Compounding problems by creating your own problems

➤ Selecting the right gun for hire

Consultants are not supermen and superwomen ready to jump into your campaign and straighten out all problems with swift, sure strokes. "Hire a consultant," when heard in a staff meeting, should be met with the following questions:

➤ What is the issue requiring outside assistance?

➤ What kind of consultant, if any, do we need?

➤ What procedures will we set up for overseeing the consultant?

➤ How can we work with a consultant to attain the most input?

Of course, consultants can be hired to define better procedures even when things are running smoothly. Often, however, consultants are hired to solve problems you've run into on your change campaign. This chapter will help you sort out the pros and cons of looking for outside help.

Defining the Problem

The closer you move to a clear, concise definition of a problem, the closer you will be to a solution. The problem with problems is that they elude easy definition. However, before you rush off to hire a consultant to solve one, attempt to narrow down the situation as far as you can.

If the overall problem is poor employee morale, what are the underlying causes? Are some employees favored over others? Are wages and benefits competitive?

Certain change campaigns inherently lend themselves to hiring someone from outside your firm. Indicators of the need for outside assistance are as follows:

➤ The magnitude or intricacy of the campaign is such that there are not enough internal time and talents to solve it.

➤ The true state of affairs can be determined only by the objectivity of someone who is not involved.

➤ The campaign may fail if outside expertise isn't retained.

➤ The campaign requires specialized knowledge to solve it.

Are We Ready Yet?

Often, change campaigns are designed to have an initial component that assesses a group's readiness to respond to change at all. For example, one sponsor at a Palo Alto–based high-tech company devised a three-part change management program.

The first part involved hiring a consulting firm to devise a change "readiness assessment tool."

The second part of the campaign involved employing the consulting firm to devise an actual change management strategy based on the data from the assessment, the company's overall mission, and the long-term and continuing perspective of the initiating sponsor.

The third component represented the actual implementation of the change management strategy for complete rollout across all departments and divisions. The ultimate goal was to achieve the following:

➤ A more uniform operating environment consisting of common tools.

➤ Consistent reporting.

➤ A shared database.

➤ Freer flow and access to company resources.

In all, the company's 7,600 people in both the home office and 16 satellite offices worldwide would be impacted, all of which was to occur with minimal disruption and downtime.

The change manager selected to work with the consulting firm on this challenging campaign had been with the organization for three and half years and had spent time at seven of the sixteen satellite installations. Although he had a technical background, he had spent time previously working with the human resources department in refining several of its systems, so he had a feel for the "people" aspect of the campaign.

Knowing the Pitfalls of Using Hired Guns

It's a common mistake to use management consultants on problems that could or should be solved internally. Consultants are best used when there are real indicators that you need outside assistance, and when the campaign can only go forward via the consultant's critical skills. Or, perhaps when a bottleneck arises, the solution can be determined only through an objective examination by someone who is not working for the company.

A big problem when using professional advisors is not retaining them early enough. Professionals outside your company can offer expertise and objectivity in a wide variety of situations—from solving specific and immediate problems to ongoing consultations and advice. However, the mere fact that someone is an outside consultant by no means guarantees he or she can help you.

Let Me Count the Ways

The setbacks that can occur with the use of outside professional help range from minor dissatisfactions (that is, your problem gets solved, but it requires far more time and money than budgeted) to major disasters (that is, not only is the desired result unachieved, but new problems emerge because of the consultant's efforts)!

Be Wary

We'd all like to feel that once we put ourselves in the hands of an "expert," we can relax and watch our problems disappear. That isn't always the case. Using outside professional help sometimes can cause more harm than good for your campaign.

The pitfalls that can occur when you decide to hire a management consultant often relate to misinterpretations of what the consultant can do for you or what you want to accomplish. Some common problems that occur in hiring and using a management consultant include:

➤ Failure to accurately identify the problem or need.

➤ Failure to determine whether or not the problem could be solved internally and how.

➤ Inability to determine what kind of consultant is needed.

➤ Failure to work with the consultant in a manner that gets the most from his or her advice.

While there are scores of specific causes for these failures, they generally divide into two broad categories: failures stemming from the outside professional versus failures stemming from inside the company relating to the outside professional.

Not Always Worth the Price

Consider this: Ten percent of all management consultants graduated in the bottom ten percent of the class. All consultants are not equally competent in handling problems within their professional purviews.

Any professional service provider can be selected for the wrong reasons.

Be Wary

It's relatively easy to hire someone who looks good and speaks well but can't deliver on a substantive basis.

Consultants you retain may be competent and have credentials and references to the high hills, but still may not be able to help you—there may not be a correct "fit" between that professional and the objectives of your change campaign or your organization in general.

Creating Your Own Problems

If you hire a management consultant but don't supply the major information needed, you can't expect even the most competent professional to successfully serve you.

Similarly, you may have proprietary problems in giving the consultant accurate information about the issues you want addressed and the needs you have. There are several reasons why change managers hold back information that could be valuable to the outside consultant. One involves the manager's own sense of power and authority. For some managers, it's difficult enough to delegate authority to in-house team members, much less to someone on the outside. So there is a temptation to hold back and not quite let the outsider *in*.

Be Wary

Information that may seem commonplace to the change manager could be a revelation to someone not as familiar with it.

Sometimes a change manager withholds information because of a failure to recognize its value. Or, he or she views consultants as omnipotent. They are experts in areas in which we have little knowledge. They know what to do, and they are hired to use their expertise.

It's easy to forget that these individuals can't do their jobs alone. They need your help in learning about the company and becoming familiar with the change issues involved.

Hidden Agendas Hurt

Rob Barnett (name disguised) started a small distribution firm that grew to 86 employees in a little more than 18 months. By the end of the second year, swamped by the dramatic increase in staff and the associated responsibilities, he hired a management-consulting firm to draft a formal employee benefit plan.

When he realized that the consultant's plan would cost his company more than he had anticipated, he was disappointed and even reluctant to pay the consulting firm's final bill. "What I expected from their expertise was some sort of economical plan that would show me where I could save on my benefits package."

When he reviewed the situation with his bookkeeper, it became evident that Barnett hadn't specifically given the consulting firm the assignment of saving money! He had simply asked them to draft a benefit plan, a task that often can result in higher personnel costs. His own hidden agenda, which he had no reason to hide, was the primary cause of the foul-up.

Although his error was inadvertent, Barnett's outcome is not uncommon among those who hire consultants and are reluctant to candidly discuss their own objectives, often because they are unclear about what their objectives are.

Proceed

One advisor to top firms recommends that companies find an appropriate consultant and then use that person as "an outside consultant-adviser" to provide ongoing advice in advance of crises and for crises avoidance. This practice can save time and money.

Crisis Mentality

A common mistake is to use a consultant only in times of immediate need or crisis. Certainly there are times when you have no choice. (See Chapter 17, "Going Cold Turkey," for more details.)

Sometimes even a CEO doesn't recognize a growing problem, but a good consultant can detect it and nip it in the bud. Prevention, however expensive, is nearly always far less expensive than finding a cure.

Proceed

Bringing a consultant into closer contact with the company and the change team at the earliest stage usually yields the best advice.

Some of the areas in which using a consultant with whom you have an ongoing relationship can make a difference include the following: timing expenditures to take advantage of tax benefits, negotiating in tricky deals with other companies, reviewing the marketing implications of change in the product line, and advising against practices that could leave the company vulnerable to competition.

Selecting Among the Hordes

Once you're ready to hire a management consultant, you still have the problem of choosing the one that will be most effective in meeting your needs. There are approximately 45,000 management-consulting firms and thousands more individual practitioners in North America alone. They can be categorized as follows:

➤ **Small firms and individual practitioners.** Many are excellent, especially in focus areas such as marketing, sales, personnel administration, accounting systems, material handling, and electronic data processing.

➤ **General management-consulting firms.** These offer advisory services to top management in functional areas ranging from energy and environment to budgeting and personnel.

➤ **Full-service management-consulting companies.** These companies are able to start with advice and carry a program right through implementation, providing an implementation team, follow-through audit, and *evaluation services.*

Don't be seduced by the name and reputation of a big firm, when a smaller, more specialized firm might be better suited. The large, well-known management-consulting firms earned their reputations through competently handling large accounts that may not bear any similarities to your needs.

Likewise, you may be tempted to fall into the trap of hiring an individual or firm that worked well for someone else you know. But, was the problem similar? As with other professionals, you need to check experience and credentials, and compare those closely to your problems and needs.

Proceed

Managers experienced in using consultants often recommend a personal visit to consulting firms under consideration.

Looking for Experience

Previous experience with similar problems should be the first consideration when searching for a management consultant. An effective consultant's experience does not necessarily have to be in the same field. A steel manufacturer does not hire a management consultant for knowledge of steel, but for broadly applicable knowledge.

You want to be able to answer as many of these general questions as possible:

➤ How old is the firm?

➤ What are the principals' backgrounds?

➤ What clients has the firm served?

➤ How much business repeats?

➤ What is the firm's general reputation in the business community?

➤ How much time will the principals of the firm spend on your project?

You need to be honest with yourself in assessing the company. Do you think you would enjoy working with this firm? Was the discussion with the firm principals sufficiently challenging that they might be a welcome addition to the change campaign?

Credentials Count

Many consultants have earned the designation Certified Management Consultant (CMC) through completing a rigorous qualifying program of the Institute of Management Consultants. The Institute's Code of Professional Conduct is a useful guide in terms of what to expect of any consultant. Here are highlights:

➤ The basic obligation of every CMC is to put the interests of clients ahead of his or her own, be impartial, and serve with integrity and competence.

➤ The CMC will guard the confidentiality of all client information. He or she will not take financial gain, or any other kind of advantage, based on inside information.

➤ Before accepting an assignment, the CMC has an obligation to confer with the prospective client in sufficient detail to understand the problem and the scope of study needed to solve it. Such preliminary consultations are conducted confidentially.

➤ A CMC will accept only those assignments he or she is qualified to perform and that will provide real benefits to the client. The CMC will not guarantee any specific result, such as the amount of cost reduction or profit increase.

➤ Whenever feasible, the CMC will agree with the client in advance on the fee or fee basis for an assignment.

Get Specific

Once you've narrowed down the field, you'll need to interview the individual(s) who would actually work with your company. That session should allow you to answer the following questions:

➤ What has the firm successfully completed that is similar to your needs?

➤ What are the backgrounds and consulting experiences of key staff members?

➤ What types of companies are clients of this firm?

➤ Does the firm have repeat business with its clients?

➤ Who in the firm will spend time on your assignment?

➤ Do the individuals involved seem to understand and take a genuine interest in your needs?

➤ What reputation does the firm have among other companies?

➤ Are the fees reasonable and fully explained in advance?

➤ Will you receive a written proposal that covers all phases of the firm's work?

Ask for a written proposal, preferably one that responds to your own written statement of work. That proposal will allow you to clearly see what you can expect and enable you to examine several firms without falling into the trap of comparing apples and oranges.

The proposal you receive should cover the following subjects:

Be Wary

If the firm "sounds good" and you like the people involved, you will be tempted to hire them on the spot. Don't. You need more data.

➤ A perception of your change issues and desired result.

➤ The objectives in solving it.

➤ The latitude needed (for example, the degree of access to your staff).

➤ The scope and nature of the engagement, including the areas to be covered.

➤ The general methods to be used.

➤ A statement of the consultant's staff who will do the work.

➤ An estimate of necessary time.

➤ An estimate of fees.

➤ How the billing will be calculated and delivered.

Which Price Is Right?

Here are four principal fee arrangements used by management consultants:

1. The per-diem or hourly fee is probably the most common. To make clients feel more comfortable with this arrangement, a consulting firm will often estimate a certain figure that its total fees will not exceed. This is called a bracket quotation.

2. The lump-sum, or fixed-amount contract, is used most frequently in consulting arrangements with governing agencies. The main attraction of this method is that it provides a firm budget. The major disadvantage lies in its inflexibility, since the scope of the work is fixed.

3. The retainer method means you reserve a certain amount of the consultant's time, usually for a year, when the work contemplated cannot be detailed in advance.

4. The contingent fee means compensation is determined on benefits accruing from the services performed, and is seldom used because consultants cannot guarantee results, but undertake only to perform to the best of their ability and skill.

If your change campaign is important enough, and it is, you want to ensure that you bring the right consultant on board.

The Least You Need to Know

➤ Consultants are not superheroes ready to jump into your campaign and straighten out all problems with swift, sure strokes.

➤ Consultants are best used when there are real indicators that you need outside assistance, when the campaign can only go forward via the consultant's critical skills.

➤ It may be advantageous to find an appropriate consultant as an outside consultant–adviser, to provide ongoing advice in advance of crises and for crises avoidance.

➤ Don't be seduced by the name and reputation of a big firm, when a smaller, more specialized firm might be better suited.

➤ Seek consultants with the designation Certified Management Consultant (CMC), issued by the Institute of Management Consultants.

Part 5

Making Change Work for You

Part 5 represents a departure from the first four parts of the book. Here you get a chance to step back and ensure that the daily job of putting out fires, that is, being a change manager, isn't getting in the way of your ability to see the big picture of where you, your team, and your organization are headed.

The chapters and issues discussed here will give you an edge over other managers who don't realize that one can be doing everything "right" and still have the campaign fail.

Chapter 19

Staying Flexible in Your Plans

In This Chapter

➤ Understanding the mega-realities of life and their ramifications

➤ Thinking through scenarios based on premises

➤ Making intelligent assumptions

Change campaigns can take the form of helping top management to decide upon strategic alternatives. When faced with three possible paths that an organization can take, for example, it's not uncommon to commission someone from within or hire an outside consultant to conduct a campaign that assesses the benefits and costs, both short- and long-term, to pursuing each of the three possible paths.

The greater the departure the paths represent from the organization's operating history, the more crucial the findings of the change manager and the change management team.

Pick the wrong path, and the company could miss lucrative opportunities or worse, find itself in dire straits. The problem with all scout work in change campaigns is that all the study, analysis, and data in the world never truly prepare a company for how it is going to be once the company actually embarks on a chosen path.

Still, all large corporations today routinely have studies under way that provide critical insights and perspectives to top managers so that they can make their best decision as to the future direction of the company. This chapter will brief you on devising scenarios that can help your organization stay flexible, meet complex challenges, and be better positioned to capitalize on emerging opportunities.

Proceed

If you are chosen to head up such a campaign, invariably it is an indicator of the trust and confidence that top executives have in you.

Five Mega-Realities and Their Ramifications

Let's look at a way of categorizing what's occurring in the world and then crafting scenarios as to what the ramifications might be.

It's no accident that virtually every working man and woman today frequently feels pressed for time. There are five present realities, or "mega-realities" as I call them, that uniformly impact each of us.

The mega-realities include:

➤ **Escalating population growth.** From the be ginning of creation to 1850 C.E., world population grew to one billion. It grew to two billion by 1930, three billion by 1960, four billion by 1979, five billion by 1987, and six billion by 1996, with seven billion en route. Every 33 months, the current population of America, 277 million people, is added to the planet. Each day, the world population increases by more than 275,000 people (births minus deaths).

➤ **Overinformation.** This moment, you, and everyone you know, are being bombarded on all sides. All told, more words are published or broadcast *in a minute* than you could comfortably ingest in the rest of your life—and America leads the world in the volume of data generated and disseminated.

➤ **Media growth.** Television now dominates the world. To capture overstimulated, distracted viewers, television and other news media increasingly rely on sensationalism. Like too much food at once, too much data, in any form, isn't easily ingested—you can't afford to pay homage to everyone else's 15 minutes of fame.

➤ **Proliferation of paper.** Similar to having too much data, or too many eyewitness reports, having too much paper to deal with is going to make you feel overwhelmed and overworked. Americans today are consuming at least three times as much paper as 10 years ago. There are two basic reasons why our society spews so much paper:

1. We have the lowest postal rates in the world.
2. We have the broadest distribution of paper-generating technology.

Worldwide paper consumption is increasing at alarming rates despite widespread use of the Internet and e-mail.

➤ **Overabundance of choices.** Having choices is a blessing of a free-market economy. Like too much of everything else, however, having too many choices leads to the feeling of being overwhelmed and results not only in increased time expenditure, but also in a mounting form of exhaustion.

Hallmark Cards offers cards for *more than one hundred* familial relationships. More than 1,260 varieties of shampoo are on the market. More than 2,000 skin care products are selling. Some 75 different types of exercise shoes are available, each with scores of variations in style, functions, and features.

Let's go a step further now and consider possible ramifications to the five mega-realities as described above.

Factoid

A *New York Times* article reported that even buying leisure time goods has become a stressful, overwhelming experience.

➤ **Escalating population growth.** The immediate impact of escalating population would include increasing population densities in urban areas, with a resulting scarcity of land, potential increase in erosion of topsoil, and an imperiled global water supply. Local city and state governments, as well as regional and national governments, would be subject to endless political jockeying to control dwindling resources.

The long-term ramifications of increasing population growth are serious. These could include the breakdown of social order, a health crisis, out-of-control pollution, and extinction of more species. There could be widespread famine, confrontation between neighboring countries, and even wars over limited resources. We might witness the rise of more diverse political parties and have to endure those who try to seize power by radical measures.

➤ **Too much information.** All around, people feel overwhelmed and abused by information. This adds to the potential for more clutter within homes, offices, and entire organizations, which results in less control. More information leads to a lack of closure in one's personal affairs, as well as in the workplace.

The long-term ramifications could include heavy reliance on specialized information vendors to help separate the wheat from the chaff. Certainly new, more powerful Internet search engines will be developed, as will new forms of gathering, storing, and, perhaps, applying information. Paradoxically, businesses will have to wade through even more information to stay competitive.

➤ **Massive media growth.** The proliferation of media growth is resulting in more news, images, and coverage of both the significant and the absurd. Some observers feel that this results in people's inability to extract meaning from the news and information they receive.

The proliferation of media has resulted in more pleasures—more entertainment, more movies, more ways to keep one's self amused. It has also produced more distractions, trivia, and nonsense. By some observations, there has also been an increasing rate of failure among firms that provide news, information, and entertainment.

➤ **Proliferation of paper.** This has resulted in an overabundance of printed materials, and yields diminishing personal control. Take a look at your typical coworker's desk these days, or your own for that matter. In recent years, paper costs have increased markedly while landfills are at overcapacity.

Those who use paper as a medium to influence others increasingly find that it is more and more arduous to make an impact. In the long term, increased dissemination of paper results in everyone's increased difficulty in handling, ferreting out, and acting upon what is significant.

There will be changes in postal rates, classification of mail, new alliances between overnight carriers, and new services springing up. Certainly, many businesses and organizations will continue the trend toward greater use of Web sites to convey information to interested parties.

➤ **Overabundance of choices.** This has had perhaps the most profound immediate impact. More options tend to result in less effectiveness—people are not as adept at choosing when facing a bewildering array of option. More people and more businesses tend to overaccumulate, squander funds, and exist in a clutter-filled state. Too many choices could be at the root of attention deficit disorder experienced by children and, increasingly, by adults. Too many choices also result in product and services failing at faster rates. (See my discussion about Sony in Chapter 2, "Change Scenarios.")

Too many choices over the long term could lead to a lack of closure, continual overwhelm, and, as Alvin Toffler long ago predicted in *Future Shock*, a state of future shock, wherein people have an inability to effectively choose.

The following table succinctly summarizes the previous discussion.

Change Master

In the long run, the proliferation of media growth will exacerbate people's inability to maintain, let alone identify, crucial issues. Mingling of the trivial and absurd with the profound and cataclysmic will heighten. The gulf between the information haves and have-nots will widen instead of narrow.

Be Wary

In the long term, an overabundance of choices all but guarantees explosive but lucrative micro-markets of a rapidly vanishing nature.

Ramifications of the Five Mega-Realities

Mega-Reality	Immediate Impact	Long-Term Ramifications
Population	Scarcity of land, high population density, erosion of topsoil, imperiled water supply, finger-pointing, political jockeying to control dwindling resources.	Breakdown of social order, serial health crisis, pollution, extinction of more species, famine, confrontation, rise of more diverse political parties, power by radical measures.
Information	Data surplus, knowledge scarcity. People feeling overwhelmed and abused by information. Lack of closure in personal affairs. More clutter, less control.	More information necessary to stay competitive. Heavy reliance on information vendors and Internet search engines. New forms of gathering and storing information.
Media Growth	More news and images, scarcity of meaning. More pleasures, more distractors. Increasing rate of failure among firms that provide news, information, or entertainment.	Inability to maintain, let alone identify, crucial issues.Mingling of the trivial and absurd with the profound and cataclysmic. Gulf between haves and have-nots widens rather than narrows.
Too Much Paper	Overabundance of printed material yields diminishing personal control. High paper costs—landfills at overcapacity. Increasingly, more difficult to make an impact.	Increased difficulty in handling, ferreting out, and acting upon the significant. Heavy reliance on Web sites to convey information. Changes in postal regulations regarding third-class mail.
Too Many Choices	More options, less effectiveness. More confusion, especially for big-ticket items. More children with attention deficit disorder. Products and services failing at faster rates.	Exploding, lucrative micro-markets of rapidly vanishing nature. Lack of closure. Overaccumulating, squandering of funds, long-term insidious stress. Continual overwhelm. Future shock.

Here's a bonus you may not have realized: Based on the kind of change campaign you're managing, the type of organization that you work for, and other particulars of your situation, the previous table could be helpful for you in terms of making assumptions about the target market or establishing design parameters for a new product or service.

Scenario Thinking Based on Varying Premises

Scenario thinking has gained popularity in many organizations that find that the rapid changes in society make long-term planning difficult. A typical approach to scenario thinking is threefold:

1. What would the scenario in your market or industry be if things went very well? Under an optimistic scenario, what would your market look like? How would you position yourself? What objectives and goals would you have?

Proceed

Let your imagination take over as you devise the potential scenarios.

2. Consider a worst-case scenario. Suppose that the market dries up. What if longstanding consumer behavior shifts, or traditional assumptions no longer hold? How would you proceed in an unfavorable climate?

3. The mid-case scenario occurs when a balance of favorable and unfavorable circumstances unfold. How would you position yourself in the mid-case scenario? What would be your goals and objectives?

Isolate the Key Question

In *The Art of the Long View,* author Peter Schwartz says, "Spinning scenarios is a highly sophisticated, singularly useful, and eminently practical way to think about the future."

When you devise scenarios, you create a vision of possible futures. Focus, however, is not to precisely determine exactly which of these scenarios will come to pass. Rather, it is to be in a ready position should any one of them come to pass.

I suggest devising three scenarios for any potential future because more than that, and well, it just gets confusing! As you map out these plausible futures, consider how prepared your organization and your team are in the event of any one of them occurring.

Peter Schwartz emphasizes the importance of isolating your decision. You don't have to figure out what's likely to happen in the future; simply focus on the key question before you. Given the change campaign that you're asked to manage, under three possible scenarios, what key decision or decisions emerge? This keeps the process much simpler.

Categorize Responses Under Three Premises

Continuing with the example of the five mega-realities discussed earlier, what kind of scenarios might be likely for the social and business environments? What might be likely institutional and individual responses under three different premises, such as ...

➤ Everyone getting back into a state of relative control,

➤ Some people getting back into control, or

➤ No one getting into control?

Use the following grid to follow the scenario analysis I am about to discuss.

THE LONGVIEW: AS THE FIVE MEGA-REALITIES PROLIFERATE

Premise	Social Environment	Business Environment	Institutional Response	Individual Response
Everyone Catches Up	*A la Star Trek*	*Balance & Control*	*Back to Basics*	*Personal Betterment*
Some Catch Up	*Declining Standards*	*Much Like Today*	*Measured Progress*	*Functionality*
No One Catches Up	*Multiphrenia*	*Constant Calamity*	*Frenzied Activity*	*Make-Do*

THE LONGVIEW: AS THE FIVE MEGA-REALITIES PROLIFERATE

Premise	Social Environment	Business Environment	Institutional Response	Individual Response
	A la Star Trek	*Balance & Control*	*Back to Basics*	*Personal Betterment*
Everyone Catches Up	**Development of social graces** Focus on family **Balance** Control	**Complete 2-way software** Sophisticated filing systems **Vacations/leisure available upon request** Feelings of competence and contentment	**Responsiveness to requests and concerns** People first **Increased wage levels** Efficiency and effectiveness	"We" first **Environmental focus** Cultural pursuits **Social pursuits**
	Declining Standards	*Much Like Today*	*Measured Progress*	*Functionality*
Some Catch Up	**Intermittent frenzy** Breakdowns seen as routine **Semipermanent overwhelm**	**Management training** Screening services **Delegating responsibility** Compensation services **Group is responsible** Defraying individual liability	**Better choice of ventures** Downsized bureaucracy **More subcontracting** Soliciting professional advice	**Choose fewer projects** Less stressed out **More leisure enjoyments** Weekends free of work **Forsaking the smothering cocoon**
	Multiphrenia	*Constant Calamity*	*Frenzied Activity*	*Make-Do*
No One Catches Up	**High stress** Constant breakdowns **Neglected children** Overwhelm **Catastrophes increase**	**Stress and burnout** Hostility **Sleepwalking** Clutter **Constantly playing catch-up** Individual responsibility	**Incentive creation** Profits first **Overburdened staff** Taking on too many activities **Trying to coordinate**	"Me" first Creature comforts **Disenfranchisement** Stuck in the rat race **Chasing your own tail** Aspiring to unrealistic goals

A sample scenario.

Premise 1: Everyone Catches Up

Under this premise, in the social environment, we might witness the development of more social graces, a stronger focus on the family, and more balance and control among individuals throughout society. I call this the *Star Trek scenario*.

In this scenario, vacations and leisure time away from work may be available upon request. People feel more competent and more content a greater amount of the time. Institutions, including organizations and governments, are more responsive to concerns and requests of their constituents. They put people first.

Individuals in this scenario may witness an increase in wage levels. Efficiency and effectiveness would certainly prevail. A "we first" mentality would prevail. People would pursue cultural and social interests. Focus on the environment would be highly important.

Premise 2: Only Some Catch Up

Suppose that the second premise prevails in which only some catch up. This is the most likely premise of the three. In the social environment, we might witness declining standards and routine breakdowns. People would be subject to a semipermanent overwhelming state. Intermittent frenzy would not be uncommon.

In the business environment, things might look pretty much like they do today. Among institutions, there would continue to be measured progress. Leaders of large organizations would continue to seek professional advice, hone and refine their decision-making abilities, constantly be on the lookout for opportunities to downsize, and rely more on arm's-length agreements and subcontractors.

Among individuals, the wise would choose fewer projects and keep themselves from getting too stressed out too often. They would more *zealously* guard their leisure time, carving out whole weekends and vacations for themselves during which they could have true relaxation.

Word Power

Anything that you do **zealously** you do avidly, eagerly, and over-enthusiastically.

Premise 3: Everyone Is Perpetually Overwhelmed

The third scenario, in which everyone in society becomes overwhelmed as a result of the five mega-realities, is not a pretty picture. It is, nevertheless, one that would be considered by a change manager whose organization offers a product or service that most assuredly would be impacted by the proliferation by the mega-realities. It would result from an inability of the general population to acknowledge, let alone manage, the impact of the mega-realities.

In the social environment, a state of multifrenzy might exist, characterized by high stress, constant breakdowns, and, unfortunately, neglect of children.

In the business environment, constant calamity might be the norm. It would be characterized by high levels of stress and burnout, and dramatic increases in the number of individuals who run up their *sleep debt*.

Institutional and organizational responses to the third scenario—no one catches up—would be a keen focus on creation of greater and sorely needed incentives for originality and innovation. Certainly, overburdened staff members and workers who are taking on too much, constantly trying to juggle activities, would have to be contended with. Some organizations might take a "society be damned" attitude, and strive simply for profits, prominence, or survival.

The individual response to the proliferation of the five mega-realities in the worst-case scenario would likely be to adopt a "me first" orientation. Many might feel disenfranchised and stuck in a lifelong rat race. They might turn to creature comforts, engaging in a level of self-indulgence rarely witnessed in history.

Create Your Own Grid

The previous discussion and model are good for an all-purpose look at society. Considering what you're managing, your industry, and other particulars of your situation, it makes sense for you to construct your own grid. At least three premises are usually advisable. (If you add far more than three premises to your grid, the analysis can get overly complex.)

Word Power

Sleep debt equals the accumulated lack of sleep of which someone has been deprived, for which the body always makes her pay in one way or another.

Factoid

Years ago, during the heyday of marijuana use, it was rumored that marijuana might be legalized for general consumption. The major tobacco companies already had undertaken scenario planning. On their drawing boards, each was planning to be among the first in the marketplace with such market pleasers as Acapulco Gold, California Clover, Lucky Seeds, and Jamaica Slims.

You're in generally good shape if you include one pessimistic scenario, one that's middle of the road, and one optimistic scenario. Then, assess those possible outcomes against two to four issues that are critical in your organization.

Change Master

After imagining your business in the aforementioned scenarios, your goal is to move into that space and marshal your resources so that you're able to be at a chosen place at a chosen previous discussion and model is good for an all-purpose look at society time.

Factoid

Several factors have prompted the declining of basic skills. Employers are reaching further into the labor pool, hiring people less ready for work. The situation is heightened by the higher capacities demanded by computerized processes and expectations that hirees will be able to tackle a wider range of skill-dependent tasks. There also appears to be insufficient student development in the public school systems.

Assembling the Puzzle

Suppose that you run a training firm dedicated to helping employees of corporate clients with business skills. Roger Herman, publisher of the weekly 'zine *The Herman Report,* states that employers are increasingly frustrated by workers' deficiencies in fundamental reading, writing, and math skills. The labor shortage is complicated by the difficulty in finding people who are qualified to work … or are at least trainable. Insufficient basic education makes business training considerably more challenging.

Alarms Sound

Upon discovering this, you begin to dig further. You encounter a study from the American Management Association (AMA)—AMA's annual survey on workplace testing, which reveals that more than 38 percent of 1999 job applicants lacked the literacy and numeracy skills required to perform the jobs they applied for. This data is astounding when compared against the figures of the two previous years: 35.5 percent in 1998 and 22.8 percent in 1997.

Scenarios of Opportunity

In your research, you uncover a gem: More companies are testing job applicants for basic skills, but only 13 percent of the companies are offering employees remedial training, which, amazingly, costs only $289 per trainee on average.

Now you begin to undertake scenario thinking: Will more employers invest in remedial education for their workers, and if so, to what degree? How will this impact your firm's prospects, and what new products or services might you offer?

The Herman Report suggests that employers "will be forced into this effort; the decision won't be easy. Once committed, however, employers will strive to provide a valuable, comprehensive, and effective educational program. This venture will be expensive, but a wise investment in attracting, growing, and retaining people who sincerely want to learn and earn. Language, culture, and life-management skills will be taught along with the basics."

Supplying Critical Resources

Where will the trainers come from? Might teachers be recruited from public school systems, which, of course, are already faced with serious staff shortages? Should you recruit teachers now, and have a "faculty" in place and ready?

Undoubtedly, companies will pay teachers more than they were making in the public school system, provide better facilities, and offer adult students the motivation to learn. Some companies might partner with school systems to award diplomas to graduates, fostering cooperative teacher-sharing arrangements.

You might also consider that school systems themselves will feel even more pressure to adjust teacher compensation, working conditions, and facilities. How might this impact your product/service offering?

It's Your Turn

For your industry and market, seek to generate at least three to five descriptors of what situations might develop, given the three scenarios you have devised, and the two to four issues worth exploring.

After you have completed your chart, at least in the draft stage, share it with others who can potentially make vital additions and modifications. Put the grid away for a few days, then come back to it when you are ready to examine it anew. Seek another round of input from knowledgeable participants.

Some Framework Is Better Than Nothing

Regardless of what you derive, you'll have a better framework for proceeding into the future and managing your change campaign than if you don't undertake the exercise at all.

Proceed

Choose sponsors, advocates, targets, friends, or relatives to review your grid as you develop it.

The Least You Need to Know

➤ The five mega-realities of today include overpopulation, excess information, media growth, too much paper, and an overabundance of choices.

➤ Scenario thinking has gained popularity in many organizations that find that the rapid changes in society make long-term planning difficult.

➤ In acknowledgment of the mega-realities, you can create three scenarios in which everyone catches up, some people catch up, or no one catches up.

➤ Considering what you're managing, your industry, and other particulars of your situation, it makes sense for you to construct your own scenario grid.

➤ The future belongs to those who effectively engage in scenario thinking and choose points in time to capitalize on the opportunities that they've identified.

Leapfrogging and Picking Spots

Combining strategies previously mentioned in this book, such as jump starting or total immersion, will give you the hours or days you need to read, study, and absorb what's occurring. It can also help you make decisions about how you'll apply new modes of doing things and new technology to your career, business, or organization. Although you can't keep up with all the changes in your industry and environment, you can periodically leapfrog over the developments of the last several months and "catch up" in a way. This chapter explains how.

You Are Not Hercules

It would be a Herculean task to respond to every change in the marketplace, or to every product and service innovation by all of the top competitors in your field. While there are a number of things you can do to maintain a managerial edge (see Chapter 22, "Maintaining the Management Edge"), sometimes you have to yield to the inevitable—neither you nor your team can stay on top of every single issue that may have ramifications for your organization as it emerges.

With that in mind and following on the heels of scenario thinking, we'll tackle leapfrogging so that you fully understand the concept. Then you'll be able to work with it in ways that are rewarding to all concerned with your change campaign.

Leapfrog Over Developments

Technology breakthroughs used to come in years, not days:

1900	Remington sells 100,000 typewriters, most for office use.
1902	The U.S. Patent Office approves the postage meter.
1912	Rotary calculators are developed.
1920	The first Pitney Bowes postage meter is placed in service.
1925	"Telephone machine" dictation is developed with the Dictaphone Telecord.
1930s	The first shredder is manufactured in Germany.
1930s	IBM introduces the first electric typewriter.
1947	Dictaphone offers a dictation machine, a plastic record replaces wax cylinder.
1949	Xerox introduces Copier Model A (first commercial electrophotographic copier).
1949	First desktop meter for small businesses is introduced.
1973	Dictaphone introduces the first mini- and standard-cassette dictation models.
1975	Savin copier gains wide market acceptance; customers buy, not lease.
1977	3M introduces first "near Group 3" fax machines.
1978	The electronic typewriter is introduced.
1979	Postage by Phone debuts.
1980s	Canon introduces first personal copiers.
1980s	Lanier introduces first digital dictation system.
1981	IBM introduces the PC.
1981	Ricoh introduces first fax machine compatible with Group 3 standard.

1983	Minolta introduces first copier with automatic zoom reduction and enlargement.
1985	GammaLink introduces first computer faxboard.
1987	Canon introduces first color copiers and develops a color copier market.
1987	Canon introduces the first plain-paper fax machine.
1989	Sharp introduces first color fax machine.
1990	Xerox introduces first successful digital alternative to offset printers.
1996	First intranet fax service is introduced.
since 1997	Nonstop breakthroughs occur in virtually all aspects of office technology.

In a world that experiences 17 technology and 200 associated services and peripheral goods breakthroughs per second, the business terrain is constantly changing. It is not only impossible to keep up in real time with every development that might impact your organization, but it is foolhardy, frustrating, and self-defeating to even make the attempt.

Make Winning Tackles

Remaining flexible or using "scenario thinking strategies," as outlined in the previous chapter, enables you to be calm and collected when forced to cope with change in a highly volatile, ever-evolving environment. This attitude will give you the confidence to leapfrog over most developments and only tackle those that will be the most beneficial to your organization.

An example of *leapfrogging* stems from the consumer electronics industry. As a manufacturer, you could find yourself literally making an improvement each day, if not more frequently, to nearly every item in your product line. You could make them lighter, faster, more modular, and more flexible. You could add a more powerful chip, use higher grade materials, or bundle items with different material.

Word Power

Leapfrogging means that you, your company, your sponsor, and your team make conscious decisions not to compete with or even address certain developments in your industry and marketplace. All attention is devoted to the pursuit of more appropriate objectives that will enable you to dominate.

Unprecedented Improvement, Choice Explosion

In consumer electronics and a number of other industries, it's relatively easy to plot the growth and development of a particular product over the last couple of decades. One can note with amazement how much more powerful and effective a given product has become.

Be Wary

In the process of making product improvements and new models, you could end up confusing many people, such as the workers in your distribution chain who handle your products, retail managers, and even consumers.

Word Power

Decentralization refers to the fact that anybody with a computer is essentially a knowledge worker, and the fruits of his or her labor easily can be distributed around the globe.

The higher levels of quality and functionality of consumer electronics over the last 10 to 20 years, however, pale in comparison to what will be developed and available in the coming 10 to 20 years. As more services become available online, the very notion of terms such as "electronics" and "appliances" will experience dramatic reinterpretation.

Skip a Beat

The acceleration of product advances points to the practicality of skipping over some developments altogether and focusing on where you want to stand as a company, as a team, and as a vendor. Entire countries have chosen this strategy.

For instance, India and Pakistan have been regarded as having third-wave, agricultural economies. Yet, they have largely bypassed the second-wave, industrial economies that most of the West experienced. Instead, they've proceeded right into first-wave, information economies. A great deal of the software written today emanates from India and acceleration of product advances points to the practicality of skipping Pakistan.

Embrace New Economy Industries

As Alvin Toffler deftly pointed out in *The Third Wave*, there was no reason for governments and prevailing institutions not to encourage their increasingly educated populations to embrace information-age economies. At the least, first-wave economies tend to be "cleaner," so they can be *decentralized*.

Don't Even Go There

To embrace the second-wave industrial economy would have meant heavy capital investment in equipment and labor. It would have also meant trying to play catch-up with western societies that had already firmly established industrial economies. Higher levels of energy usage, potential degradation of the environment, and years of "ramp-up" time would have resulted.

Cater to Specific Tastes

On a nontechnical, less sweeping basis, Powell's Bookstore, the bricks-and-clicks store based in Portland, Oregon, has leapt over competitor marketing strategies, picked its spot, and profited.

With competitors in the form of corporate giants such as Amazon.com and Barnes & Noble's online division, who wouldn't be amazed that Powells. com can keep afloat in the online bookstore market? How can Powell's turn a profit against those giants? It's relatively easy. Powells.com bypassed Amazon's marketing model and targeted a different market altogether. While the big guys make traditional merchandise offerings, Powell's bookstores and online business cater to more specific literary tastes.

Change Master

India's and Pakistan's massive leapfrog from agricultural to information-based economies enables governments and entrepreneurs of both countries to essentially ignore concerns about industrial developments in the rest of the world with which they could not possibly compete. All the while, they could position themselves to be able to effectively compete for years to come in the new economy.

On average, Powell's advertising costs each year are only 1 percent of its sales. Forsaking the approach of advertising all over, Powell's targets the intellectual readership of publications such as *Mother Jones* and the *Utne Reader*. In comparison, Amazon spends 10 percent of sales on advertising in their attempt to reach the masses and a pretty penny on fulfillments costs. Thus far, Amazon has lost money each year, while Powell's turns a decent profit.

In time, giants may choose to emulate elements of Powell's marketing strategy, and hence Powell's might have to "leap" and "pick" again.

Leaping and Loving It

Leapfroggers acknowledge developments in the marketplace and decide not to compete against them. Instead, their "change campaign" focuses on what *they* want to offer and to whom, and sets realistic deadlines by which they can offer such services.

Ideally, at the point of launch, the marketplace is already amenable to their new product or service.

Proceed

Success comes in finding a lucrative niche. Once you pinpoint a market, you can provide your customers with what they want and therefore make a profit. With lower overhead and advertising costs, Web-based businesses have the ability to target a particular niche with fewer expenditures than ever. The more narrow the target market, the lower the marketing and advertising costs.

Change Master

Effective leapfrogging is analogous to the consumer who scratches his head and says, "Why doesn't somebody come up with a way to XYZ?" Lo and behold, your company happens to have developed a product, service, or delivery system that converts the consumer's pipedream into a reality.

Read, Study, Absorb, and Strike

Leapfrogging over an existing industry or market developments doesn't mean that you can be completely oblivious to them. You need to be aware and selectively choose to ignore certain developments.

While you can't stay abreast in real time of every single innovation, it is highly desirable, if not mandatory, to understand broad-based trends, target market wants and needs, and who's serving whom. Does it make sense to read and study about developments in your industry and in the marketplace? Most definitely!

The Internet Helps a Lot

Visiting any of a number of helpful sites can quickly get you up to speed on some of the activities of other companies. Here are some great sources of corporate and business information:

➤ **www.hooversonline.com:** Maintains a database of company profiles.

➤ **www.altavisita.com:** A search engine specializing in business sites.

➤ **www.google.com:** The biggest, broadest, fastest search engine of them all.

➤ **www.dowjones.com:** Company data in many formats.

➤ **www.edgar-online.com:** Information from 10K filings.

➤ **www.vault.com:** 3,000 company profiles.

➤ **www.rileyguide.com:** Information on researching companies.

➤ **www.findarticles.com:** From key words offer hundreds of articles.

➤ **www.refdesk.com:** Offers a huge variety of vital reference sources.

Certainly, it helps to know what has transpired in your industry and in your marketplace, both long ago and recently. The further back you research, the greater insights you will acquire for the future. More importantly, this will help you understand how needs and wants are changing.

Anyone Can Innovate

Is it primarily startups and new ventures engaged in leapfrog-type thinking that are forcing others in their wake to catch up to them? Often yes, yet even companies in operation for decades can engage in leapfrog developments. The *Encyclopedia Britannica* published a hard copy, multivolume edition for more than 130 years, and then scrapped it for 100 percent online operations.

Sensing that the production of a voluminous set of books would be deemed out-of-date almost immediately upon publication in the Internet age, the company decided to go completely online. *Encyclopedia Britannica* offered its basic online services for free, generating revenue primarily through advertisers on their site. They have since added a yearly subscription fee for more in-depth services only.

Cyber Showroom

In the auto industry, CarMax popularized offering a huge assortment of used vehicles heavily promoted in full-page newspaper advertisements. Consumers didn't even have to physically walk the lot because they could use computers in the showroom to search the cars CarMax had available. They could also designate age, price, color, model, make, and all other parameters with a click of the mouse.

On-site consumers were intrigued by the idea of being able to visit a multiacre CarMax lot day or night since the cars were now illuminated by floodlights.

Factoid

CarMax began listing every single vehicle at every single lot across the country online. Therefore, if your local CarMax does not have the exact car that you're looking for, you now have the option of searching CarMax's lots across the country.

Factoid

The CarMax founders thoroughly researched the auto industry prior to launching this venture. They scouted for, identified, and then deeply understood consumer frustrations and pet peeves. Then, they designed a sales system that addressed those frustrations.

Price Haggling Eliminated

CarMax went a step further by indicating precise cost information right up front. No negotiation, no haggling, no special favors, not a second wasted on whether you could have gotten a salesperson to come down in price. The prices were there for anybody to see. You either wanted to buy, or you thought you could get a better deal elsewhere. However, the mystery was completely removed.

Change Master

Despite the size of your company, the market share that you acquire and the market position that you develop may prove to be substantial indeed.

Be Wary

Operating a business in society today is frustrating. The hyper-accelerating number of technological breakthroughs all but ensures that you can't know, let alone predict, how an innovation will occur or who will be responsible for it. It will be even harder to know when a business entity is going to make a dramatic impact on your revenue by inventing a unique means of fulfilling a market need.

Not Easily Emulated

A venture of such large magnitude cannot be easily replicated by others due to the capitalization considerations, never mind acquiring the real estate, developing the inventory, installing the management system, and integrating the entire network so that anyone can research any car on any lot at any time.

You can make your mark in smaller, local markets as well. Your leapfrog over the competition may not be as grand and your competitive advantage may not last as long as in the previous example, but you can lead for a while in the revenues that you generate.

Study the Competition

Competition is sometimes "cooperation in disguise." While you don't want to emulate everything that one or more of your competitors are doing, as mentioned earlier, it's still prudent to have knowledge of their operations.

Sometimes, a twist or a turn on what a competitor is doing adds up to an innovative breakthrough in your organization. Or, if two competitors have similar aspects to their products or services, you may be able to devise a new strategy that far supersedes what anyone else is doing in the industry by straying from their example.

Peril from Afar

Problems often arise from competition that originates in other industries. For example, in the years 2000 and 2001, the biggest competition for the CD manufacturing industry was Napster and other MP3 file-swapping and file-sharing Web sites, along with the associated technology that made them possible.

Scary and Hairy

It is indeed a scary world out there, particularly from a competitive standpoint. Hence, it pays for you or your emissary to attend tradeshows and symposiums outside of your immediate industry.

While it's important to focus mainly on your close competitors, choose a number of companies whose products and services are similar to, but not in competition with, your own, and study their markets as well.

It also makes sense to employ a researcher who does nothing but peruse the Internet, scouting developments high and low that have the potential to impact your world.

Even the most spectacular breakthroughs, however, still yield some type of advance warning. A journal article, a newspaper feature, or statements from conferences often add up to the clues and cues necessary for your researcher to make further inquiries.

Pick Your Spots

The key to picking your spots is pinpointing what you want to achieve and choosing a deadline for doing so—the perfect climate for pursuing a change campaign. The specific language that you use both mentally and verbally can make a difference.

Language Leads

In his book *2020 Vision*, author Stanley Davis concludes that many of the world's successful leaders developed a future-perfect attitude. Such leaders would not merely think in terms of "if we came to

Proceed

In the age of the Internet, staying on top of what the known competition is doing has probably never been easier.

Change Master

If a single technology innovation can turn your industry on its heels and it has the requisite financial backing, the chances are that it will.

Proceed

To leapfrog over what is already being done both internally and externally, pick a specific position to strive for, that is market leadership, industry dominance, or highest rating.

power," but rather, "by this time next year we will have accomplished XYZ." This use of language may seem subtle, but it yields a dramatic change in actions and mindset.

"We will have accomplished …" signifies to the revolutionary leader, the sponsor, the first lieutenant or field captain, and the change manager a type of "living into the future." For a specific product or service, it is helpful and encouraging to offer thoughts in a manner such as: "By the third quarter of this year we will have attained market leadership in the sales of XYZ …."

Change Master

Pick your spots in the future—say, in six months—whereby you want to have a new product or service introduced, have some new technology fully integrated into your operations, and so forth. You can't digest every development in your field, but by picking certain spots, you can handle these.

Word Power

Singularities is the term that astrophysicist and cosmologist Steven Hawking uses to describe a one-time event in the universe.

They Come, They Go

Inherent in such use of language and, by extension, such thinking, is that other developments within the industry or marketplace may come and go during that time. Nonetheless, the desired goals will be reached.

Some developments may have to be given short shrift or otherwise be ignored. However, the company and the change team are focused precisely on how and where they will stand at their chosen point in the future.

The Pinnacle: Singularities

It takes vision to choose a spot, guts to announce it, energy to initiate the campaign that will achieve it, and fortitude to see it through. Repeatedly, however, we have witnessed dramatic leapfrogging and picking of spots that, once achieved, have resulted in *singularities*.

Walt Disney's development of Disneyland, Walt Disney World, and all the related products and services that followed not only superseded the amusement and theme parks that came before it; as of early in the twentieth century, it created entertainment and goods that can't be duplicated.

In summary, the process of leapfrogging and picking spots is most appropriately regarded as a series of cascading campaigns designed to maintain long-term health and viability of the organization.

The Least You Need to Know

➤ You cannot keep up with all the changes in your industry and environment, but you can periodically leapfrog over the developments and "catch up" in a way.

➤ Leapfrogging means that you decide not to address certain developments in your industry and marketplace and instead pursue appropriate objectives that will enable you to dominate.

➤ Success comes in finding a lucrative niche. Once you pinpoint a market, you can provide your customers with what they want and therefore make a profit.

➤ Sometimes, a twist or a turn on what a competitor is doing adds up to an innovative breakthrough in your organization.

➤ The key to picking your spots is pinpointing what you want to achieve and choosing a deadline for doing so.

Chapter 21

Understanding the Importance of Negotiation

In This Chapter

➤ Examining what you want to get out of a negotiation

➤ Understanding the tactics and strategy of negotiation

➤ Looking at positional versus principled negotiation

➤ Teaching yourself to negotiate

Almost everything in life is negotiable. Negotiation is all around us, in all situations. Local government officials bargain with each other to keep streets plowed of snow, enact changes in zoning laws, build a shopping mall in the area, or assess property taxes. State and federal government officials debate what will be spent on your children's education, your community's drug rehabilitation programs, and, again, the amount of taxes you will pay.

This chapter discusses using negotiation in a change campaign. Often the best way to get what you need is to ensure that the others who impact your campaign get what they need. There is no magic formula for successful negotiation. Solving other people's problems or having them believe you've done so probably comes the closest.

There Is No Substitute for Preparation

All skilled negotiators do their homework. Authors and seminar leaders Chester Karrass, Ph.D.; Gerald Nierenberg, Ph.D.; and other top negotiation trainers agree that the best negotiators are well prepared prior to participating in a negotiation. They first establish an objective by asking "What do I seek to accomplish?" although the answer may be obvious.

Examine your strengths—what advantages do you have? Think financial, strategic, perceptual, geographic, and so on. Then, determine in advance what you want to get from the negotiation, and for what you will settle. The other party may be receptive to your ideas; hence, they are negotiating tools.

The Tactics and Strategies of Negotiation

How can a change manager negotiate successfully to get what he or she wants? Effective negotiators make tactful decisions before entering the negotiation process, one of which is to negotiate as an individual or as a team. You may have only yourself to rely on, but if you can draw upon your sponsor or your staff, you may benefit.

Going Solo

The advantages to negotiating alone include the following:

➤ You can prevent a "divide and conquer" strategy by others.

➤ You can demonstrate that you have complete responsibility.

➤ You can eliminate a weakening position resulting from differences of opinion among team members.

➤ You can facilitate on-the-spot decision making, particularly for granting or receiving concessions.

United We Stand

The advantages to employing a group to negotiate include the following:

➤ Group members can play to each member's strength.

➤ The group is less likely to be swayed than a single negotiator.

➤ The collective stamina of the group can be extensive.

➤ A variety of tactics, such as time-outs and stalling, become more tenable.

Picking the Players

The members of your team should be able to work together to achieve success. When selecting a negotiating team, each member should have a specific function. All members need to know the group's strategy and objectives, and demonstrate confidence in performing their respective duties. And everyone plays a significant role on a negotiating team; potential conflict or misunderstanding must be overcome well in advance of the negotiation.

Don't Reveal Your Hand

When you begin negotiating, it's unwise to reveal the exact terms that you desire. Instead, both parties usually strive for and request unrealistic goals at the outset. This way, once the negotiation begins, each party is more likely to be satisfied after compromising to reach a mutually agreeable position.

Be Aware of Counter Tactics

Roger Dawson, author of *You Can Get Anything You Want, But You Have to Do More Than Ask,* observes the importance of becoming proficient in the fundamentals of negotiation. Otherwise, you probably won't be effective because you'll be subject to the negotiating, training, and techniques of others.

Here is a list of key negotiation tactics that your opponents may know:

➤ **The double flinch.** If you quote a price, the other party has been taught to say "Holy cow" or its equivalent. If your opponent is part of a team, several members will say it slowly and distinctly ... so that you can hear it!

➤ **Avoiding discussion of price.** Another strategy that opponents may throw at you is not addressing the issue of price, particularly after you have made an initial offer. This tends to raise your anxieties and put pressure on you. The opponent knows what price you quoted and that you are interested in getting some kind of confirmation. His or her measured reluctance in giving you that confirmation is all part of a master plan.

➤ **Your bottom line.** One way to avoid the other party's negotiation tactics is to predetermine your walk-away terms, which refers to the point at which you would leave the negotiation rather than stay and accept far less than desirable terms. So, before entering the

Proceed

Don't settle for your opposition's first offer. Recognize that compromising increases your chances of attaining your *initial* unrevealed position.

Be Wary

If you're not aware of these types of tactics, you are likely to buckle under on your price or on some other major provision, perhaps only moments before you were about to get what you asked for.

negotiation, it's absolutely crucial to determine the terms or limits you cannot accept if doing so would impede the change campaign.

➤ **Take this.** The negotiator who comes to the table with a useful counterproposal often saves a failing deal and receives a feather in his cap. Always be ready to present a counterproposal!

➤ **Timing can be everything.** Sometimes it isn't how you negotiate, but when you negotiate. In 1989, with the reunification of Germany days away, garbage collectors in East Germany went on strike to protest wages. They were paid in nonconvertible Communist Bloc currency that was far below its Western counterparts. After only three days of negotiations—not long for such a complicated situation—their demands for 33 percent raises were met.

Negotiation trainer Herb Cohen suggests that one of the best tactics for assuring a successful negotiation is to figure out, or estimate in advance, the time constraints or deadlines that your opponent faces.

Change Master

People are more agreeable when facing a tight deadline. However, don't reveal to your opponent that you know his or her deadline.

Be Wary

People who take a firm position and bargain from that one stronghold tend to box themselves into a win-lose situation.

Positional Negotiation and Its Consequences

A classic example of the most common type of negotiation, called positional negotiation, is represented in union or labor-versus-management negotiations. Each person or group takes a position, argues to defend that position, and makes concessions to reach a compromise. Positional negotiation does not always result in a workable solution for either party, although it is one of the most pervasive types of negotiation practiced.

In the last couple decades of the twentieth century, some unions, from air traffic controllers to bus drivers, lost ground using rigid positional negotiations. Many companies also went into bankruptcy as a result of union strikes on top of their financial problems and poor management.

Positional negotiation forces people to focus on the mechanics of the process and not on the underlying issues impacting each side.

Take a Cue from Captain Kirk

One of the attractions of the television series *Star Trek* was that the episodes often contained elements of logic, debate, and positional negotiation. Nearly each show involved Captain Kirk or Mr. Spock opening communication with intergalactic pirates or aliens. The *Enterprise*'s position, as mandated by Starfleet Command, was not to interfere with the inhabitants or strange life forms.

If attacked or challenged, the Enterprise responded with caution. Mr. Spock's logical responses were often likened to the three-dimensional game of chess he liked to play. Of course, each negotiation took as long as a one-hour show with commercials. Imagine a professional chess match or contract negotiation taking a single hour—it doesn't happen.

Factoid

Positional negotiation is akin to chess—it takes a long time to complete the moves as each side successively takes and then gives up a series of positions until one side wins.

Listen and Attack

Good negotiators both have notes prepared and take notes during the negotiations. Trainer Neil Rackham says that the best negotiators carefully listen to the points presented by the other side. Then, they attack those points, indicating that they listened and understood what the other side said. They show that they agree in part with some of the points made, but they disagree with "X, Y, and Z" and "here is why"—Captain Kirk's method.

This is far more efficient, believes Rackham, than politely listening to the other party and then launching full-scale into what you want to say without addressing and sticking with what your opponent has just said.

Change Master

The best negotiators choose words and tone of voice carefully, and pose questions in an inoffensive manner.

Unyielding, Unending

Maintaining an unyielding stance damages the chances for a long-term relationship between both parties as the negotiation protracts. Consider the conflicts that have raged for years between the Catholics and Protestants in Northern Ireland, or the Jews and the Palestinians in the Middle East, to see that each group's rigid stance strains the possibility of reaching a compromise.

Be Wary

With more than two parties, negotiation can be even more complicated and confusing.

From Positional to Principled Negotiation

In *Getting to Yes: Negotiating Agreement Without Giving In,* authors Roger Fisher and William Ury explain how their method, principled negotiation, is more effective than positional negotiation.

Principled negotiation has four facets:

➤ It addresses not only the problem, but also the people behind the problem.

➤ It focuses on satisfying the underlying interests of both parties rather than examining positions.

➤ It encourages brainstorming by both sides to generate a variety of possibilities before making any final decisions.

➤ It recommends the use of objective criteria to reach a fair solution that is agreeable to both sides.

Separate the People from the Problem

It's easy to get emotionally involved when pursuing something important to you. For example, a developer wants a zoning law changed to be able to build a new shopping center. She wants to do the job efficiently, inexpensively, and without complications. The developer also believes the shopping center will be beneficial by bringing goods and services closer to a densely populated area.

The people, however, may feel the new shopping center will also bring traffic, crime, noise, and higher taxes. A city council meeting can get heated when the emotions of both sides come into play. In principled negotiation, you proceed by acknowledging the parties involved are real people, not "a developer" or "the community."

Proceed

Separate the people from the problem by putting yourself in their shoes. Practice writing down or repeating orally to others your understanding or perception of how they feel.

Put Yourself in Their Shoes

If you were a developer trying to do your job, how would you go about it? If a shopping center was built next door to your home, what would you do?

If the community perceives a developer as cold and money-hungry, then the developer needs to take every opportunity to portray himself or herself as warm, caring, and concerned about the quality of life in the community.

By making people in the community a part of the process early on, the developer can help them feel that they have a stake in the outcome. She could attend community meetings early on to reveal the shopping center plan and ask for input. By taking the initiative and making the first step to include the other side, she builds a working relationship and reduces the likelihood of future problems. A solution may be as simple as putting up a roadside wall to cushion the sound, or adding more parking spaces devoted to commuter parking.

In the movie *Five Easy Pieces* there is a negotiation scene in which Jack Nicholson, seated in a diner with three others, asks a veteran waitress for a special order. The waitress balks, saying there are "no substitutions." Because the waitress condescends to him, Nicholson treats her as he does other authority figures. He insults her, hoping to get his wheat toast with no butter. If the two characters had considered themselves as people and separate from the problem, he might have gotten his order the way he wanted it, and she would have avoided having to deal with an unhappy customer.

At times, saying "I understand how you might feel that way," and then explaining how you feel can lead to a mutually satisfactory conclusion. Allow people on the other side to express their emotions, but don't attempt to react to any wild outbursts.

Listening Works Wonders

Communicate by first listening to what is said, and then acknowledge both the words and the emotion behind the words. You may even restate them by saying, "Let me understand this. What you're saying is …," and then listen for their confirmation of your understanding.

Proceed

When you negotiate, speak to be understood. Actively seek the understanding of negotiating opponents by asking them to restate what you have said.

Focus on Interests, Not Positions

In separating people from their problems, analyze the other person's position to discover his or her interests. While each side has many interests, the most significant ones can be boiled down to the basic needs everyone has: to be secure, to be recognized, and to have a sense of belonging.

Suppose you're on the senior management team of a large corporation with many retail locations across the United States. After five years of decentralization, the president decides that the management system is not working out, and is looking to his senior managers for a new direction.

Your Side; Their Side

You're the change manager in charge of decentralization and feel strongly attached to the position, not simply because the failure of the decentralization might reflect badly on you. You feel that decentralization is the only way for the company to keep costs down and stay competitive in the retail market.

Others on the senior management team feel that the tide has shifted and they want to jump on the centralization band wagon, knowing it will mean more responsibilities—and power—for them. What do you do?

Look beyond your position, and the opposing one, to the interests of the people and the company involved. Common interests can often be found behind opposing positions. In supporting decentralization, you're interested in saving the senior managers at the headquarters from time-consuming, day-to-day management concerns. You are also interested in reducing overhead costs, such as headquarters staff, so that more profits can be realized.

In favoring centralization, the other senior managers are interested in more control. They want to keep a tighter handle on problems in the field so that a resolution can be achieved quickly and decisively. They are also interested in saving money, however, so that more profits can be realized.

Proceed

There are often several ways to satisfy one interest.

Win-Win

Having examined the interests of both positions, you might suggest a solution that would meet both interests: proposing a network of computers at each work location, linked by satellite, that would allow better communication between the headquarters and each store.

The result would be better information and control from the top, without centralization, and immediate response to problems in the field—such as better inventory control and uniform pricing—to keep costs down and profits up.

Generate a Variety of Possibilities Before Deciding

Suppose you're on a change team (a committee) to hire a new chancellor for a major university. There are extreme pressures on your team to find the right person because the university is facing major issues that may impact its survival.

Change Master

The more you can brainstorm about a situation before you sit down at a bargaining table, the more options you'll have to offer the other side that may benefit both negotiating parties.

The qualified candidates seemingly number in the hundreds, and you and your colleagues have spent several months weeding through resumés and references, interviewing people, and bringing them back to your university for additional questioning.

The field is finally narrowed down to the top five candidates. How does your committee choose one person, especially if the vote is split evenly between two or three of the candidates? After months of involvement, brainstorming is a good way to see the candidates in a different light.

Away from the Rabble

Choose a setting other than your regular meeting place, and make it informal. As the group brainstorms, have someone act as facilitator to write down each committee member's pros and cons for each of the candidates. Match these pros and cons against your final criteria on what the job of chancellor entails.

On paper, put each of the five candidates in a number of challenging situations and predict, based on the information gathered in your interviews, how he or she would react. What if the university faced an educational crisis? What if a major contributor pulled his or her financial support? What if in-state enrollment suddenly dropped? Your top candidate will eventually emerge and the final vote will be much more decisive.

Proceed

If you're having trouble deciding between several candidates for a position, create a number of scenarios (see Chapter 19, "Staying Flexible in Your Plans") that may occur, and imagine each candidate handling them.

Stay Objective

Because there will always be differences and conflicts in the way you and another person in a negotiation view things no matter how much you attempt to understand the other's feelings, insist that the result of the negotiation be based on objective standards or criteria.

For example, you are a change manager working with a limited budget to automate record keeping for your company. The plan calls for you to complete the first phase by a certain date. However, once you begin the job, you discover hidden obstacles to completing the first phase—things that the department head knew but didn't tell you during planning.

The more you bring your honesty and expertise into the open to solve a particular problem, the more likely you will deliver a system that is exactly what the client wants, within a reasonable time period. Better yet, develop the objective criteria and write it into your change campaign plan from the outset.

Change Master

You could compromise the quality of your automation program and deliver on time, or you could begin to communicate that concessions have to be made. Commit yourself instead to reaching a solution that is based on an objective, mutually beneficial standard, not on pressure to complete a job by an arbitrary contract date.

Teaching Yourself How to Negotiate

Principled negotiation is an effective alternative to positional negotiation. The best way to get what you want, however, is to discover your own style. Most effective change managers do their best learning and self-improvement while observing others.

Proceed

Pinpoint those achievers you consider to be expert negotiators, and study their techniques.

Take every chance you get to try your hand at striking increasingly better deals as you proceed on your campaign. When in doubt, focus on interests rather than positions. If you look for the concepts that the other person values, such as cost-containment or quality, and try to relate to those values, you will be much more successful at negotiation than if you perceive the other person as being on the other side of a wall that you are trying to knock down.

After all is said and done, the fastest way to master negotiation skills *is to actively begin looking* for the multitude of opportunities that occur each day to negotiate for more favorable terms and to start giving them your best shot.

The Least You Need to Know

➤ Before negotiating for anything, determine your objective.

➤ After deciding on your objective, devise a strategy, including creating counter-tactics, establishing a bottom line, and considering your timing.

➤ In positional negotiation, each side chooses its position and argues for that stance.

➤ Principled negotiation focuses on the other side's position while considering the people and factors behind both sides.

➤ Learn from watching others, but ultimately determine your own style of negotiating to be successful.

Maintaining the Management Edge

James Madison was the fourth president of the United States. At five feet three inches, he was small in stature but an intellectual giant and a deep thinker who profoundly influenced the course of U.S. history.

Madison studied democracies and republics throughout the centuries. He noted a common denominator among many. The revolutionaries always believed that after they assumed power, society would be different. People would change. There would be a new epoch in humankind. Yet, repeatedly, people reverted to exactly the way they had been, except now they had a new government. This chapter initially draws upon the wisdom of James Madison to show you how to maintain the management edge.

The Wisdom of James Madison

In applying the lessons of history to the American colonies, Madison made the basic assumption that once America defeated the British and installed its own form of government, people would be relatively the same as they had been prior to British rule.

No New Epoch

All of his thinking was directed toward devising a system of government with checks and balances, a constitution, and then amendments that acknowledged no new epoch in humankind. Madison never presumed that the U.S. Constitution was perfect or that it could remain unchanged. The first 10 amendments to the constitution, the Bill of Rights, represented a broad-sweeping and dramatic indication that the Constitution required continual adjustment and modifications as the times rolled on.

Factoid

In nearly 220 years since the Bill of Rights, 17 more amendments have been added—an average of about 1 every 13 years—although they have come in clumps as opposed to an even distribution.

Counting on Human Nature

Here is the essence of effective change management that we can glean from the wisdom of James Madison: Avoid the erroneous notion that after a change campaign is complete and the desired objective is fully realized, people will be fundamentally different. Human nature will remain the same.

Perhaps people will be more cheerful, effective, or profitable because of organizational structure that allows them to be at their best. Perhaps the company will enjoy an increase in market share, a more loyal customer base, or some other operating advantage.

Proceed

Presuming that there will be no new epoch, no grand sweeping change in human nature, altruism, or heroics, and that, in the long run, nothing out of the ordinary will come from a change campaign, represents a rather reasonable assumption.

Empower Your Staff

A Fortune 500 company was experiencing a dilemma. Traditionally, the company maintained a strong hierarchy, wherein decisions flowed from the top down. As more and more of the organization's employees were essentially knowledge workers, dealing with the transmission of information as opposed to actually working with physical products or on an assembly line, it became apparent to top managers that decision-making ability would have to be pervasive throughout all levels of the organization.

242

The mission was to empower the staff to be able to make decisions on the spot and become more accountable, without consulting supervisory level managers.

The initiating sponsor knew that empowerment programs in many corporations were mere *euphemisms* for half-hearted initiatives that ultimately had no impact. True empowerment, as she understood it, would entail giving frontline staff the opportunity to make continual decisions. This initiative carried risk, but the risk of weighing down operations by maintaining cumbersome approval procedures could prove far more costly.

Word Power

A **euphemism** is a nicer, or at least more flattering, way of saying something, and it can often become misleading.

The change manager commissioned to tackle this challenge recognized that a multifaceted approach would be necessary, including:

➤ Helping supervisors become more comfortable with allowing their workers to proceed without getting constant approval.

➤ Providing first-line staff with the range of decision-making issues that were now their responsibilities.

➤ Hiring new staff members who had the capability and inclination to proceed effectively with little direction from supervisors.

➤ Establishing a system of more frequent, shorter, informal performance reviews so that front-line staff received regular appropriate feedback, while not feeling encumbered by such reviews.

➤ Enabling front-line staff members to make self-assessments as to the effectiveness of their decisions, and, in that regard, increasing their level of accountability.

The change campaign lasted nearly six months, although it was originally planned to last four months. During that time, several painful adjustments were made. All the while, the change manager kept his eye on the desired end result: an organization of decision-makers and self-accountable employees on every level.

Stimulate Creative Thinking

If more empowered team members are more valuable to the campaign, what about more creative team members? A pervasive notion in change management literature holds that solutions are often facilitated by creative thinking. Whether or not this is true, stimulating your creative thinking, and that of your team, is rarely disadvantageous.

Are there methods to stimulate the creative thinking among participants in your change campaign? Affirmative! Here are a number of ways to get the creative juices flowing.

Change Your Venue

When you change your *venue* and the scenery, you open up new vistas. When you do this for some of your tasks (especially tasks that require conceptualization or creative thinking), you'll be more productive than ever before.

Begin to identify the places in your life that are welcome retreats to which you can go and work—a library, parking lot, or even a shopping center. When you change where you're working, you can benefit immensely and immediately.

Schedule Brainstorming Sessions

Brainstorming is a great process by which you get a wonderful array of ideas that you might not have otherwise had. You can brainstorm with yourself, or (preferably) with others. Have you ever gone to lunch with a colleague and discussed ways to approach a topic at work? After a few minutes, perhaps you both are deep in conversation, coming up with all sorts of great ideas.

When the waiter comes to take your order or bring your check, however, what usually happens? The conversation dies down. When you both go back to work, often those ideas are forgotten or just put on a back burner. If you consciously schedule a meeting, the sole purpose of which is to brainstorm, you'll grab control of your time and get some of the most productive sessions that you've ever had.

I used to meet with a mentor once a month. At his dining room table, we sat across from each other, each with a tape recorder, and discussed problems and issues we faced and ways to overcome them. We both retained our respective copies of the tape, took them home, made notes from them, and then *captured* those ideas—instead of letting them die.

Word Power

A **venue** is a setting, place, or locale.

Factoid

When you come in contact with other people, you're exposed to whole new worlds—*their* worlds.

Narrow Your Focus

If you want to do your best work, allow your brain to concentrate on one activity—focus on one thing at a time. It sounds simple enough, but this advice goes against the grain of a society telling you to do many things at once in order to be more efficient. People double their activities in an effort to make things easier and better.

Alexander Hamilton once said, "All the genius I have lies in this: When I have a subject at hand I study it profoundly. Day and night it is before me. I explore it in all its bearings. My mind becomes pervaded with it. Then the effort which I have made is what people are pleased to call the fruit of genius. It is instead the fruit of labor and thought."

As I discussed in my book *The Complete Idiot's Guide to Managing Your Time,* airline reservation attendants set good examples in the middle of pressure situations. Suppose a plane is going to be leaving in a matter of minutes, and several passengers just arrived. Rather than dealing with three or four passengers at once, the ticketing agents deal with one person and one ticket situation at a time, often not even raising their heads from the computer monitors. They ensure that the reservation and ticket will be correct once the ticket is printed. (The same observation can be made of bank tellers, good bus drivers, or construction workers walking on scaffolding five stories above the ground—they focus on the task at hand.)

Understand Workplace Dynamics

No matter how diligent your team members are, the unintended consequences of rapid change at work can wreak havoc. Many ambitious managers up the task loads of their staffs without understanding the dynamics of their situations. As a result, not just for those who work in highly competitive or high-tech industries, but across a broad swath of industries, many workers report that stress levels increased within the last several years.

You Want It When?

The common lament from employees is that there is too much to do and too little time in which to get it done.

David Gamo, a corporate trainer based in Mountain View, California, says that "when you feel under stress, you find your mental wheels spinning, you work mechanically rather than creatively. Tasks that would normally take a few minutes of time sit unfinished for days because you lose the capacity to prioritize and you put off the larger, important projects that take more energy and concentration."

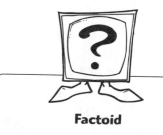

Factoid

Employee surveys cite that workers are feeling too much pressure from constant deadlines.

Too many companies, however, simply stick their heads in the sand over such issues. They believe that the issue will blow over, and no management intervention is necessary. In some businesses, this viewpoint strains credibility as pace of work and expectations constantly rise, and the only plateaus are of a highly fleeting nature.

Unbless This Stress

Gus Steiber, director of business development at VMC Behavioral Health Care Services in Gurnee, Illinois, observes that companies admire energetic, ambitious managers who take on huge projects in attempts to motivate their staffs to put in extra effort. The stress on workers, however, can be incredible.

"To assess the level of stress in the workforce," he says, "companies should measure whether essential work is getting done, whether workforce levels are sufficient, whether they are losing people, and whether projects are failing."

The answers are often abundantly clear. Businesses need to ask themselves if high levels of stress among workers result in lost business or employee *attrition*—both "costs" that are too high to sustain. "If they take an honest look at that, they will see that they need to change."

Word Power

An **attrition** means a reduction or a decline.

A Business Issue

Robert Ostermann, Ph.D., the Executive Director of COPE, based in Paramus, New Jersey, believes that the most appropriate way to address workplace stress is for companies to concede that it's a business issue. Further, companies need to assume responsibility to provide support to employees.

Ostermann, whose company deals exclusively with executive health, observes that much of the stress that employees exhibit on the job is attributable to things that happen outside work. There is "a commonality with the kinds of problems that cause stress at work and the kinds of problems that employees are probably dealing with in their lives," he says.

Be Wary

Often, top executives and managers with vested interests in the success of a company work at a pace that exceeds what workers can muster. These executives have little clue as to how their staffs may be responding to long hours and rapid changes. The executives themselves seem to thrive on it.

Time Out

So ... to be an effective change manager in any industry, in any situation, seems to require that you periodically offer your staff an adult form of "time out." I'm not talking about vacations or time off. Time out, in this context, means several consecutive days during which the work pace is less than unrelenting.

Staff members can consolidate what they've learned, organize their space, files and information, have time to reflect, and recapture the spirit and vitality that comes with feeling that one is indeed in control of his or her work situation.

Fair Is Fair

People have an inborn sense of equity. When they feel that they're being worked too hard, they seek compensating mechanisms.

> ➤ They appropriate "perks" that are not part of company policy or their job status.

> ➤ They use company resources liberally.

> ➤ They are more likely to engage in rationalizing behavior when it comes to, say, padding an expense report, acquiring company supplies for personal use, and allocating their work time in rather frivolous ways when not being directly observed.

Encourage Staff Participation in Task Scheduling

One excellent way to keep staff members from becoming too stressed, in turn, preventing problems for your campaign, is to allow them to be flexible with their schedules. For example, if I am on your team, and as one of my tasks I have to round up 225 case histories, I might make a goal of doing it in three days instead of four, or assembling them over four days while concurrently completing something else.

Rebellion or Realization?

Take the case of Kristen. Kristen won't transcribe tapes late in the day or any time on Friday. She established a personal work pattern in which specific tasks will be undertaken throughout the course of

Be Wary

The unintended consequences of too much change coming too quickly, even when it's highly appropriate and timely, is a mentally, if not physically, frazzled work force. Such a work force is less likely to exhibit creativity or spark, less likely to be loyal, and more likely to engage in behaviors unsupportive of the company.

Factoid

In some companies, increased personal use of the Internet, e-mail, phones, and other forms of communication rise to troubling levels.

the week. Amy, the change manager on the same campaign, rarely interferes with Kristen's way of doing things unless a deadline is pending. Is Kristen an obstinate team member who undermines production? Is Amy a poor manager?

On the contrary, Kristen is an effective member of the staff, and Amy manages the campaign skillfully. Kristen determined her own personal production peaks and valleys, and she now works according to these. Amy recognizes this, and for all but urgent matters, works with Kristen's personal production cycle.

Staff-Established Cycles

Proceed

Good performers, such as Kristen, need to be recognized and allowed to work within their personal cycles.

Good team members should be afforded the opportunity to establish their own productivity cycles, and within reason, to undertake assignments in a manner that best suits them. Unfortunately, some employees devise countless ways to diminish productivity, such as stretching out the time it takes to complete assignments.

Allowing productive people to establish their own schedules means that they will be less fatigued. Productive team members, when allowed to pace themselves, can accomplish more and remain more vibrant while doing so.

Working with Your Staff

Given that all staff have personal productivity cycles, how can a change manager use this to his or her advantage? Here are some suggestions:

➤ Provide numerous and varied assignments within the campaign to accommodate various cycles. This allows the staff to, in effect, "plan their own days," with the ultimate goal of being the most productive possible.

➤ Be flexible with deadlines and due dates whenever you can. Again, this provides flexibility to the employee. Good staff will complete tasks in a timely manner. What's more, when trusted, they'll often go beyond what is called for or asked of them.

➤ Avoid late afternoon and "surprise" assignments. Almost all workers have a "lag" near the end of the day. Don't assign anything new if you can help it; wait until the next morning when both of you are more alert.

If need be, the cycle of productivity of a good team member can be altered to meet the needs of the campaign. For example, if a crucial important report has to be completed within four days, good employees will forgo their desired sequence of assignments, write the report, and do what it takes to succeed. This is a short-term challenge, but one any employee can (or should) meet.

Prepare for the Unexpected

Maintaining the management edge when directing a change campaign is almost synonymous with being in a ready state to deal with the unexpected. To close the chapter, here is my personal list of recommendations for being able to better the unexpected issues that change campaigns, and life in general:

1. **Be here now.** The catch phrase of the 1960s is more valid now than ever. Being in the present is a rare capability in today's world of overinformation and preoccupation. It is viewing each day and each moment as new, ripe with possibilities, and not necessarily tied to the past. Being here now means being ...

   ➤ Aware of the cues and the stimulus in your immediate environment.

   ➤ Open to what is said.

   ➤ Receptive to new ways of doing things as opposed to proceeding based on predispositions.

2. **Be well-rested.** Managing change is not a responsibility for the exhausted

3. **Be alert.** Being alert involves connecting the dots—surmising how pieces of a puzzle fit together. The more well-read you are, not simply in your own industry literature, but in seemingly unrelated industries as well, the greater your ability for identifying new opportunities.

4. **Be physically fit.** Everything in medical science confirms that the benefits of physical fitness extend to the mental aspect of your life as well. As author Edwin Bliss once said "If you're too busy to stay fit, you're too busy."

5. **Be ready to abandon old procedures.** When approaching a change situation, often being steeped in rules or rituals can hinder your progress. Recognizing that true innovation

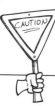

Be Wary

Forcing a good worker to reprogram his or her cycle for an extended period of time isn't recommended. The extended variation soon becomes an imposition, and can upset the delicate balance by which the good employee remains productive.

Be Wary

Being alert requires more than simply physically keeping your eyes wide open or slugging down another cup of coffee or caffeinated soft drink.

often represents a break from the past and is not simply an extension of what came before necessitates that you allow for the possibility of new ways of proceeding not necessarily based on a time-honored formula.

6. **Allow for some slack in your schedule.** When every moment of your day is accounted for, you diminish your capacity for reflective, creative thought. By having as little as five or ten minutes of slack in your schedule, the odds are in favor of actually increasing that day's level of productivity and being more open and receptive to new ideas and procedures.

Finally, whether it's working with your sponsor, advocates, or targets of change, keep attempting to understand situations from their perspectives. You can't know everything another person experiences, but you can surmise a great deal, and the exercise will give you greater perspective when interacting with that person.

The Least You Need to Know

➤ After a change campaign is complete and the desired objective is fully realized, people will not be fundamentally different. Human nature will remain the same.

➤ Every day, let each team member know in one way or another that, despite the travails, the campaign has great merit.

➤ Stimulating your creative thinking, and that of your team, is usually advantageous.

➤ If you want to do your best work, allow your brain to concentrate on one activity—focus on one thing at a time.

➤ Allowing productive people to establish their own schedules means that they will be less fatigued and therefore accomplish more.

Chapter 23

Keeping a Keen Eye on the Competition

In This Chapter

➤ The danger of complacency

➤ Fighting back

➤ Strategic inflection points

➤ Keeping an eye on unexpected competitors

The day may soon come when everything in your company is working optimally. The moment will arrive when you've positioned yourself well and are profitably serving the needs of your target market. You will have allocated your marketing resources wisely and have an effective after-marketing program in place.

Yet, like snowflakes that melt on your windowsill, the golden moment is fleeting. Within the coming year, the next month, week, or even minute, some crucial factor in your business environment is likely to shift.

In Chapter 2, "Change Scenarios," I discussed how companies de-accent the effects of competition and essentially carve their own paths. The odds are, however, that keeping a keen eye on the competition will be important to you. To round out Part 5, "Making Change Work for You," I'll discuss the subtle and not-so-subtle effects of competition.

The Complacent Supplier

In my previous hometown of Falls Church, Virginia, in the Bailey's Crossroad section, Southern Office Supply was the premier office supply store. It was well-located in the L-shaped shopping center at the intersection of Columbia Pike and Leesburg Pike. Both roads were major commercial highways and commuter thoroughfares. There was ample free parking in front of the store. The store itself was appropriately located next to a low-to mid-quality department store and high-volume chain drugstore.

At approximately 1,000 square feet, the interior of Southern Office Supply was more than adequate. As office supply stores go, it was doing well. Over the years, it built up a mailing list and distributed a high-quality, four-color, four-page monthly flyer announcing specials and bargain buys. The personnel were helpful if not entirely knowledgeable about the products offered. The *atmosphere* was one of dedication and seriousness. It was low-key, almost somber.

Word Power

Atmosphere in a business context means how an environment appeals to consumers. An atmosphere can be friendly, serious, busy, frenetic, nurturing, tranquil, and so on, and may well combine several attributes.

Be Wary

Remaining complacent in your industry could result in surprise encroachment by competitors.

Just Looking

You came, you looked around, you made your purchase, and you left. A trip to Southern blended in with the rest of your day, and, certainly, the rest of your errands. It was but one stop along the way.

Its prices were reasonable. Except for the advertised monthly bargains, one would consider the store's prices to be competitive, definitely not outrageous. Southern's major competitors were Miller Office Supply, Ginn's, and Jacobs-Gardner. All three companies had numerous outlets throughout Northern Virginia.

Coming Out of Nowhere?

From what must have seemed to Southern's management to be out of nowhere, Staples arrived in town. Staples took the corner on the right of the L-shaped shopping strip. The location's previous tenants included Circuit City, which moved to an even larger location; Warehouse Foods, which failed miserably; and Bill's Carpets.

From its first month of operation through the end of the year, Staples caught on like wildfire. The store was at least four times the square footage of Southern, and contained four times the inventory. When you first entered, you had the magical feeling that it was no ordinary office supply store. The selection was vast and deep. It is doubtful that any office supply purchasers in the area had ever experienced anything like Staples. It was clean, bright, and bustling. The sign said, "The Office Super Store," and the outfit lived up to it in every way.

No Ordinary Office Supply Store

Staples' prices were unlike anything the area had experienced. Notebooks, pads, paper, and computer supplies often sold for as much as 40 percent less than at other office supply stores. If you happened to have a Staples card, and this was encouraged at all checkout counters and by all employees, you could save another 10 percent.

A One-Stop Center

In addition to the traditional items you might expect, Staples also provided accessory office products. Bargains were offered on coffee, juice, business magazines, business literature, and reference books. Staples was a one-stop center. Along the left side of the store were office copying machines so you could make your own copies. There were also engraving, laminating, and other related services.

Superior in Every Way

More than just being a physically superior store both inside and outside and having showroom lighting, showroom displays, and shelf talkers that said, "Buy me," Staples' employees had a completely different attitude than those of competitors. They held a "We are in business to serve you" attitude.

Visiting Staples was a memorable, if not pleasurable, experience. Each time you entered the store you felt as if you were in partnership with it. Many customers commented that the prices were so low they wanted to stock up as much as possible on the first few trips. They wanted to make sure these kinds of bargains, whether they lasted or not, were experienced now.

Up Against the Wall

Along the wall facing customers at checkout was a six-by-twenty-feet bulletin board with clear plastic pockets to hold business cards. Across the top were major categories such as real estate, secretarial services, consultants, temporary services, and so forth. In a few months, hundreds of patrons had put their cards in the plastic sleeves and become part of the Staples family.

Southern had actually maintained a similar technique. Its bulletin board, however, was three-by-four-feet and cards were held in place by a pin or thumb tack. On its best day, there were never more than 60 to 70 cards on Southern's bulletin board. By contrast, Staples displayed well over a thousand cards in an organized, helpful manner.

Various activity checks throughout the day showed that Staples averaged between eight and sixteen patrons in the store at any given moment, while Southern had fallen off to a little less than two patrons at any given time. By the year's end, Ginn's and Jacobs-Gardner, as well as Miller's Office Supply, were feeling the impact of Staples' clearly superior methods and marketing capabilities.

Who Was That Masked Man?

Let's step back now and examine how Staples positioned itself for success in the Northern Virginia market, and how Southern Office Supply, with no inclination to scout market changes, met its predictable fate.

Staples was already successful throughout New Jersey, Philadelphia, Boston, Long Island, and the metropolitan area of New York. Its expansion into the Washington, D.C., area was logical and perhaps even foreseeable.

Doing Their Homework

Prior to opening in the Bailey's Crossroads area, the owners visited each of their potential competitors and examined how the shelves were stocked, as well as the prices, ambience, and quality of employees. They determined that there were more than 15,000 workers within a two-mile trade radius and thousands more residents who demographically fit their target niche.

There is little brand loyalty for office products; a notepad is a notepad and a printer cartridge is a printer cartridge. Significant price savings were able to separate Staples from its competitors. Staples placed full-page ads in the back of community newspapers and journals, highlighting some of the store's best bargains. Experience in other store openings showed that significant word-of-mouth advertising could be generated.

Superior by a Wide Margin

In every way, Staples was more customer-oriented. It opened earlier and closed later. The employees answered the telephone within two rings. They prepared a store layout map for distribution to all customers, which detailed where each item in the store could be found. Experts directed customers to appropriate aisles.

By contrast, Southern and many of its competitors were miserable at orienting themselves to the customer. Clerks were frequently put off and even acted as if they had been disturbed when asked about the location of specific items.

In paying for items at Staples, one had a choice of three different cash registers including an express check-out line. When exiting any competitors' stores, room to set down your goods was scarce.

One could go on and on about the superior distribution and marketing techniques employed by Staples. Its ability to move into the market and quickly establish itself as an office supply store to be reckoned with is now a matter of record.

While Rome Burned

What about the top management at Southern Office Supply? Where were they? Here is what they apparently did not do:

➤ **Attend trade shows and conventions, and pay attention to the latest developments in the industry.** It seems impossible to believe that Southern's top management had neither heard of Staples nor had any inkling that the company was in an expansion phase.

➤ **Subscribe to and read industry journals, insiders' newsletters, and association reports.** An organization as well-run and well-functioning as Staples does not and, in fact, cannot go unnoticed within its industry. Indication of its existence and progress included its own press releases, endless reports, and a series of grand openings.

➤ **Tour Staples and other competitors' stores.** On an ongoing basis, Southern's management should have been visiting the stores and showrooms of all competitors within its own region and beyond. While Staples was originally not present in the Northern Virginia area, it was operating successfully in the New York and New Jersey metropolitan areas. Its progress should have been cause for alarm for Southern's top management.

➤ **Communicate with the original equipment manufacturers, wholesalers, and distributors.** Many of the items offered in Southern's outlets also appeared in Staples' outlets. In many instances, the two chains were served by the same original equipment manufacturers or their distributors.

Staples' expansion outside the New York metropolitan area was known within the industry long before the actual grand opening in Northern Virginia. Southern's top management, its business analysts, and, indeed, all personnel above the clerical level would have access to this information via the host of distributors and suppliers with whom they may have come in contact.

Suppose for a moment, though, that Southern was aware of Staples' expansion, particularly into the

Change Master

It is important to study your market, as well as your competitors, and communicate with those involved in order to stay ahead in your industry.

Bailey's Crossroads area. What could Southern have done in the short and long term to try to compete and protect its market share? Stated more clearly, how could Southern have positioned itself to remain a viable force in the market?

➤ On a short-term basis, Southern could have advertised several items at bargain prices and competed head-on with Staples by vigorously promoting those items.

➤ Through its monthly circular to customers, Southern could have announced a price slashing or a "we-meet-the-competition-head-on" campaign, which would have increased store traffic temporarily. Such a campaign may have encouraged bulk buying.

➤ It would have made excellent sense for Southern's managers to visit Staples to determine what it was lacking and become especially proficient in stocking those items.

➤ As a long-term strategy, Southern could have billed itself as provider of "XYZ," the XYZ representing whatever Staples was not offering and giving Southern a unique draw.

➤ While store renovation is costly, in the short term, Southern could have increased in-store illumination so that it would not appear cave-like compared to the professional showroom atmosphere that Staples offered.

➤ Southern could have redesigned its store-front displays, changing them from the tired array of unexciting products to an eye-catching, customer-drawing, professionally crafted and designed display.

➤ Requiring even less ingenuity, Southern could have made use of in-store shelf talkers, signs that say "bargain," "X percent off," "sale today," "red tag special," and so forth.

Crushing the Competition

By mid-year, Staples was often ringing up more business in an hour than Southern was generating in a day. While Staples was advertising for more help, Southern had cut its staff. Staples' entire product offering was discounted, while Southern continued to distribute the same monthly flyer and generate less and less response.

Even with its neighbor a mere 200 feet away, and more visible marketing clues than one could ask for, Southern went on, set in its ways, not adopting any of the high-power marketing techniques Staples had mastered.

Instead, Southern embarked upon the course examined critically above.

➤ Did they have a large base of commercial accounts that they believed would remain loyal in the face of overwhelming price reductions?

➤ Did they believe that customer loyalty transcends outrageous savings?

➤ Did they embark on some other failed strategy that was not apparent to observers?

It is easy after reading what has been described earlier to regard Southern's management as inept, inflexible, or swamped by change. Faced with outrageous competition on all sides, however, there are always options for profitably providing products or services in a manner that outflanks the competition.

Battered by the Waves of Change

As this book is being written, one of the Internet pioneers of the mid and late 1990s is facing its moment of truth—a virtual no-choice, cold-turkey change-management situation.

In the latter half of the 1990s, Cisco Systems was regarded as one of the premier technology companies in the world. For more than three and a half years running, its quarterly earnings exceeded estimates. The company could not hire talented staff members fast enough. Its stock was considered one of NASDAQ's darlings. For several years, annual revenue grew by more than 50 percent.

Factoid

CEO John Chambers was on the cover of all the top business magazines and was widely lauded in the accompanying articles. Cisco routers, in demand to fuel the Internet worldwide, captured 85 percent of the router market.

All Fall Down

In the course of a year, things began to unravel. The company started downsizing, reducing its work force by 15 percent. Quarterly earnings estimates were reduced to reflect more sobering times. The company's market capitalization dropped by a staggering 70 percent. How could the company be caught flatfooted so quickly?

Many financial and business analysts believe that Cisco didn't respond to change quickly enough and actually found itself in the wrong business. Cisco was the premier manufacturer of both the hardware and the software that fueled the Internet. It created high-ticket black boxes that smoothly integrated software, processed chips, and were wired in a way that no other competitor could approach.

Factoid

Suddenly, Cisco found itself crunched between the emerging potential of fiber optics and the onslaught of cheap, effective microchips.

When Bandwidth Was Plentiful

Cisco's original claim to fame was recognizing the explosive need for bandwidth. Prior to the Netscape browser in 1994, most people used their telephones relatively sparingly by today's standards. There was significant *bandwidth* compared to demand.

Factoid

In recent years, with more than 200 million kilometers of optical fiber in place worldwide, optical network companies can send thousands of distinct messages through a single fiber strand far more efficiently than anything Cisco ever did, even on its best day.

The explosion of the Internet, cell phones, Web browsers, and "the killer app" e-mail was poised to swamp the voice-optimized telephone network. It was backed by copper wire configurations that simply couldn't handle the load.

Cisco was ready with a solution that was more than timely. It devised a system that divided up messages into packets and gave each packet a destination, but allowed for many potential routes. At the end of the path, the packets could be reassembled coherently and seamlessly for both sender and receiver. Cisco's network essentially eliminated circuits between users while drawing upon all available bandwidth to create virtually instantaneous, continuous communication.

Enter the Explosion

Cisco's lightening-fast data processing quickly became passé. Optical networks today merely change the direction that light travels, a mega-leap over Cisco's workman-like systems that continuously examined data packets and sent them on their way.

All of the central routing operations, including Cisco's, simply do not have the capacity to manage the second wave of data.

Word Power

Bandwidth is the capacity for data bits. The wider the bandwidth, the greater the data flow per unit of time.

Businesses located in urban centers are connecting directly to optical fiber networks, which relay messages even faster than broadband cable or copper DSL networks. In some cases, residential markets can benefit from the system as well.

Cisco and other massive central routing system providers lack the optical capacities to partake in the bandwidth explosion.

Not Flatfoot, but Not Sprite

While Cisco wasn't caught completely flatfooted and had made some strategic acquisitions, it found itself at a competitive disadvantage with optical fiber firms that are already on to second-generation capabilities.

Cisco will endure for the short term, as routers and switches, as well as electronic terminals, are still needed within networks. As microchips are now getting smaller and more powerful, a variety of firms are fashioning a single silicon chip that can provide the same functions as Cisco's clunky router boxes. If routers themselves can be replaced by a single chip, the brunt of Cisco's business will largely be lost.

Flourish or Fail

The crux of the issue facing this once highly innovative market leader is that unless the company makes dramatic, sweeping changes and converts to all optical networks, it will simply become a footnote in early Internet history.

The magnitude of such a conversion is a marvel to contemplate. Tens of thousands of employees at installations around the world are, in many respects, having to forsake what they're doing and embrace new processes, products, methods of delivery, competition, and price structures.

What business is not constantly in need of keeping pace?

Competition from Unexpected Quarters

Change Master

It is apparent that only immediate immersion into the fray, in this case optical networks, will give Cisco the fighting chance it deserves to remain viable as the second-generation Internet emerges. In a few years hence, it will be a perfect case study for business school students who aspire to be effective change managers.

Be Wary

The tendency of market leaders to give short shrift to innovations in the industry, and to both regard them as being insignificant and having little potential to make a ripple in the marketplace, ends up causing problems for the market leaders.

Sometimes the changes confronting a company originate from the least suspected sources. In *The Innovator's Dilemma,* Clayton Christensen discusses how rapidly an innovative new technology or a unique market strategy on the part of a new or smaller business can affect leading companies within an industry.

The Meek May Rise

Christensen's findings point to an all too common phenomenon. If the new approach satisfies a market demand, if the product or service offering adequately serves some segment of the market, and if the market's response is one of acceptance, then even the smallest players within an industry can prompt significant changes for industry leaders.

In the 1970s, the emergence of small steel mills offering specialty goods to customer segments in the steel market began to impact the large multiprocess steel mills, Christensen observes. At first, the small mills offered products that were relatively low in quality but good enough for the low end of the market.

Change Master

Time and time again, weak competitors who start on a shoestring gain experience, hone and refine their products and services, make nearly undetectable inroads into more profitable segments of a marketplace, and, suddenly, cause the whole industry to change.

Word Power

Stratify refers to the process of offering specific products/services and strategic price points to specific market segments.

Ignore at Your Peril

The major players in the industry basically ignored the small mills and were content with letting them have the low margin, low end of the business. As years passed, the small mills incrementally improved their overall quality. Soon, the small mills were able to compete in every segment of the steel market, including the high-end, high-margin steel plate segment.

Can you blame top management in leading firms within an industry for ignoring the low-profit segment of their own industry?

PC Prices Take a Holiday

In personal computers, low-end models had been available for many years, but most buyers ultimately upgraded to models that offered greater functionality and capabilities. Nevertheless, low-cost PCs hung around and, during the mid to late 1990s, moved from less than 5 percent of the U.S. desktop market to more than 20 percent.

With decreasing prices for memory chips and increasing performance and functionality, low-cost desktop PCs soon caught on. The top-line industry vendors realized that they'd have to *stratify* their product offerings, such as high-end, high-functionality PCs, along with lower-cost, lower-functionality PCs.

Of late, top-line manufacturers adapted their marketing strategies even further, allowing customers to go on the Internet and hand-pick the array of components they want to be included within their system. So, one can acquire a Dell, Compaq, or IBM with the latest processor, biggest hard drive, fastest CD-ROM writer, and all the other peripherals, or simply acquire a bare-bones model costing a fraction of the high-performance, high-functionality prices.

Monitoring the Business Joneses

Vendors who weren't responsive enough to the change in the late 1990s might have been stuck offering one basic level of PC. Their more forward-thinking competitors were already offering an array of choices. When industry leaders like Dell began offering customers the ability to customize and order their systems over the Internet, the entire industry marketing model changed again.

In the PC industry, as well as in many others, keeping up with the business Joneses is no easy feat. The marketplace quickly grows to understand, accept, and, eventually, demand innovations.

Be Wary

The alternative to keeping pace in one's industry is being swamped by new product and new service offerings and customer-friendly ordering systems.

The Least You Need to Know

➤ Today, innovations are an integral part of all businesses and industries.

➤ Faced with outrageous competition on all sides, there are always options for profitably providing products or services in a manner that outflanks the competition.

➤ Sometimes, the changes confronting a company originate from the least suspected sources.

➤ When industry leaders ignore the emergence of smaller companies, the smaller companies gain an advantage and often succeed in obtaining customers.

➤ The alternative to keeping pace in one's industry is being swamped by new product and service offerings and customer-friendly ordering systems.

Part 6

Broadening Your Understanding

In this part, I'll offer insights from management experts who have intently studied change and how it applies in organizations. I'll also discuss some of their change models and basic philosophies about managing change, all of which can impact and enhance your individual approach to change management.

Constant change has become the order of the day and the hallmark of our lives. Less than smooth sailing is the ever-present reality for a change manager. I'll conclude with a discussion of the ever-changing environment and what it means for change managers everywhere.

Chapter 24

Change Strategies from the Gurus

In This Chapter

➤ Practicing total quality management

➤ Managing the quality of change

➤ Using methodical approaches

➤ Plotting your style

With the proliferation of change in the last 100 years came a new breed of social theorists: the change experts. In the twentieth century, perhaps for the first time in history, society needed people who could help individuals and organizations manage change, a part of life that previously was taken for granted.

Some of these experts specialized in organizational quality issues and addressed change as part of their quality work. Others focused more exclusively on change, whether describing it theoretically or managing it practically. Let's look at what some of these leaders in business and academia have to say about change, how to manage it, and how not to manage it.

The Quality Club

Early work on managing change was a byproduct of the "quality revolution." In years past, people simply didn't talk about things like "quality improvement" or

Word Power

Total quality management is an attempt to maintain the merit of an entire project, rather than focusing on its individual parts.

Change Master

One cannot guide a system of smaller systems toward quality improvement without the precise knowledge of the organization's processes and products.

Factoid

Deming became renowned for his "14 Points for Management," a set of all-purpose rules to apply to any organization seeking to improve customer satisfaction by improving quality.

"zero defects." Today, the phrase *total quality management* has overcome buzzword status to become holy doctrine at many organizations.

Three significant experts on changes in the way companies are run include W. Edwards Deming, Joseph Juran, and Philip W. Crosby.

W. Edwards Deming, Ph.D.

W. Edwards Deming (1900–1993), an educator, lecturer, author, and consultant, is acknowledged as the grand master of the quality movement. His ideas had a sweeping and profound impact on virtually all areas of American business.

Deming's theories also found a home in the public sector and in organizations around the world. In fact, Deming is probably most famous for his work in Japan, where he taught managers and engineers methods for managing and improving quality.

Honors Abound

Deming is the author of *Quality, Productivity, and Competitive Position* (1982); *The New Economics* (1984); and *Out of the Crisis* (1986), among other works. His ideas made such a positive contribution to the post–World War II Japanese economy that he received a medal of honor from the Japanese government. Decades later, after his ideas became popular in the United States, President Reagan honored Deming with the National Medal of Technology in 1987.

The Customer Defines Quality

According to Deming, quality was not anything that needed to be defined in concrete terms. He viewed quality as a concept that could only be defined by the customer. Nevertheless, Deming took a systematic approach to quality management. He taught that organizations are systems that are composed of networks and hierarchies of smaller systems.

Deming's Fourteen Commandments

Deming felt that sound statistical information, painstakingly gathered and correctly interpreted,

266

would be crucial in guiding the organization's quality-improvement efforts. Specifically, he focused on the reduction of variation among processes and products as keys to the improvement of quality.

Management Leads and Embraces Change

His crucial second point read as follows: Adopt the new, current philosophy of your industry. We are in a new economic age. Western management must rise to the challenge, learn its responsibilities, and accept leadership for change.

This point emphasized that all responsibility for change should fall upon the shoulders of management, which should not only manage change, but also lead it. Deming's fundamental attitude toward change was that it should not be avoided—change should be sought out and created in the form of quality improvement. After all, change is implicitly tied to change.

Deming denounced time changes and changes that only seldom occur. He taught that improving quality (change) must occur on a continual basis to ensure success for the organization.

Proceed

Although Deming's admonition to improve "constantly and forever" may seem like an impossible goal, he regarded it as an ideal that every company must strive to attain.

Constantly and Forever

Deming's fifth point states: To improve quality and productivity, and consequently cost, constantly and forever make changes to the system of production and service.

Deming believed in an aggressive approach to instituting, leading, and managing the types of change that would make an organization stronger, healthier, and more adaptable.

Joseph Juran

Nearing age 100, Joseph Juran holds degrees in electrical engineering and law. He has worked as an engineer, industrial executive, government administrator, university professor, corporate director, and management consultant. After working with Western Electric for 21 years, Juran quit his job in 1945 to devote his time to developing and promulgating the study of quality in business.

Factoid

In 1954, after nine years of research on the topic, Juran was invited to present his findings to Japanese business leaders. Soon after, it was evident that his work had contributed to the overall synergistic impact of quality theory on the Japanese economy, and, like Deming, Joseph Juran was eventually honored by the Japanese government for his contributions.

Improvement Requires Change

In 1979, Juran founded the Juran Institute to continue with the study of quality in business. While Deming's work is often categorized as "quality improvement," Juran's work is categorized as "total quality management."

Juran's books include *Juran on Planning for Quality* (1988) and *The Quality Control Handbook* (1988). Juran defined quality as "fitness for use." Quality was viewed in terms of "breakthroughs," which are dynamic, decisive movements to new and higher levels of performance.

Be Wary

Control activities have a short-term focus and won't lead to improvement or innovation. Only breakthrough activities can enable organizations to achieve the improvements in quality that lead to success.

Change Master

Constant change might be unnerving or irritating to many, but Juran regarded this process as absolutely crucial to total quality management. Only by regularly instigating significant change would an organization be able to improve its quality and maintain its competitive drive.

Striking a Balance

Juran recommended striking a balance between the effort and time focused on developing a product's special features versus attempting to eliminate all flaws of a product. He advocated a project-by-project approach to quality improvement and management.

While it is important for managers to strive for breakthroughs, they must also use control to maintain current levels of performance, or when necessary, prevent harmful changes. Juran believed that all management activity was directed at either capitalizing on breakthroughs or applying controls.

With industry breakthroughs come changes, and inevitably, managers often resist by increasing their control, even when the changes would lead to greater prosperity. Breakthroughs could lead to improvements in leadership, solutions to field problems, and an enhanced public image for the organization.

The Highs and Lows

Juran believed that breakthroughs and controls were analogous to the continuous cycle of highs and lows in performance. Like Deming, he advised managers to promote beneficial changes on an ongoing basis. While he was aware that it was both easy and comforting to remain ensconced in the status quo, he advised that the constant cycle of highs and lows needed integration into an organization to manage and improve the quality of an organization.

To Juran, change and quality were inextricably linked. His approach to managing change included accepting change as an element of the quality-improvement process, and managing it accordingly.

Philip B. Crosby

Philip B. Crosby, an engineer and quality expert, is most famous for popularizing the "Zero Defects" concept. This concept originated at the Martin Marietta Corporation, where he worked for 14 years in the 1960s as Director of Quality and Corporate Vice President of ITT Corp. His books *Quality Is Free* (1979), *Quality Without Tears* (1984), and *Leading* (1990) became bestsellers and established Crosby as one of the world's foremost quality consultants.

Conformance to Requirements

Crosby defined quality as conformance to requirements. He proclaimed that quality either does or does not exist; there are no intermediate levels. Managers must measure quality by regularly calculating the cost of making mistakes.

To help managers quantify this cost, Crosby developed the following formula:

Cost of Quality = Price of Conformance (the cost of doing things right the first time) + Price of Nonconformance (the cost of waste incurred by error)

The price of nonconformance, and thus the overall cost of quality, can be reduced if products and services are made or done correctly the first time. His "Zero Defects" idea called for a commitment from every individual in an organization to strive for perfection the first time around.

Like Juran and Deming, Crosby felt that constant change, which ultimately improves quality, should be instituted and managed in every organization. His theory was unique, however, because he focused on preventing errors rather than finding efficient means of fixing mistakes.

Make Expectations Clear

In Crosby's view, solutions to seemingly unpredictable setbacks could be provided in advance. For example, companies can create service and quality standards that would eliminate late deliveries or decreases in production. Crosby argued that such problems only occurred when employees lacked clear expectations for the quality of their work. Realistic, rational requirements result in well-functioning processes that produce the needed result.

Proceed

Expending the effort to do things right the first time will save you considerable time, energy, and money in the long run.

Change Master

If you clearly communicate your expectations for quality of service and production, you will be more likely to see your desired results.

Because inappropriate requirements can backfire, causing decreases in production or quality and unnecessary stress on workers, owners and managers need to monitor the effects of such requirements.

Change Model Makers

While the quality experts introduced earlier primarily dealt with change-management issues related to quality, other experts followed different paths. These theorists create models of change to describe its nature and how it manifests itself in organizations and society. Three of the most prominent change model-makers include the afore-mentioned Kurt Lewin (mentioned in Chapters 7, "The Normative-Reeducative Approach," and 11, "Leading Your Team Through Change"), and Robert Blake and Jane Mouton.

Kurt Lewin, Ph.D.

While most psychologists study the behavior of individuals, Kurt Lewin (1890–1947) was among the first psychologists to study the behavior of social groups. Lewin's pioneering work in this area has earned him a generally recognized title as the "Founder of Modern Social Psychology."

Lewin is noted for viewing the process of change as a series of psychological events. He tackled the question "What exactly causes change?" He taught that motivation to change is not enough to guarantee change.

The Field of Force

Lewin understood that all the data and information in the world wouldn't be useful unless translated into action, which is exactly what change managers need to do.

Factoid

Change managers found force field analysis to be particularly useful for delineating the forces at work behind or within a given change, especially when those forces are not immediately apparent.

Because of this, he developed force field analysis, a tool for diagnosing organizational situations. Force field analysis is the process of studying the catalysts of changes within an organization, as well as focusing on those factors that benefit and disrupt the changes.

Drivers and Restrainers

The basic assumption of force field analysis is that two kinds of forces, driving forces and restraining forces, influence change in any situation. Driving forces push elements of a situation in a certain direction.

If you were evaluating your organization's productivity, factors such as productivity targets, work incentives, and pressure from supervisors would all be driving forces.

Restraining forces oppose the action of the driving forces. Employee apathy, poor management planning, and insufficient equipment maintenance represent restraining forces. When the forces are roughly equal, the organization could be said to be in a state of *equilibrium*.

If an organization needed to institute a certain change, such as updating technology, introducing a new product, or revising workflow requirements, Lewin's force field analysis could help indicate which factors would resist and support that change.

The Forces Within

Lewin used force field analysis to describe how change works on individual levels. He theorized that the stability of human behavior was founded upon each individual's state of equilibrium, which was based on the interplay of his or her own set of driving and restraining forces.

For change to occur on the individual level, the driving and restraining forces would have to have a new relationship to one another. An apparently easy way to tweak this relationship is to add to the driving forces. Any increase in driving forces, however, is usually immediately met with a compensatory restraining force in an attempt to preserve equilibrium. Humans generally cling to their equilibrium, maintaining the status quo even when it's less than desirable.

Because of the instinct to resist change, Lewin ended up theorizing that the equilibrium might be more easily achieved if one reduced the restraining forces instead of increasing the driving forces.

Anxious While You Learn

Long-term observation led Lewin to believe that the key to producing change was dealing successfully with learning anxiety, a key restraining force. Today, many successful change managers take a page out of Lewin's book by employing a wide range of techniques for reducing *learning anxiety,* such as:

Word Power

Equilibrium is the state in which the driving forces and restraining forces are roughly equal.

Factoid

Restraining forces are harder to manipulate, especially on an individual level, because they often take the form of entrenched psychological defenses.

Word Power

Learning anxiety is what most of us feel to some degree when we're compelled to learn something new. It is the main restraining force that opposes both learning and change.

➤ Having people work in groups.

➤ Providing practice situations.

➤ Actively encouraging learners.

➤ Making constant help available.

Blake and Mouton

Years ago, Robert Blake, Ph.D., and Jane Mouton developed a model for describing leadership styles by graphing managerial traits on a grid. Blake and Mouton began marketing their grid tool through Scientific Methods, a company they founded in Austin, Texas, in 1961. They published their first book, *The Managerial Grid: Key Orientations for Achieving Production Through People,* in 1965. Other books followed including *The Managerial Grid III: The Key to Leadership Excellence* (1985), and *Change by Design* (1989).

Blake-Mouton Managerial Grid

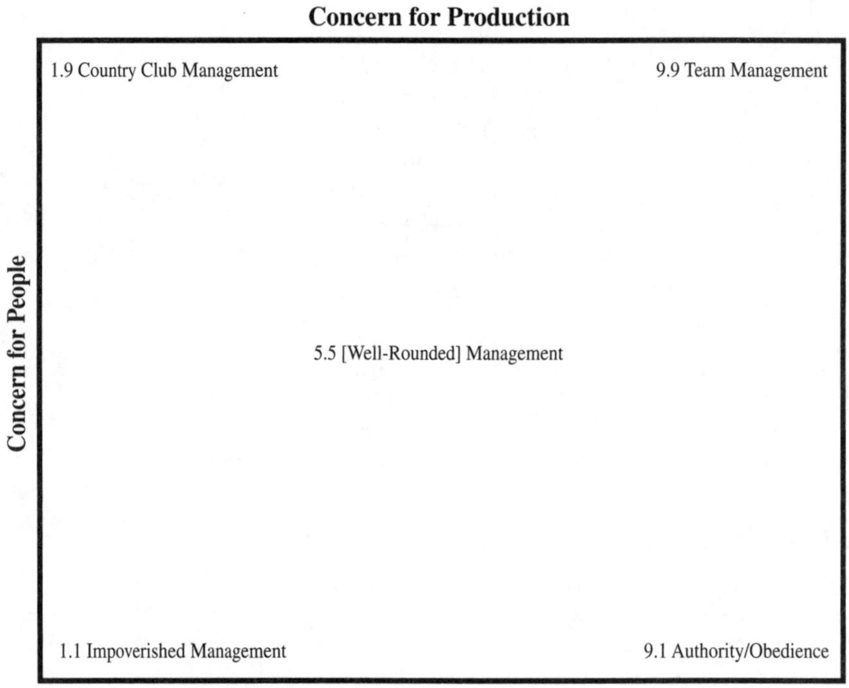

Concern for Production

The managerial grid.

272

Blake and Mouton's now famous managerial grid has since achieved widespread attention and has greatly influenced corporate America.

Grid, Grid on the Wall

To begin using their grid to describe a particular manager's style, one must have administered a questionnaire to the manager. The questionnaire is designed to measure the level of the manager's concern with two principal areas of management responsibility: people and production.

After the manager answers the questions, he is scored. A score of 1 on either the people or productions scale shows that the manager places little or no importance on the construct being measured. Similarly, a score of 9 in either area shows that the construct is highly important to the manager.

The manager's two scores are then plotted on the grid, thus describing the manager's leadership style.

Four Corners

Blake and Mouton's grid allows four possible extreme scores on the grid, as well as mid-range scores, such as 5.5. In the descriptions that follow, the first number rates the manager's concern with production, and the second number rates his or her concern with people.

➤ **1.9 Country Club Management:** Thoughtful attention to needs of people for satisfying relationships leads to a comfortable, friendly organization atmosphere and work tempo.

➤ **1.1 Impoverished Management:** Exertion of minimum effort to get required work done is appropriate to sustain organization membership.

➤ **5.5 Well-Rounded Management:** Adequate organization performance is possible through balancing the necessity to work with maintaining morale of people at a satisfactory level.

➤ **9.1 Authority/Obedience:** Efficiency in operations results from arranging conditions of work in such a way that human elements interfere to a minimum degree.

➤ **9.9 Team Management:** Work accomplishment is from committed people; interdependence through a "common stake" in organization purpose leads to relationships of trust and respect.

Self-Deception Abounds

If you think you know where you'd fall on this grid, think again. "Most of us would not be self-conscious enough to be able to place ourselves on such a grid," Blake commented. This lack of self-awareness has direct implications for change managers.

273

Factoid

Developing accurate self-assessments is not an easy undertaking. Blake conducted week-long grid seminars to help managers make such determinations.

In excerpts from a conversation with Robert Blake, he commented, "If you're unable to face yourself objectively, you place yourself in the 9.9 corner, deeply concerned for production but equally concerned about people, which is not where you are in fact. A tremendous amount of self-deception enters into this raw, naive self-examination. And as long as you are deceiving yourself, any plan of personal change is likely to be invalid" (*Healthcare Forum Journal*, 1992; 35).

A Beneficial Tool

Over the years, Blake and Mouton's grid has helped thousands of change managers develop a more realistic understanding of their leadership styles. This is a crucial step in managing any kind of change.

Rooted in Reality

What all of the theories presented in this chapter have in common is a stubborn insistence on *accurate perception of reality*. You can't manage change if you don't know what's really happening around you, and knowledge of self is a great place to start.

The Least You Need to Know

➤ W. Edwards Deming proposed that managers aggressively institute and lead scientifically targeted changes.

➤ Joseph Juran found that regular instigation of rationally targeted change is an inextricable element of total quality management.

➤ Philip W. Crosby emphasized elimination of harmful changes through prevention of the errors that lead to those changes.

➤ Kurt Lewin developed force field analysis as a tool for change by preventing use to determine which forces support and oppose a particular change.

➤ Blake and Mouton's managerial grid showed change managers what kinds of leaders they really were, as opposed to the kinds of leaders they thought they were.

Chapter 25

Gurus with Academic Ties

In This Chapter

➤ Recent theorists' impact on change management

➤ The role of learning organizations

➤ Change according to the chaos theory

➤ Organizations as living organisms

In this chapter, I will deal with some change-management experts in the business world with strong academic ties. Most of their work is more recent than the work of gurus cited in the previous chapter and throughout this book. These gurus focus on a variety of change-related issues, many of which will lend keen insights to your understanding of managing change.

Peter Senge's Learning Organization

Peter Senge, Ph.D., a senior lecturer at the Massachusetts Institute of Technology, ignited a revolution in organizational thinking with his 1990 book *The Fifth Discipline: The Art and Practice of the Learning Organization*. Senge's work transforms the ideas of systems theory into tools for understanding and managing organizational change.

Senge, who holds a Bachelor of science degree in engineering, a Master of science degree in social systems modeling, and a Ph.D. in management, is chairman of the

Society for Organizational Learning. This society is an organization of corporations, researchers, and consultants dedicated to the interdependent development of people and their institutions.

Continually Expanding Capacities

The Fifth Discipline introduced the core idea of the "learning organization," an organization in which people continually expand their capacities and absorb information. New and expansive patterns of thinking are nurtured. Collective aspiration is freed. People continually learn how to learn together.

Senge teaches that businesses must become learning organizations if they are to survive the ever-accelerating business world. His five "disciplines" that must be adapted to create a learning organization are …

➤ Systems thinking

➤ Personal mastery

➤ Mental models

➤ Shared vision

➤ Team learning

Senge's Vision

Senge's idealistic view of the future includes the transition of businesses to humane institutions that are centered around learning. To enable such a transition, he addresses the need for a decentralization of leadership within the organization to better enable all employees to work productively toward common goals. He also emphasizes the importance of respecting human values within the workplace.

Change Master

When the organization is viewed as a living entity, its richness and complexity can be properly taken into account. Such a view puts any strategic initiative for change on much better footing.

Senge holds that the task of making change happen requires business leaders to modify the way they think about organizations. "We need to think less like managers and more like biologists," Senge maintains. (See Chapter 2, "Change Scenarios," for the parallel to Senge's findings.)

It is this view of companies as living entities—because companies are composed of people who are living entities themselves—that Senge insists business leaders adopt to create initiatives for change. He believes that most strategic initiatives for change, which are driven from the top, are only marginally successful at best because they use the machine as a metaphor of the functioning capabilities of the company.

Chaos Theory: Margaret J. Wheatley, Ed.D.

Author and consultant Margaret J. Wheatley also views organizations as living systems, an idea that she integrated into her *chaos theory*.

Since it is the randomness and complexity of events that seem to hamstring so many promising change initiatives, change managers find great value in Wheatley's work.

Organization and Physics

Wheatley, who obtained her doctorate in administration, planning, and social policy from Harvard, is probably best known for her 1992 book, *Leadership and the New Science: Learning About Organization from an Orderly Universe*. Wheatley currently is a partner in Kellner-Rogers & Wheatley, Inc., and the nonprofit Berkana Institute, two Utah-based institutions that study new ways of organization.

Wheatley grounds her teachings in the latest discoveries of quantum physics. These discoveries seem to point to a fundamental relationship among phenomena, even when there is no apparent means for the occurrence of such a relationship.

Scientists and philosophers interpreted this relationship to mean that the world is not a collection of individual particles that are colliding, combining, fusing, or exploding. Rather, the universe is one infinite interrelationship in which all things are somehow connected.

Word Power

Chaos theory is the body of ideas that attempts to explain both the randomness and the complexity of events and processes.

Consult Your Heart

Wheatley advises that corporate managers should be given permission to change the way they make conscious business judgments. Such judgments are usually made only in the brain, but Wheatley says the heart should come into play as well. When the heart is involved in business decisions, relationships usually have a larger stake in the decision-making process. Such consideration is a crucial element that the majority of decision processes too often lack.

The business world, as Wheatley notes, is typically characterized by stylized and static rituals and

Change Master

In conjunction with her experience as a consultant, Wheatley has concluded that relationships are the most important elements of successful organizations because relationships allow organizations to flexibly respond to change.

processes that leave the function of evaluation to a select elite. There is a slowly growing movement toward changing that situation by allowing more members of the group to be evaluators. However, most organizations are not set up for that mode of operation on a structural level.

Reconnecting Relationships

Wheatley is interested in seeing organizations adopt methods that provide access to intellectual participation for all members, as well as a conscious social reconnection. She maintains that the reconnection of social patterns is a necessity for any organization.

Change Master

Wheatley argues that organizations that can change their relationships to allow greater degrees of connectedness will be rewarded with greater degrees of success.

Perhaps Wheatley's most radical proposition is as follows: "Love, in organizations, is the most potent source of power we have available." When Wheatley consults with an organization, she examines its interpersonal relationships more carefully than its tasks or hierarchies. She notes that power within organizations can be given either a positive or a negative charge depending on the quality of the relationships within which power is wielded.

Universal Principle of Life

Wheatley focuses on a significant universal principle: Life and living organisms are constantly moving of their own accord toward higher and more sophisticated levels of self-organization. Because human organizations are composed of living organisms (that's you and me), our organizations are also constantly making this upward trek toward higher states of organization.

Like Senge, Wheatley also encourages a style of thinking about organizations that allows for their richness, complexity, and, yes, even chaos. This viewpoint provides the best framework for an organization's healthy growth and development.

Proceed

People who coerce rather than negotiate, or who operate from a position of disregard for others, will create negative energy; those who relate with a quality of openness and respect will generate positive energy.

Management by Objective: Peter Drucker

If you've ever heard the phrase "management by objective," then you've come across insights first introduced by Peter Drucker. Drucker, a long-time professor at Claremont Graduate University in California, is also a consultant and author whose books include *The Practice of Management* (1954), *The Age of Discontinuity* (1969), *Innovation and Entrepreneurship* (1985), *Drucker on Asia* (1997), and *Management Challenges for the 21st Century* (1999). His emphasis on seeing change as an opportunity and a goal provided a radically different perspective of change from most managers.

Born in Vienna, Drucker moved to the United States in 1937 to work in political science. He believed that capitalism's failure to give "status and function" to the individual had paved the way for European fascism. In the 1940s, Drucker forsook political science to begin studying corporate management, a new field at that time.

Drucker's Landmark Concept

General Motors commissioned Drucker to write a policy report for the company. While analyzing its policies, he created his landmark book *Concept of the Corporation* (1946), which challenged conventional corporate structure and cited *decentralization* as a crucial element missing from most organizations.

GM managers were not receptive to Drucker's book because he contended that employees should be viewed as resources rather than costs. Nevertheless, over the next six decades, Drucker became a highly sought-after adviser to CEOs in the United States, and his viewpoints about managing people and change enjoyed widespread acceptance.

Be Wary

Managers and other leaders too often strive to maintain the status quo at all costs, which stifles the organization's natural progression toward higher organizational levels. When the organization's evolution is choked off in this way, potential improvements are never realized, and tremendous amounts of energy are wasted.

Change Is Normal

Drucker has analyzed many organizations, and he has been uncanny in his ability to accurately identify emerging trends among them.

Drucker observed that most organizations view change much like one views death and taxes: undesirable but inevitable, things to be postponed for as long as possible. He maintains that this reluctance to change is a fundamental error in today's business environment because change is the norm.

Word Power

Decentralization also refers to giving power and control to the separate parts of a structure instead of dispensing power and administering control from a central source.

Successful organizations can't restrict themselves to merely seeking to survive or even to manage change. Organizations must lead change in this time of rapid, constant, and widespread structural alteration.

Organized Abandonment and Improvement

According to Drucker, being a change leader means more than simply doing new and different things. It entails being willing and able to change what already exists. "Abandon yesterday," Drucker advises, meaning that every organization should have a policy of *organized abandonment.*

Word Power

In **organized abandonment,** change managers examine products, services, processes, and all other elements of the organization on a regular schedule to determine whether they should stay, go, or be adapted.

Organized abandonment must be conducted on a regular and systematic basis; it will never happen otherwise because letting go of the status quo is usually not a popular activity. The few companies that have instituted organized abandonment have reported significant growth.

Drucker also recommends the continual systematic improvement of anything an organization does. If these continual improvements are targeted at a preset annual rate, such as 3 percent, they will eventually transform the organization. Innovations in products and services will result, as will the creation of new services, products, and businesses.

Innovation Means Opportunity

Druckerbelieves managers need to focus on innovation to most successfully manage change. But *simple* innovation is not what's needed. *Systematic innovation* is the key to invigorating your organization's commitment to managing change.

Word Power

Systematic innovation is the process of continually seeking out improvements and breakthroughs in the way one operates.

Systematic innovation is vital because, eventually, it produces the mindset necessary for an organization to lead change, namely, to conceptualize change as an opportunity.

A Fresh Perspective: Rosabeth Moss Kanter

Rosabeth Moss Kanter, a professor of Business Administration at Harvard Business School, is a leading expert on organizational change.

Kanter is a former editor of the *Harvard Business Review* and a consultant to major corporations around the world. She is the author or co-author of 13 books, including *The Challenge of Organizational Change: How Companies Experience It and Leaders Guide It* (1992).

Beware of the Bold

Certain kinds of organizational changes, Kanter observes, such as reorganizing a unit or allocating resources for new product development, are quite simple for managers to bring about. Yet, this kind of bold stroke is often a defensive maneuver to avoid dealing with more fundamental issues, while making managers feel good about having instituted noticeable change!

Kanter says long-term, sustainable change is not supported by bold strokes of change, but rather by long marches toward change. These long marches have to take place at every level of the organization in the form of personal commitments by every member.

Be Wary

When organizations lack concepts, competence, and connections, people in the organization typically react defensively because they see change as a threat driven by a crisis, not an opportunity driven by evolution.

Traits of the Adept

Kanter says that change adept organizations possess three crucial traits: concepts (the imagination to innovate), competence (the professionalism to perform), and connections (the openness to collaborate).

These traits, Kanter points out, are not programs or policies, but a reflection of ingrained habits. When these traits are interwoven throughout an organization, people tend to react to change much less defensively. They do so because concepts, competence, and connections make people confident that they can handle change. Indeed, they can shape it and even lead it.

Change Master

Leaders need to be prepared to question their own assumptions (and the assumptions of others) and be open to different ways of looking at a problem or a proposed solution.

The Role of Leaders

Kanter maintains that organizational leaders possess the ability to transform their organizations into "change-adept" enterprises. However, executives often employ ineffective leadership tactics, such as haphazardly assigning tasks to people and hoping they get them right.

Proceed

Perhaps the most important skill of a leader is the ability to persevere in the middle of a change project, the point at which the excitement of the beginning has worn off but the payoff of completion has not yet arrived.

Be Wary

Leaders often launch a change project with great fanfare only to walk away from it later. Abandonment of the change effort suggests to the rest of the organization that change isn't important.

Leaders who want to foster change must be willing to embrace it as extensively as they expect their employees to do so. To lead the organization into a mode of being responsive to change, leaders must have certain classic skills, Kanter says. For instance, leaders must be tuned in to their environments. They should actively collect information that will inform them about what's going on, both inside and outside the organization. They should challenge the prevailing conventional wisdom in their organizations.

Lead with Conviction

Kanter says leaders cannot enlist people in a change project, or any other kind of project, without communicating genuine conviction. Genuine conviction is one of the few ways (besides using brute force) to discourage resistance to change.

Leaders also need to build coalitions with people who have the resources to make things happen within the organization. "Coalition building is probably the most neglected step in the change process," Kanter says.

Emphasize Steady Change

Leaders should send the message that personal effort, innovation, and perseverance will pay off in the long run with success and growth. By collecting information, questioning assumptions, building coalitions, and using other classic skills, leaders can position their organizations to respond to change adaptively and lead change in an innovative way.

Organizations As Living Systems: Arie de Geus

Consultant and author Arie de Geus is widely credited with originating the concept of the learning organization, a term that was later popularized by Peter Senge. He has advised many public and private institutions all over the world. Like Margaret Wheatley, he regards organizations as living systems. He holds that the current typical view of corporations as machines is dangerous as change accelerates in the twenty-first century.

De Geus is a consultant member of the Society for Organizational Learning (of which Peter Senge is chairman) and a board member of both the Center for Organizational Learning at MIT's Sloan School of Management and the Nijenrode Learning Centre in the Netherlands. He is also a visiting fellow at the London Business School.

The Biology of Management

De Geus's book, *The Living Company* (1997), uses biological metaphors to analyze corporate management. If we think of corporations as species, the average life expectancy of the corporation is only 12 years in many industrialized countries. Yet, there are corporations that have thrived and have been in business for centuries.

Factoid

A living work community is much more able to harmonize itself with the ever-changing world around it because of the marvelous ability of all living organisms to adapt themselves to their environments.

How is it that some corporations are so short-lived, while others seem to exist forever? De Geus maintains that the crucial difference is how the long-lived companies run their organizations as "living work communities" rather than as pure economic machines.

Unlike an organism, a machine cannot adapt. It can be renovated, retrofitted, or torn apart and re-built, but this requires much more effort due to the machine's inherent inertia.

Traits for Longevity

Long-lived companies, those that thrive for centuries, will manifest the following traits of living organisms, according to de Geus:

➤ **Sensitivity to the environment.** Enduring companies maintain an awareness of their surroundings and can act accordingly.

➤ **Persona.** They have a cohesive sense of identity based on a shared community.

➤ **Tolerance.** Power and decision-making authority are decentralized and widespread. The organization is tolerant of noncore activities on the periphery because they may become tomorrow's core.

➤ **Frugality.** They are conservative with money.

Adaptations and Communication

De Geus often uses biological metaphors to describe business behavior and to impart lessons about the nature of organizations. One story he tells in lectures uses the behavior of birds as a metaphor.

283

In the early 1900s, milk was delivered to every home in the country in glass bottles with open mouths. The internal organs of two birds, the robin and the titmouse, soon adapted the ability to digest milk after the birds repeatedly stole sips from the early morning deliveries.

Then, in the 1930s, milk distributors began sealing the tops of the bottles with aluminum. The titmouse soon learned to penetrate the seal to continue getting milk, but the robin never learned how to do this. De Geus believes that because the titmouse is a flocking bird, it had an advantage over the robin.

Titmice only display territorial behavior for two months out of the year; the rest of the time, they flock with other titmice. This flocking allows titmice to promulgate learning, such as penetrating the aluminum milk seal, to other members of the flock. The robin, however, is territorial all year and never travels in flocks. Thus, robins are unable to propagate learning widely.

Factoid

Flocking allows titmice to promulgate learning. Birds that do not flock have no way of informing others in their species of their discoveries.

Learn to Flock

Institutions that want to be learning organizations must possess the following three traits, according to de Geus:

➤ They must have plenty of individuals on hand to increase the pool of available innovators.

➤ Those individuals must engage in innovative activities.

➤ The results of innovation must be widely shared through good flocking activities.

Good flocking can take a variety of forms on the organizational level. People should maintain a continuous variety of new contacts, for instance, and develop opportunities to talk with them. Bringing people together from different units could constitute another flocking activity, as could job rotation.

Change Master

Develop your own approaches to change management, while gleaning useful techniques from today's change theorists. By using their ideas, solutions to the problems within your change campaigns may become more evident.

Through flocking and other biological lessons, de Geus points the way to a new conception of the corporation that could make widespread extinction a disaster of the past.

The Least You Need to Know

➤ People continually expand their capacities to create the results they truly desire.

➤ In learning organizations, there is a need for decentralized leadership to better enable all employees to work productively toward common goals.

➤ According to Rosabeth Moss Kanter, change requires personal commitments of all who are involved.

➤ Unlike an organism, a machine cannot adapt. It can be renovated, retrofitted, torn apart and rebuilt, but this requires much more effort due to the machine's inherent inertia.

➤ Leaders must be prepared to initiate change, lead by example, and give attention to followers.

Chapter 26

Managing Through the Maelstrom

Suppose that as change manager, you've done every single thing you can to accomplish your goal. You expended your resources carefully; helped to identify, assemble, and manage a winning team; and, all along, you monitored your progress.

You continually stayed on top of the day-to-day and even the hour-to-hour details of the change campaign in your quest to achieve the desired outcome. You stayed flexible, you rolled with the punches, and you developed a good framework for handling the unexpected.

After all that, developments can still occur from what seems to be outer space, or at least left field, that fundamentally change or derange your campaign efforts. What are some of these developments, and what steps can you rapidly implement in the face of such sudden intrusions?

Changes Related to the Authorizing Party

Despite being 70 percent of the way to your desired objective, humming along smoothly for weeks or months, and getting kudos from everywhere (even the top management of your organization), fundamental changes involving the role of the authorizing party frequently translate into dramatic project shifts, or even project termination.

If such a turn of events befalls you, but you happen to have a personal, professional, or emotional stake in seeing the campaign to completion, your assignment is clear: you need to resecure sponsorship. In this case, the sponsorship comes from whatever authority now prevails; this person should be someone you can reach and favorably influence.

Sheer logic would dictate that if you have already been on a campaign for months, tied up the time and talents of several team members, expended funds in at least the high five-figure area, and are making definite progress, your organization would not want to impede or jeopardize the campaign. Too often, this is exactly what happens.

Be Wary

If the initiating sponsor interest in the campaign has his or her role somehow fundamentally altered or leaves the organization, your change campaign may be in jeopardy!

Change Master

The larger the organization and the deeper its pockets, the greater the chance that a midstream disheveling of authorization can lead to abandonment of the change campaign.

When the Deck Gets Reshuffled

Corporations are like poker players at a table. If the player has stayed in for a hand when the stakes were raised repeatedly, but now realizes that he can't win, he'll fold his cards, consider that round as sunk costs, and retreat so as to be prepared to play another round.

Your campaign may be viewed in such a light. To you, it may make perfect sense to continue. You have come so far, turned over so many stones, stayed focused on the change campaign objective, and you know in the marrow of your bones that you can achieve the desired outcome.

To the higher-ups, however, your project is one of many, and with a new power alignment, perhaps it's not high on the priority list.

Resell or Be Gone

The key to reselling an existing change campaign is to avoid the reflexive tendency to overemphasize ...

➤ How well the campaign has been managed,

➤ How far you've come, and

➤ How much you've achieved thus far.

As nice and important as those items are, to a dispassionate or disinterested authorizing body, they may merely represent sunk costs.

The focus of your argument, key to campaign continuance, is to sell what greater good is in store by adhering to the established course. In essence, you need to relate three things:

1. Why the amount left in the budget to expend on this campaign still represents an excellent value for the organization, one that would be hard to emulate by allocating the money elsewhere.

2. How the original objects and desired outcomes continue to fit into the overall picture of what the organization is trying to achieve. Specifically, how failure to achieve the desired outcome will result in undesired consequences for the company, perhaps significantly affecting other departments and divisions.

Proceed

Your ability to *resell* the change campaign to those newly in authority becomes crucial.

3. Why you and your team are the appropriate people to continue in your respective roles, how the skills and experiences you are developing will further benefit the organization, and how the overall campaign experience can translate into insights and lessons learned that may rival the value of achieving the desired outcome.

Not Home Free Yet

If you do a good job on the resell, that is if you get authorizing parties to actually contemplate the continuance of the campaign, you still are not home free.

Be Wary

Chances are that any new authorizing party is going to want to make some changes—everybody does.

Any one or more of these developments may ensue. So, do as the scouts say—be prepared:

➤ **Your timeframe may be shortened.** You may have had three months to go, and you might now only have six weeks. This may necessitate working late into the evening and on weekends, a scenario which you have worked to avoid for both you and your team. Still, if the end is in sight, and it means that much to you, it makes sense to go for it. A finite time period—say, six weeks or less—goes by fast, especially when you are working like a mad dog around the clock!

Be Wary

Unfortunately, whether it is slashing the timeframe or the funds, the end result is often the same. You are working later into the evening and on weekends, so you are confronted by some of the same kinds of issues discussed above.

➤ **Your budget may be restricted.** As carefully as you meted out the available funds for this campaign, and however much you were counting on the remaining funds to see you through to the end of the project, don't be shell-shocked if you find you will have to continue with half or less of the remaining earmarked funds.

➤ **Your staff size may be reduced.** Suppose the authorizing party says that it's okay to complete the campaign, but with only 75 percent of your staff. If you are managing eight people, now you are down to six. This leads inevitably to—you guessed it—working longer and harder.

Continue, but Not Like Before

Another type of course modification, somewhat different from those discussed above, may result as well. The authorizing party decides the campaign is worth continuing, but fundamentally alters it. For example:

➤ The scope of your work is dramatically increased and perhaps without additional time, funds, or staff.

➤ Your campaign objective is altered so that you have to undertake significant backtracking to achieve the new desired outcome.

➤ Your campaign is combined with another one or becomes a subset of someone else's larger campaign.

In cases like these, you have a whole new set of challenges regarding timeframe, budget, and staffing. Mixing and matching teams, or being merged into a larger campaign, brings with it challenges of ...

➤ Reassembling a winning team,

➤ Keeping the team motivated,

➤ Keeping conflicts to a minimum, and

➤ Keeping everyone focused on the objective (which, in this case, has changed!).

The Unanticipated Happens

Despite these or other possible developments, as a change manager and career professional, you need to strive for objectivity. These kinds of occurrences go on all the time in the working world. No one is necessarily out to get you. Campaigns shift, people move on, technology advances, competition stiffens, customers change their minds, organizations evolve, needs change, directions vary, and some days it feels like it all falls down on you.

Even in the most basic settings—for example, if you're a project manager for a construction project—external factors such as the weather can wreak havoc on your plans. *Contingency planning* counts! You can run into zoning problems, equipment or material shortages, accidents, and any one of a number of other developments.

All the contingency planning, chart plotting, built-in slack in the system, emergency preparation, and back-up systems that you have in place cannot see you through the times when some itty-bitty, fundamental, unanticipated change occurs.

Flying High: The Iridium Network

Imagine 70 satellites circling the globe. The Motorola Corporation allocated millions of dollars, thousands of workers, and many, many years in the pursuit of a desired end result. They wanted to create a global communication system that would enable anyone virtually anywhere on the planet to be in phone contact with anyone else.

As the venture passed the halfway point, some surprising challenges surfaced. Construction, launch, and placement of the satellites were not the issue.

Word Power

A **contingency plan** is a backup course of action to be initiated in the event that the original course of action encounters significant barriers or roadblocks.

Factoid

This grand dream captured the imagination of top brass within the organization, its shareholders, and the business, as well as popular media. *Forbes, Fortune, Business Week,* and *The Wall Street Journal* all carried multiple features on the venture, luring readers with tales of how this wondrous communication system would transform the planet.

The major bugaboo occurred *on land*. The "phone" communication device was cumbersome. It would have a high per-unit cost, on the order of $250. Operation was awkward.

Downed by Practicality

Who wanted to buy a $250 clunky phone system so you could make a one-minute call to the Gobi Desert for $5? Negative articles started to appear in the very same publications that years earlier had lauded the venture. The company was looking to sell out, but, alas, no one with a few extra billion dollars stepped up.

What is the status of the venture today? The satellites are in place, forming a wondrous network in the heavens. For now, the concept of person-to-person global phone communications any time, anywhere on the planet remains a dream.

Longevity and Failure

The issues addressed thus far can have heightened impact on particularly *long* duration change campaigns.

"Projects can invariably develop needs for resources that were not originally allocated," say authors J.R. Meredith and Samuel Mantel in *Project Management*. "Arguments between functional departments over the command of such resources are very common." The acquisition of resources can be costly, especially when they relate to plants and equipment.

Be Wary

All other things being equal, the longer a campaign is scheduled to run, the more time is available for both internal and external events to develop that represent supreme challenges to the continuation of the campaign.

You probably know from personal experience that when you actually start a project, even some solo effort, halfway through you inevitably discover needs that are crucial for success.

Consider the times you decided to fix something in your house, assembled all your tools, and, lo and behold, in mid-fix, you found that you still had to make a trip to the hardware store to get something. Or, you were getting ready to throw a party, and, in the middle of preparations, you found that you were short on several items.

It is no different for a change campaign involving significant time, labor, and funds. If anything, the probability is higher that such campaigns will require additional resources that were not originally allocated. Still, chances may be reasonable that your request for additional resources will be honored.

The Path to Derangement

A survey of 36 companies revealed that among terminated research and development projects, technical issues often prevailed (probably unanticipated technical issues). Of responding companies, 34 percent cited low probability of achieving technical objectives or commercializing results as the primary reason for termination.

Other technical issues included manufacturing problems that could not be resolved with available research and development skills (11 percent) and the emergence of other or higher priority projects requiring research and development, labor, or funds (10 percent).

Factoid

Companies also reported too much time required to achieve commercial results as being a reason for termination (6 percent), in addition to a project having negative affects on other projects or products (3 percent), and patent problems (1 percent).

Companies reported that economic and market issues sometimes lead to termination as well. Of survey respondents, about 23 percent reported that "low profitability or return on investment" led to termination, followed by "too costly to develop an individual product" (18 percent), low market potential (16 percent), and changing competitive factors or market needs (10 percent).

While you may not be managing a research and development project, plenty of other prevailing factors may spell the degradation or termination of your campaign.

1. **Does the campaign remain in alignment with overall organizational objectives?** While objectives of organizations tend to change slowly, they do change. Changes are more frequent within departments and divisions of organizations.

2. **Is the change campaign practical, useful, and applicable?** This may seem like a strange question to ask once a campaign has commenced, and stranger still if you ask it late in the life of a campaign. All too often, however, after being viewed with a longer term perspective, some campaigns that seemed so worthwhile at the outset are deemed far less so later on. If you are committed to the campaign and still regard it as highly valid, here is where your reselling efforts must prevail.

Be Wary

Being too far ahead of the technology curve is the curse of temporary society. The woods are full of companies that developed products too many years in advance of market acceptance for the original developer to make a profit. Think of early models of videophones, electric cars, flat computer screens, or portable (barely luggable!) computers.

3. **Does the campaign represent too great of an advance for current technology?** It is one thing to be on the leading edge, but no one wants to be on the bleeding edge. Organizations with deep pockets can sustain losses from a number of change campaigns, knowing that only a small minority needs to have big payoffs to remain profitable.

4. **Has the team remained vibrant and alert, or has it become stale and lethargic?** It happens to the best teams, particularly on long campaigns. How long can you maintain a sharp focus? How long can you expend the brunt of your energy and effort in a single focus area? Increasingly, the answer in these high-distraction times is not very long.

   These days, it seems that people continually need new challenges. How many would be willing to devote countless hours, over many years, to try more than 8,000 potential filaments for the electric light bulb as Edison did? Who would lie flat on his or her back for 8 or 10 hours a day over several months catching paint drips in the face while painting the Sistine Chapel as Michelangelo did? While these may be historical and dramatic examples of the necessity of concentration and focus, the point is that the attention span of workers today is at an all-time low, and it's dropping.

5. **Is support for the campaign dissipating within the organization?** Maybe the sponsor is still in place, and the funds and timeframe are secure, but the organization has initiated other change campaigns, and, by default, the interest level in yours has dropped dramatically.

6. **Has the organization suffered a financial downturn?** What once was a highly viable campaign during a period of sustained growth and revenues may be a marginal campaign at best during a period of retrenchment. Once again, recall your domestic projects. Depending on your level of income and savings, you're likely to tackle different projects when money is tight than when you are more financially secure.

7. **Can the change campaign be subcontracted without diminishing its prospects for success?** As top management continually reassesses organizational objectives and how best to allocate resources, sometimes campaigns that were initiated in-house are deemed more suitable to be handled by contractors. For some change managers, having their projects farmed out represents a supreme loss of face. Others simply see it as "just business," while still others are relieved to no longer be involved with it!

8. **Is communication between staff members breaking down?** The change manager beset with staff members who can't work with each other, or who cannot adequately manage the team, has a decent shot at having the campaign withdrawn from him or terminated altogether.

Sometimes it's a case of the change manager being ill-equipped to handle the reins, the luck of who happens to be assigned to the campaigns, and irreconcilable differences do occur among otherwise well-meaning professionals.

9. **Is a key team member departing, or has a critical member already gone?** People come and go within organizations, as they will among change-management teams. In most cases, the departing team member can be replaced. His or her skills are widely available within the organization.

What about when his or her skills are unique and very difficult to replace? This is particularly true for technical projects in which a team member was chosen specifically for his or her area of expertise. Sometimes the campaign carries on, begins to sputter, and then runs aground. If so, top managers can quickly get the message that staff and budget resources set aside for this project could be used best if reallocated.

Be Wary

As top management looks for ways to tighten operations, conserve costs, and propel the organization forward, rumblings of dissension from one particular change campaign may be all that's necessary to have the plug pulled on it.

10. **Has a critical deadline been missed?** With the sophisticated project management scheduling software available today and your steadfastness in continually monitoring the project, the incidence of this happening is less than it would be for your management counterpart of a generation ago. When your team misses a critical deadline, perhaps missing it widely, and perhaps not even being able to quickly get back on track, the entire campaign itself may be in jeopardy. This could be cause for the authorizing party to withdraw further sponsorship.

11. **Is the external environment changing?** As time passes, this is inevitable. Changes that can spell immediate termination of your campaign include the following:

   ➤ A competitor beating you to the marketplace so convincingly that it does not pay to continue.

   ➤ Legislation or regulation that severely hampers or restricts your progress.

   ➤ A lawsuit, lean, or entanglement that forces your organization or critical players to divert their focus.

   ➤ Development of a new process or technology that renders your budget obsolete. Think of a team empowered to design a higher quality eight-track tape player in the face of breakthroughs in cassette tapes, compact disks, and DVD players.

If your progress to date is good, the sponsor is still fully committed and achievement of the desired objective is still deemed highly worthwhile within the organization, then, despite other setbacks, the chances are reasonable that you'll continue on!

The Least You Need to Know

➤ All things being equal, the longer a change campaign's duration, the greater the chance that something will occur to quash the campaign.

➤ One of your unanticipated duties may be that of reselling the change campaign midstream as new developments threaten its continuance.

➤ Among research and development campaigns, termination most often occurs when there is a low probability of achieving technical objectives or commercial results.

➤ Be on guard if your organization suffers a financial downturn.

➤ A campaign may be terminated for many reasons, most of them unrelated to the skills and capabilities of the campaign manager. Try not to take it personally.

Chapter 27

Tomorrow Will Be Different

In This Chapter

➤ The folly of linear predictions

➤ Small shifts, huge impact

➤ The value of doing "something"

➤ Stay loose and adjust

Early in the twenty-first century, I saw an article highlighting a collection of predictions:

➤ **Mix-and-match religions.** A growing number of people combine, say, Jewish customs with Zen principles and Quaker decor.

➤ **Spirituality breaks.** On the job, employees can walk into a chapel at work and take a few moments for themselves, or schedule to have the company's visiting chaplain drop by.

➤ **Trophy families.** As typified by Hollywood public relations machines, people from John and Jane Doe to Madonna getting married so as to enhance their images.

Who can say if these forecasted social trends are already in formation and will take hold in a significant way?

Futuristic Folly

Despite considerable efforts, the technology futurists most often get it wrong. Pick up some leading guru's book from 10 years ago depicting how things will be today, and it almost reads like folly.

Even in the strict confines of the business world, the leading thinkers of the day, the "captains of industry," if you will, are often so wrong in retrospect as to be amusing:

➤ The well-known British mathematician and physicist William Kelvin assured everyone back in 1895 that heavier-than-air flying machines were impossible.

➤ Although he was cited as being the first to isolate the electron and measure its charge, in 1923, Nobel Laureate and physicist Robert Andrews Millikan declared that man could never tap the power of the atom.

➤ In 1943, Tom Watson of IBM said that there was perhaps a market for five computers in the whole world.

➤ Bill Gates in 1991 wildly underestimated the coming impact of the Internet.

The all-time erroneous observation, one that makes me wonder how he rose to his post, was uttered by Charles H. Duell, director of the U.S. Patent Office in 1899. Duell solemnly proclaimed, "Everything that can be invented has been invented."

I lived in New England for the first 26 years of my life and there was a popular expression there about the weather. It was said that if you don't like the weather, wait a minute. In the Midwest I was told that if you don't like the weather, walk a mile.

On the West Coast, up around San Francisco Bay, I figured out that if you don't like the weather, dress in layers because that is the only way you will be ready for the extremes to which you may be subjected at any given moment. When it comes to predicting the weather, you're better off anticipating a change!

Why do so many otherwise knowledgeable and well-meaning people fail so miserably when it comes to predicting tomorrow? Why, too, do change managers of all stripes proceed as if tomorrow will be pretty much like today, perhaps with a few little differences here and there?

The short answer is that too many people base their predictions of the future on linear progressions of the present and near present. It's like watching the stock market rise a couple dollars every day, and predicting at the month's end that the total increase will be $60.

All you are doing is assuming a linear progression, a simple mathematic equation, based on a few recent

Factoid

Throughout history, even the best and the brightest, along with the mediocre and the dim, have made prognostications that not only didn't come to pass, but, as they say, weren't even close.

data points. You are not calling the turns, those critical junctures in a change situation in which a dramatic rise or fall irrevocably impacts what everybody thought was the predictable trend line.

The Trap of Unintended Consequences

In *The Complete Idiot's Guide to Managing Your Time,* I refer to the "revenge effect," or the trap of unintended consequences. Professor Edward Tenner of Princeton says, "The revenge effect is the curious way the world has of getting even, defeating our best efforts to speed it up and otherwise improve it."

One of the all-time most unintended consequences has to be the mushrooming growth of kudzu, which vanquishes other plants around it. This very green, quickly growing vine imported to the United States from Japan in the 1930s was supposed to help control soil erosion. Instead, it is growing out of control across many southern states. As Stephen Gillon observes in his book, *That's Not What We Meant to Do,* kudzu has come to symbolize the effect of unintended consequences.

The Government Steps In

The Federal Government in particular has experienced more than its share of unintended consequences. Gillon sites examples of social reform legislation that were supposed to make society more fair and equitable, but, instead, turned out to create situations that still plague us today.

The Community Mental Health Act of 1963, designed to offer structure and a measure of equity in dealing with the nation's mentally ill, ended up de-institutionalizing many of them, offering lots of structure, little equity, and little support.

Good Intentions, But ...

The Civil Rights Act of 1964 was designed with the best of intentions—to end long-term, socially pervasive racial discrimination. Yet, 38 years later, the "strange career" of affirmative action, based on the numbers, has yielded little in the way of tangible results, has created backlashes in many sectors of society, and has widely been viewed as an experiment with limited results at best.

The Federal Election Campaign Finance Reform Act (wow; that's a mouthful!) of 1974, as strange as it seems, was designed to introduce a new measure of

Factoid

All the New Deal programs established in the 1930s were designed to give the Depression-strapped workers of the day a chance to stay afloat, do some good for the nation, and eventually get back to self-sufficiency. Instead, many people found themselves trapped in the cycle of poverty for decades, even up to the present day.

financial reform to the way politicians raised funds for federal elections. Yet unforeseen loopholes have created federal election funding nightmares, which have impacted every election since and remain one of the top priorities of the United States Congress to this day.

Minor Influence, Major Impact

Sometimes the slightest influences end up significantly impacting events in a seemingly unrelated industry or arena. Consider the Federal Communications Commission's decision to deregulate television programming in the mid 1980s. In the interest of promoting competition and free trade, and letting the market decide what types of programming would succeed and what types should fall by the wayside, the *Pandora's box* of television programming was opened.

Word Power

Pandora's Box is a tale from Greek mythology that today equates to opening or initiating something of an undesirable nature that you can't stop.

Deregulation is a fine principle in theory, designed to foster true competition, lower prices, and better choices for citizens. Milton Friedman, in his book *Freedom to Choose,* argued that by keeping markets unrestricted, competition would flourish and the ultimate beneficiary would be the consumer or end user.

In practice, deregulation seems to work well for a variety of consumer goods. When it comes to entertainment—movies, television, CDs, and video games in particular—the lack of effective government control has arguably propagated new problems for society.

Cornell West, Ph.D., and Sylvia Ann Hewlett observed in *The War Against Parents* that when the FCC relaxed its standards relating to the use of violence, profanity, and adult situations on television, the result was wave after wave of programs that increasingly push the envelope.

Be Wary

Few people are able to link FCC deregulation with the phenomenon. As violent media infiltrates other societies, most notably Japan, inexplicably violent acts on the part of teenagers are beginning to occur at too frequent intervals.

Changes You Were Hoping For?

The threads of change from an initial change wave often waft through the years leaving their marks in ways that dumbfound the masses. In your own organization and your own change-management campaign, sometimes the smallest new procedures end up having repercussions widely disproportionate with "predicted" impacts.

Morale Boost Busts

Suppose your campaign is charged with finding ways to increase employee morale throughout your company. Morale has been declining for several quarters, since the company ...

➤ Cut staff levels by 10 percent,

➤ Dropped one of its product lines,

➤ Replaced a highly popular top manager, and

➤ Suffered some damaging press coverage.

Turnover has been higher than usual, and it has become increasingly more difficult to attract top new talent to the company. Among many of the strategies that your change team institutes is an employee of the month award.

Dr. Aubrey Daniels, in *Bringing Out the Best in People,* says, "Surprisingly, even the honored person may react negatively. Annual awards often work just as poorly."

Appropriate Incentives to Prompt Change

There is nothing wrong per se with giving recognition to outstanding performers. However, anytime a reward is for "best," "first," "most," or "most improved," by design, the number of individuals who could participate in the process is limited. "With an effective recognition system," Daniels says, "everyone is acknowledged in some way for their efforts. Ideally you take nobody or no improvement for granted."

Daniels finds that too many companies, particularly the sales divisions of companies, have a "forced distribution of rewards." For example, only 5 percent or 10 percent of the work force can earn an outstanding grade. "With zero sum appraisal systems, one person's outrageous success forces others into the mediocre or failure category." Worse, most performance appraisal systems introduce *unhealthy competition* into the workplace.

Be Wary

Too often, one person is reinforced for his or her accomplishments while everyone else either remains unaffected or is even negatively reinforced by not being selected.

Word Power

Unhealthy competition in the workplace represents any instance of one person's success diminishing another's success, or the catalyst for someone's motivation being the catalyst for someone else's demotivation.

Anxiety-Provoking Appraisals

"It's no wonder," says Daniels, "that performance appraisal is an anxiety-provoking activity that is dreaded, misunderstood, and often bungled by managers; feared by and upsetting to employees; and rewarding to no one."

Here we witness the classic situation: a small change, such as instituting an employee of the month award, which is designed to alleviate a particular problem only partially or superficially, fails to address the problem *and* actually creates an altogether different kind of challenge.

Proceed

When you're behind in the final seconds of the basketball game, if you don't foul someone to stop the clock, you surely will lose the game. Doing something, even if it spawns a new problem, often is preferable over holding pat.

Word Power

A **career path** within an organization is a somewhat formal progression of promotions, raises, and responsibility for high-achieving employees.

Nowhere to Run

By now, you may have concluded that change management is scary stuff. Why get involved at all if you don't have to? You institute one little procedure and it snowballs into something that no one had any idea was coming! Yet, in the face of stiff challenges, the odds are with taking action. Goethe said, "Boldness has genius, power and magic in it."

With low staff morale, to do nothing is to shirk the issues and pretend that the problem will go away on its own. How many more months do you want to endure high employee turnover, or be unable to attract talented new staff? How long can you wait before the problem gets so critical that the survival of the organization is in jeopardy?

As you detect any demotivating workplace factors, you can design other programs that may have a more appropriate impact.

Career Development Without Career Ladders

A large corporation in the Midwest was facing a crisis. It needed to retain key staff members; yet, a variety of changes that had impacted the organization over the last decade demanded abandonment of a career ladder. As a result of downsizing, outsourcing, restructuring, and merging, there was no true *career path* for veterans of the organization, and everyone knew it.

An initiating sponsor believed the best solution would be to create an office of career development within the organization. A change campaign was initiated to determine what form, role, and responsibilities such an office would have. How would it be staffed, and how would it serve the needs of both the organization and individual employees?

Survey to Discover Needs

The designated change manager recognized that he needed to survey hundreds of people to understand how to formulate a new department within the organization that would have legitimacy and efficacy in the face of challenges to retaining key staff members.

One of the issues that surfaced as a result of his exploration was the need among employees to acquire career development skills. Such skills would help them manage the big picture of their own careers within the context of staying with the organization.

Factoid

The employees needed specific strategies and tactics to survive and prosper in an ever-changing workplace environment.

Risk for the Staff's Sake

The change manager presented these interim findings to the sponsor. Such initiative would carry some risk. After all, if you provide employees with instruction and insights on how to manage the big picture of their own careers, as well as impart survival skills, you run the risk of having them depart for greener pastures when the going gets tough.

Alternatively, the pain of the status quo—letting good staff members simply dangle as constant shifts in organizational structure further negate any semblance of a career ladder—was regarded as highly undesirable.

A Payoff Benefiting All

At this critical junction, the change campaign was refocused on empowering staff members for the good of their own careers. Top management was willing to take the risk of providing staff with tools that might ultimately hasten its members' departure.

In the coming months, the initiative yielded positive results. Personnel turnover decreased over that of comparable quarters in previous years. Many staff members came to realize that providing such services showed that the organization really did care about the direction and viability of their careers.

This realization helped engender higher levels of loyalty. Moreover, empowered with the knowledge and skills to more effectively manage their own careers, it appeared that many employees were exhibiting a newfound sense of self-confidence.

The Few Key Factors That Count

As some theorists have observed, you can't really undertake market research in an area that is totally new. If you are charged with overseeing some innovation within your company, chances are that you're not going to get it completely right on the first try. Situations arise that no one could surmise. Concurrently, problems that were anticipated to be large and especially challenging prove to be minuscule.

The more factors in a change situation, the harder it is to predict the impact of any particular procedures you may put in place. This isn't an all-purpose excuse for not proceeding!

You have to have the mental and emotional strength to let go of the "also rans." You can't keep your fingers on everything all the time. When you stay attuned to the larger, more critical factors, the small ones often fall into place.

Move the Rocks, Then the Pebbles

In his books and lectures, Steven Covey, Ph.D. illustrates the wisdom of concentrating on the critical issues you confront you by using an analogy about filling a glass jar with rocks, pebbles, and sand. If you begin to fill the jar with the pebbles and sand, you run the risk of not being able to get all the rocks into the jar. If you put the rocks in first, followed by some of the smaller pebbles, and then sprinkle in the sand, *voilà!*—everything fits into the jar.

Suppose the rocks represent factors critical to your change campaign. The pebbles represent secondary issues, and the grains of sand represent minor tasks. When you deal with the rocks, that is, primary issues first, a magical thing happens: You still find room for the secondary and tertiary issues. They fit in and around the spaces available.

Change Master

Many of the change campaigns you might be commissioned to manage could be exceedingly complex and contain many variables, the interaction of which is very difficult to predict. Your mission becomes identifying the few key factors out of the many that are likely to be most cogent in the successful resolution of the campaign.

Change Master

If a small factor proves to have a large ramification over time, as a change manager, you have to play the percentages. Identifying what seem to be the most critical factors is your primary concern. Worrying about the long-term ramifications of every little thing that may have an impact is an energy-draining and largely unrewarding exercise.

If you attempt to do it the other way around, too often you end up giving short shrift to what is truly important and squandering your energy and efforts on minutiae.

Look Back, Then Look Forward

There are ways to help ensure that the assumptions and predictions you make have viability. One way is to take a longitudinal look at the issues at hand. If you only go back three months into your company's history, you're not likely to have a wide enough purview.

Richard Nixon, when he was president of the United States, as well as throughout the rest of his life, drew upon the lessons of history to guide him in making decisions. Nixon believed that the more you knew about what happened in the past, especially if you were proposing to institute a new tax or regulation, the more adept you'd be at understanding the potential ramifications in the present. This is quite different than linear extrapolation.

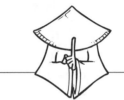

In one case, Nixon reviewed the strong, negative public reaction to legislation enacted in Europe in the early 1800s. As a result, he declined to support a somewhat parallel act proposed during his administration.

Change Master

The further back you can see, the further ahead you can see.

Use a Wider Lens

Beyond taking a long-term view of your organization's history and experience, viewing your current challenge with a wide lens also bears fruit.

When videocassette recorders (VCRs) started to become popular throughout the United States, the Disney Corporation viewed both VCRs and movies on video as a threat to its existence. Disney's top management believed that the theatrical movie business, in which Disney was one of the chief players, would suffer debilitating revenue losses.

Curiously, Disney is the largest and most successful vendor of home videos.

What took place between Disney's loss of the lawsuit and its leadership position in home video sales? Disney broadened its view.

Recognizing that it couldn't stem the VCR tide, Disney embraced it. Focusing on its strength, the

Factoid

Disney initiated a major lawsuit against VCR manufacturers. The suit was long and costly, but Disney felt that one of its main sources of revenue was in jeopardy, and so it persevered. Eventually, Disney lost the suit and today, VCRs are fixtures in the majority of U.S. households and are a popular entertainment device throughout the world.

children's market, Disney produced a flourish of high-quality entertainment programming. Products include longtime classics; original productions for the movie theatre, which would then be packaged as videos; and live theme park entertainment captured on video for sale in the home market.

Walk into any household today with children, and the odds are there is at least one, if not a dozen, Disney videos near the TV.

Look Once and Look Again

Another measure to ensure that your assumptions and predictions remain valid is to take a constant look at them. Rather than falling in love with a study that was undertaken by your organization or provided by an outside consultant, keep charting the waters. If you end up reaffirming what you had already concluded, fine. The exercise was still worthwhile.

If you note significant changes in what you see from your examination of, say, last week or last month, then you have a strong reason for probing even further. You may find that some basic assumptions need to be rethought, as well.

Creating New Positions for New Challenges

When Levi Strauss and Company felt it needed to focus more sharply on global revenue opportunities, the company created the position of vice president of global marketing. This first vice president assembled a global marketing team consisting of six members.

The team's mission is to transport new product ideas and advertising messages across borders so the various divisions within Levi Strauss's far-flung empire can benefit from organization-wide synergy. The team is reviewing the organization's worldwide media mix and hiring and firing new advertising and communication agencies to announce and promote its products. It is also building new Web sites to attract customers.

Expand and Refine the Focus

While expanding the company's traditional focus, the global marketing team also holds bench-marking sessions outside the apparel business with other global marketers. In other words, the team finds out what the best and most innovative marketers in other industries are doing, and then looks for parallels within its own industry.

Recent results indicate that Levi's 501S jeans, selling at 10 to 15 percent higher rates than Lee or Wrangler jeans, are the product leader in Europe. Rather than fall in love with some survey or study, the global marketing team seems to live by the credo "Tomorrow will be different."

Your tomorrow will be different as well, and you have the insights and capability to meet the challenges head-on!

In mastering change, recognize that virtually all career professionals are up against many of the same hurdles as you are. This generation of professionals, in particular, faces challenges unlike any generation before it.

Those who succeed learn to be resilient. They understand that economics are at the root of all social interactions. They learn to compete effectively, or, better yet, create a niche so as to reduce the need to compete. They learn to take things in stride.

The Least You Need to Know

➤ Throughout history, even the best and the brightest have made forecasts that not only didn't come to pass, but weren't even close.

➤ Too many people base their predictions of the future on linear progressions of the present and near present.

➤ Sometimes, the smallest new procedures end up having repercussions widely disproportionate with the "predicted" impact.

➤ Doing something, even if it spawns a new problem, often is preferable over doing nothing. As Goethe said, "Boldness has genius, power and magic in it."

➤ The further back you can see, the further ahead you can see.

Further Reading

Ackoff, Russell. *Redesigning the Future*. New York: Wiley, 1974.

Ashe, Arthur. *Days of Grace*. New York: Ballantine Books, 1994.

Barker, Joel. *Future Edge: Discovering the New Paradigms of Success*. New York: Morrow, 1992.

Beer, Michael, and Nitin Nohria. *Breaking the Code of Change*. Cambridge, MA: Harvard Business School Press, 2000.

Bennett, John. *Leading the Edge of Change*. Morrisville, NC: Pawprint Press, 2000.

Bennis, Warren, et al. *The Planning of Change*. New York: Holt, 1969.

Bion, W.R. *Experiences in Groups*. New York: Ballantine, 1959.

Blake, Robert, and Jane Mouton. *Change by Design*. Houston: Gulf Publishing, 1989.

Block, Peter. *The Empowered Manager*. San Francisco: Jossey Bass, 1987.

Bridges, William. *Managing Transitions*. Cambridge, MA: Perseus Press, 1991.

———. *Transitions*. Cambridge, MA: Perseus Press, 1991.

Carpenter, Phil. *Ebrands: Building an Internet Business at Breakneck Speed*. Boston: Harvard Business School Press, 2000.

Champy, James. *Reengineering Management: The Mandate for New Leadership*. New York: HarperBusiness, 1995.

Chappell, Tom. *Managing Upside Down: The Seven Intentions of Values-Centered Leadership*. New York: Morrow, 1999.

Chin, R., and K. Benne. *The Planning of Change*. New York: HRW Press, 1972.

Christensen, Clayton. *The Innovator's Dilemma*. Cambridge, MA: Harvard Business School Press, 2000.

Collins, James, and Jerry Porras. *Built to Last: Successful Habits of Visionary Companies*. New York: HarperCollins, 1994.

Conner, Daryl. *Managing at the Speed of Change*. New York: Villard, 1993.

Covey, Stephen. *The 7 Habits of Highly Effective People*. New York: Fireside, 1990.

Crosby, Philip B. *Quality Is Free*. New York: Mentor Books, 1979.

———. *Quality Without Tears*. New York: McGraw-Hill, 1984.

———. *Running Things: The Art of Making Things Happen*. New York: McGraw-Hill, 1986.

Daniels, Aubrey. *Bring Out the Best in People*. New York: McGraw-Hill, 1999.

Darwin, Charles. *The Origin of the Species*. New York: Grammercy, 1998.

Davenport, Thomas. *Process Innovation*. Boston: Harvard Business School Press, 1993.

Davidson, Jeff. *The Complete Idiot's Guide to Assertiveness*. Indianapolis: Alpha Books, 1997.

———. *The Complete Idiot's Guide to Managing Stress*. Indianapolis: Alpha Books, 1999.

———. *The Complete Idiot's Guide to Managing Your Time*. Indianapolis: Alpha Books, 1999.

———. *The Complete Idiot's Guide to Project Management*. Indianapolis: Alpha Books, 2000.

———. *The Complete Idiot's Guide to Reaching Your Goals*. Indianapolis: Alpha Books, 1998.

———. *The Complete Idiot's Guide to Reinventing Yourself*. Indianapolis: Alpha Books, 2001.

———. *The Joy of Simple Living*. Emmaus, PA: Rodale, 1999.

Davidson, Jeff, and Dave Yoho. *How to Have a Good Year Every Year*. New York: Berkley Books, 1991.

Davis, Stan. *2020 Vision*. Reading, MA: Addison-Wesley, 1999.

Davis, Stan, and Christopher Meyer. *Blur: The Speed of Change and the Connected Economy*. Reading, MA: Addison-Wesley, 1998.

Dawson, Roger. *You Can Get Anything You Want, But You Have to Do More Than Ask*. Lighthouse Pub., 1985.

De Geus, Arie. *The Living Company*. Cambridge, MA: Harvard Business School Press, 1997.

Deming, W. Edwards. *The New Economics*. 1984. Cambridge, MA: MIT Press, 2000.

———. *Out of the Crisis*. Cambridge, MA: MIT Press, 1986.

———. *Quality, Productivity, and Competitive Position*. Cambridge, MA: MIT Press, 1982.

———. *Statistical Adjustment of Data*. New York: Wiley, 1943.

DePree, Max. *Leadership Is an Art*. New York: Dell, 1989.

Drucker, Peter. *The Age of Discontinuity*. New Brunswick, NJ: Transaction Publishing, 1992.

———. *Concept of the Corporation*. New York: Transaction Publishing, 1946.

———. *Drucker on Asia*. Boston: Butterworth Heinmann, 1954.

———. *Innovation and Entrepreneurship*. New York: HarperBusiness, 1985.

———. *Management Challenges for the 21st Century*. New York: HarperBusiness, 1999.

———. *The Practice of Management*. New York: Harper, 1954.

Eisenberg, Howard. *Creative Thinking Tools for Innovation*. Stowe, VT: Syntrek, 1994.

———. *Fundamentals of High Performance Teamwork*. Stowe, VT: Syntrek, 1995.

Fisher, Roger, and William Ury. *Getting to Yes: Negotiating Agreement Without Giving In*. New York: Penguin USA, 1991.

Fritz, Robert. *The Path of Least Resistance*. San Francisco: Berrett-Koehler, 1999.

Galbraith, John Kenneth. *The Nature of Mass Poverty*. Cambridge, MA: Harvard University Press, 2001.

Galpin, Timothy. *The Human Side of Change*. San Francisco: Jossey Bass, 1996.

Gillon, Steven. *That's Not What We Meant to Do*. New York: Norton, 2000.

Gleick, James. *Chaos: Making a New Science*. New York: Penguin, 1987.

Hammer, Michael, and James Champy. *Reengineering the Corporation*. New York: HarperCollins, 1993.

Huczynski, Andrzej. *Management Gurus: What Makes Them and How to Become One*. London: Rutledge, 1993.

Imai, M. *Kaizen*. New York: McGraw-Hill, 1986.

Juran, Joseph. *Bureaucracy: A Challenge to Better Management*. New York: Harper, 1944.

———. *Juran on Leadership for Quality*. New York: Free Press, 1989.

———. *Juran on Planning for Quality*. New York: Free Press, 1988.

———. *The Quality Control Handbook*. New York: McGraw-Hill, 1988.

Kanter, Rosabeth Moss. *The Challenge of Organizational Change*. New York: Free Press, 1992.

———. *The Change Masters*. New York: Simon & Schuster, 1983.

———. *Evolve!: Succeeding in the Digital Culture of Tomorrow*. Cambridge, MA: Harvard Business School Press, 2001.

Katzenbach, Jon, and Douglas Smith. *The Wisdom of Teams*. New York: HarperBusiness, 1994.

Kostner, Jaclyn. *Knights of the Tele-Round Table*. New York: Warner Books, 1994.

Kotter, John, and James Heskitt. *Corporate Culture and Performance*. New York: Free Press, 1992.

Kriegel, Robert. *Scared Cows Make the Best Burgers: Developing Change-Ready People and Organizations*. New York: Warner, 1997.

Kuhn, Thomas. *The Structure of Scientific Revolutions*. Chicago: University of Chicago Press, 1962.

Larkin, T. J., and Sandra Larkin. *Communicating Change*. New York: McGraw-Hill, 1994.

Leavitt, Harold. *Corporate Pathfinders*. New York: Penguin, 1986.

Lemberg, Paul. *Faster than the Speed of Change*. San Diego: Akiba Press, 2001.

Levering, Robert, and Milton Moskowitz. *Hundred Best Companies to Work For in America*. New York: Plume, 1994.

Lewin, Kurt. *The Philosophy of Ernst Cassirer*. New York: Tudor Publishing, 1945.

Machiavelli, Niccolo. *The Prince*. New York: Bantam Classics, 1984.

Meredith, J.R., and Samuel Mantel. *Project Management*. New York: Wiley, 1995.

Meyer, Christopher. *Fast Cycle Time: How to Align Purpose, Strategy, and Structure for Speed*. New York: Free Press, 1993.

Newell, Allen, and Herbert Simon. *Human Problem Solving*. Englewood Cliffs, NJ: Prentice Hall, 1972.

Nolan, Richard, and David Croson. *Creative Destruction*. Boston: Harvard University Press, 1995.

Oden, Howard. *Managing Corporate Culture, Innovation, and Intrapreneurship*. Westport, CT: Quorum Books, 1997.

Oldham, Greg. *Work Redesign*. Reading, MA: Addison-Wesley, 1980.

Osborn, Carol. *The Art of Resilience*. New York: Three Rivers Press, 1997.

Pascale, Richard, Mark Mallemann, and Linda Gioga. *Surfacing the Edge of Chaos: The Laws of Nature and the New Laws of Business*. New York: Crown Publishing, 2000.

Pasmore, William. *Designing Effective Organizations*. New York: Wiley, 1988.

Peppers, Don, and Martha Rogers. *The One to One Future: Building Relationships One Customer at a Time*. New York: Currency Doubleday, 1993.

Porter, Michael. *Competitive Advantage*. New York: Free Press, 1998.

Quinn, Robert. *Change the World: How Ordinary People Can Achieve Extraordinary Results*. San Francisco: Jossey Bass, 2000.

Reid, Robert. *Architects of the Web: 1000 Days that Built the Future of Business*. New York: Wiley, 1997.

Robbins, Tony. *Awaken the Giant Within*. New York: Fireside, 1993.

Rogers, Everett. *Diffusion of Invasion*. New York: Free Press, 1983.

Rosenberg, Nathan. *Inside the Black Box: Technology and Economics*. Cambridge, MA: Cambridge University Press, 1982.

Schon, Donald. *The Reflective Practitioner*. New York: Basic Books, 1983.

Schwartz, Peter. *The Art of the Long View*. New York: Currency Doubleday, 1996.

Scott-Morgan, Peter. *The Unwritten Rules of the Game*. New York: McGraw-Hill, 1994.

Selye, Hans. *The Stress of Life*. New York: McGraw-Hill, 1956.

Senge, Peter. *Fifth Discipline: The Art and Practice of the Learning Organization*. New York: Doubleday, 1990.

———. *The Fifth Discipline Fieldbook: Strategies and Tools for Building a Learning Organization*. New York: Currency Doubleday, 1994.

Senge, Peter, et al. *The Dance of Change: The Challenge to Sustaining Momentum in Learning Organizations*. New York: Doubleday, 1999.

Smith, Douglas. *Taking Charge of Change*. Reading, MA: Addison-Wesley, 1996.

Tertouzos, Michael. *Made in America*. Cambridge, MA: MIT Press, 1989.

Thomas, James. *Organizations in Action*. New York: McGraw-Hill, 1967.

Tichy, Noel, and Stratford Sherman. *Control Your Destiny or Someone Else Will*. New York: HarperBusiness, 1999.

Toffler, Alvin. *Future Shock*. New York: Bantam Books, 1991.

———. *The Third Wave*. New York: Bantam Books, 1991.

Toushman, Michael. *Winning Through Innovation: A Practical Guide to Leading Organizational Change and Renewal*. Cambridge, MA: Harvard Business School Press, 1997.

Vance, Mike, and Diane Deacon. *Think Out of the Box*. Franklin Lakes, NJ: Career Press, 1995.

Wacker, Watts. *The Visionary's Handbook: Nine Paradoxes That Will Shape the Future of Your Business*. New York: HarperBusiness, 2000.

West, Cornell, and Sylvia Ann Hewlett. *The War Against Parents*. New York: Mariner Books, 1999.

Wheatly, Margaret J. *Leadership and the New Science: Learning About Organization from an Orderly Universe*. San Francisco: Berrett-Koehler Publishers, 1992.

Wheelwright, Stephen, and Kim Clark. *Revolutionizing Product Development*. New York: Free Press, 1992.

Williamson, Oliver. *Markets and Hierarchies*. New York: North-Holland, 1975.

Wilson, James Q. *The Moral Sense*. New York: Simon & Schuster, 1997.

Womack, James, et al. *The Machine That Changed the World*. New York: Ross and Associates, 1990.

Woodward, Harry, and Steve Buckholz. *After Shock: Helping People Through Corporate Change*. New York: Wiley, 1987.

Zuboff, Shoshana. *In the Age of the Smart Machine*. New York: Basic Books, 1988.

Glossary

accommodate   To tolerate the situation as the only alternative.

adaptable teams   Groups of people in a purposeful state of flux to meet the ever-changing requirements with which they are tasked.

adaptive organizations   Establishments led by top management who are committed to improving operations, empowering the staff, and increasing shareholder value.

antsy   Agitated or overly excited.

askew   Off-center, titled, or lopsided.

assimilation   The process of adapting a new idea to a process already in progress.

atmosphere   In a business context, how an environment appeals to consumers.

attachment   In the workplace, the perception that existing customs or procedures cannot be improved upon without risking negative effects.

attrition   A reduction or a decline.

aura   An atmosphere or a climate, and, on a personal basis, an air or undercurrent.

bandwidth   The capacity for data bits.

calling the turns   Predicting when a trend is going to break or reverse itself.

capacity to change   The ability of an organization to initiate and successfully achieve change on an ongoing basis.

capitulate   To relent, succumb, or surrender.

career path   A somewhat formal progression of promotions, raises, and responsibility for high-achieving employees within an organization.

chaos theory   The body of ideas that attempts to explain both the randomness and the complexity of events and processes.

closure   Completion.

cogitation   Contemplation or mental reflection.

contingency plan   A backup course of action to be initiated in the event that the original course of action encounters significant barriers.

creative sabotage   The process by which an organization discontinues popular products or services in order to meet the ever-changing needs of the marketplace.

de facto   How something is, independent of laws, formal rules, or written guidelines.

decentralization   Giving power and control to the separate parts of a structure instead of dispensing power and administering control from a central source.

decoupling   Detaching or removing something.

diffidence   Reluctance or caution.

disconfirm   To recant or cancel.

disenfranchised   Cut off from the mainstream or having no power.

empower   To commission to take action on one's own.

engender   To help produce, bring about, or make so.

equilibrium   The state in which driving forces and restraining forces are roughly equal.

euphemism   A nicer or at least more flattering way of saying something.

Eureka effect   An effect that occurs when you have a breakthrough idea at a time when you weren't focusing on the issues leading up to the idea.

fathom   To grasp or comprehend an issue.

force field analysis   The process of studying the catalysts of changes within an organization, as well as focusing on those factors that benefit and disrupt the changes.

Gantt or PERT/CPM charts   Traditional project planning and management tools, useful for a wide variety of applications.

germination   A growth or sprouting, budding or blooming that occurs once the seed of a plant or of an idea is rooted in firm soil.

grand strategy   A plan that incorporates the relevant aspects of different approaches to best tackle the matter at hand.

heliotropic   Literally, growing in the direction of the sun; within organizations: stimulating learning, innovation, and enthusiasm.

homeostasis   A state in which an entity's relationship to the environment is stable.

hone   To sharpen or file to a fine edge.

impetus   Momentum.

inadvertent   Something that is unintentional.

leapfrogging   Making conscious decisions not to compete with or even address certain developments in your industry and marketplace.

learning anxiety   A restraining force that most of us feel to some degree when we're compelled to learn something new and which opposes both learning and change.

martinet   A dictatorial, autocratic type of person.

objectivity   Clear, impartial, and neutral focus.

old saw   An old saying, usually conventional wisdom, passed on over time.

organized abandonment   Process in which change managers regularly examine products, services, and every other element of the organization to determine whether they should stay or go.

palatable   The quality of being agreeable, enjoyable, or tasty.

Pandora's Box   A tale from Greek mythology which today equates to opening or initiating something of an undesirable nature that you can't stop.

passivity   Listlessness or lethargy.

plethora   Something that flows in abundance or that there is a surplus of.

postulate   To surmise, assume, or guess.

procure   To buy, acquire, or otherwise get possession of something.

quality   According to Juran, fitness for use.

rationalize   To justify or mentally minimize the negative aspects of a situation.

reintegration   Reassimilation or reconsolidation.

replicate   To repeat or duplicate.

rightsizing   Determining the appropriate staffing levels within an organization based on both a short, and a long-term perspective.

sanctions   Penalties or punishments.

semantic   Of or relating to words or word choices.

singularities   Term that astrophysicist and cosmologist Steven Hawking, Ph.D., uses to describe a one-time event in the universe.

sleep debt   Person's accumulated lack of sleep.

social psychology   The study of how individuals act in relation to others.

stratify   To offer specific products/services and strategic price points to specific market segments.

synergy   The whole equals more than the sum of the parts.

systematic innovation   The process of continually seeking out improvements to the way one operates.

total quality management   An attempt to maintain the merit of an entire project, rather than focusing on its individual parts.

transition   The process of an individual deciding to accept change and work on its behalf.

unhealthy competition   In the workplace, any instance of the success of one person diminishing the success of another's.

venue   A setting place or locale.

vernacular   Everyday spoken language.

vicissitudes   The up-and-down variations in an event or observable phenomenon.

vindictive   The quality of being spiteful, vengeful, or vicious.

walk-away terms   The point at which you would leave the negotiation rather than stay and accept far less than desirable terms.

wanton   Reckless use.

zealous   Avid, eager, and overenthusiastic.

Index

widgets, 8-9
wildlife, societal views, 7
Wills, Maury, 102
Wilson, James Q., 87-88
Wolfgang, Johann, 180-181
women, societal views, 6-7
work groups, 108
work-related issues, failing tasks,
    55-56
workforce, companies, 246
workplace
    dynamics, change managers,
        245
    issues, overworked, 247
    stress, 246-247
    testing, AMA, 216
    unhealthy competition, 301
wudgets, 8-9